TRANSFORMING LEARNING AND TEACHING

Professor Barbara MacGilchrist is Deputy Director at the Institute of Education, University of London and an Associate Director of the Institute's International School Effectiveness and Improvement Centre. She has been a teacher, a head-teacher, local education authority inspector and chief inspector, and has substantial experience of professional development and school improvement programmes. She is the author of *Managing Access and Entitlement in Primary Education* (Trentham, 1992) and co-author of *Planning Matters* (Paul Chapman Publishing, 1995) and *The Intelligent School* (Paul Chapman/Sage Publishing, 1997; 2004). She has published a wide range of articles for practitioners in professional journals and on the National College for School Leadership website. In 2003 she was awarded an OBE for her services to the 'education and professional development of teachers'.

Margaret Buttress is the Headteacher of Highlands Primary School in the London Borough of Redbridge. Prior to this she was a teacher and deputy headteacher in the outer London Boroughs of Merton, Hillingdon and Ealing. She has led and managed two successful amalgamations, including Highlands, where she has been Headteacher since 1997. Awarded a Research Associateship by the National College for School Leadership in 2001, she has disseminated the transformational learning from the 'Learning to Learn' project locally, nationally and internationally. She has been a member of groups developing revised school self-evaluation and monitoring frameworks for Redbridge. She is also contributing to the Department for Education and Skills' pilot schemes and consultation exercises on the New Relationship with Schools.

TRANSFORMING LEARNING AND TEACHING

'we can if … '

Barbara MacGilchrist
and
Margaret Buttress

P·C·P
Paul Chapman
Publishing

First published 2005

P·C·P
Paul Chapman
Publishing

Paul Chapman Publishing
A SAGE Publications Company
1 Oliver's Yard
55 City Road
London EC1Y 1SP

SAGE Publications Inc
2455 Teller Road
Thousand Oaks, California 91320

SAGE Publications India Pvt Ltd
B-42, Panchsheel Enclave
Post Box 4109
New Delhi 110 017

Library of Congress Control Number: 2004106433

A catalogue record for this book is available from the British Library

ISBN 1 4129 0055 7
ISBN 1 4129 0056 5 (pbk)

Typeset by Dorwyn Ltd, Wells.
Printed in Great Britain by Athenaeum Press, Gateshead

Dedicated to Gareth Brooke-Williams

an inspirational and charismatic headteacher who always believed *'we can if ... '*.
(1952–2001)

Contents

Acknowledgements

This book reflects the learning journey of five primary schools and is a celebration of primary practice in the London Borough of Redbridge.

In writing up the 'Learning to Learn' project we have tried to encapsulate the deep learning that took place within our learning community. Particular thanks are extended to the headteachers for their unwavering leadership, support and collegiality during the project:

Lesley Hagon, Headteacher, Ilford Jewish Primary School
Helen Marchant, Acting Headteacher, Oakdale Junior School
Judith Skelton, Headteacher, Churchfields Junior School
Dinah Smith, Headteacher, Parkhill Junior School.

The outstanding contributions, and engagement, from staff and pupils in all five schools have been instrumental in translating the aims of the project into practical reality. The support of parents and governors was a vital part of this process. Judith Skelton's organization and collation of the children's views about learning was greatly appreciated.

Special thanks are extended to the staff, pupils and governors of Highlands Primary School, for their enthusiasm, forbearance, and continued support whilst the authors were writing this book. Outstanding contributions from Jean Durr, Ian Bennett, Sue Barnes and Angela Sparkes in their leadership, challenge and support have been especially appreciated, as has the very practical support provided by members of the office staff.

The vision, creative foresight, courage and tenacity of our mentor, Melanie Foster, enabled the learning journey to happen for *all*. Lisa Starr, through her unstinting support, kept us on track.

We wish to thank Jackie Lee for her endless patience, goodwill and endurance in helping us to type and retype our story, and Bob Percival for his work in producing the data.

We also wish to thank the following for their individual contributions. Martin Coles, Janice Eacott, Anne Farmer, Claire Griffiths, Sue Hyett, Rachel Jackson, Vicky

Jones, Roz Levin, Isobel Madhani, Samim Patel, Mary Robinson, Maninder Sagoo, Jes Da Santos, Robeena Shah, Linda Snow, Geoff Southworth, Mick Taylor, Jo Wakefield, Saira Yakub and Meena Zaverchand.

Last, but not least, Barbara would like to thank her husband, Bob, and Margaret would like to thank her husband, Patrick, daughters, Jessica and Martha, and her mother, Margaret, for their support and encouragement.

Barbara MacGilchrist
Margaret Buttress

Introduction – 'we can if ...'

We introduce this book by describing:
- what the story is about
- how the story is told
- how it can be used.

The story

This book tells the story of how a group of primary schools transformed learning and teaching. It is a 'warts and all' story, which provides a fascinating insight into the day-to-day realities of trying to bring about school improvement. The book describes the wide range of practical strategies the schools used for supporting and enhancing:

- children's learning
- teachers' learning
- the schools' capacity for learning.

It describes how the focus on learning led to significant improvements in children's motivation, behaviour, engagement in learning and learning outcomes. It also illustrates how, through teachers learning with, and from one another, the schools' capacity for sustained improvement was strengthened.

The book is based on an action research project entitled 'Learning to Learn' which concentrated on the development of children's understanding, skills and attitudes about themselves as learners, and about the learning and thinking strategies they were currently using, and could use in the future.

Throughout, the book gives the children's perspective on the impact that the project had on them. It describes what worked for the schools, and what did not. It draws out the main lessons learned for:

1

- children
- teachers
- support staff
- headteachers
- parents
- external consultants.

It raises issues about the transfer of learners from primary to secondary school.

The story told by the schools is an important one. It reminds us that there is much more to education than a narrow concentration on target setting and league tables. It tells the story of a group of schools committed to: inclusive education for all; the provision of a rich, broad curriculum, and the development of young people's confidence, self-esteem and the skills and attitudes needed to become lifelong learners.

How the story is told

The story begins in Chapter 1 with a brief description of the 'Learning to Learn' project and those involved in it, to provide a context for the chapters that follow. Chapter 2 describes – warts and all – how the 'Learning to Learn' headteachers and their mentors came together, developed a learning orientation and brought their staff on board. Chapter 3 recounts how the schools developed their teaching practice to develop pupils' learning.

Adults learning to learn take up the following two chapters. Chapter 4's account of how the schools supported teachers as learners and researchers, is followed, in Chapter 5, by how the schools provided leadership for learning, and the different people involved in that process.

The spotlight then refocuses on the children. Chapter 6 deals with the strategies the schools used to accelerate learning and Chapter 7 with how the schools kept track of children's learning.

The impact of the 'Learning to Learn' project is summarized in Chapter 8 in respect of:

- children's levels of achievement in English, mathematics and science, and how these outcomes compared with other schools in the borough and with schools nationally
- teachers and their teaching practice
- the headteachers
- parents
- those who work with the schools.

The progress made by the schools is affirmed in Office for Standards in Education (Ofsted) inspection reports. The children's own story about the growth of themselves as learners and about their learning journey follows in Chapter 9.

The different strands of the 'Learning to Learn' story come together in Chapter 10. The lessons learned and the implications for future practice in schools and LEAs are identified. The story does not end here however. The schools are continuing to work together and have now been joined by some more primary schools and a group of secondary schools to form an enlarged 'Learning to Learn' network. This network of schools is building on the work of the original group of five to ensure that the lessons learned by them inform the next stage of their learning journey together.

How the book can be used

The book is intended for school leaders and practising teachers in primary and secondary schools, and for those who work in an advisory or consultancy capacity with schools. It will also be of interest to those training to be teachers and to their teachers.

Theme headings are highlighted at the beginning of each chapter. Subdivisions of each heading are similarly marked, to enable the reader to see the big picture at a glance. Most chapters end with a concluding section in which we review what we did, and reflect on what we learned. These reviews and reflections can be used as a starting point for individual, group or whole-staff learning and professional development. In the last chapter, arising from the lessons learned, we identify some key principles that need to underpin the transformation of learning and teaching. We conclude with a series of questions to promote discussion amongst practitioners and policy-makers.

Throughout the book there are practical examples of the 'Learning to Learn' project in action, which it is hoped practitioners will find informative and useful for enhancing their own practice. For those involved in networked learning communities, or about to be, the book offers practical strategies for maximizing the effectiveness of such groups.

In using the book it is important to bear in mind the strapline – 'we can if … '. This was our guiding mantra because it signified our belief that *all* children (and adults for that matter) can learn. It underpinned our commitment to inclusive education for all in the context of a broad and balanced curriculum for the twenty-first century.

Barbara MacGilchrist
Margaret Buttress
April 2004

1

Setting the scene

Effective educational leaders are continuously open to new learning because the (leadership for learning) journey keeps changing. (Stoll et al., 2003, p. 103)

We set the scene by describing:
- the 'Learning to Learn' project
- the LEA context at the beginning of the project
- the schools
- our guiding mantra – *'we can if ... '.*

This chapter describes the rationale for the 'Learning to Learn' project and gives an outline of how the project was designed. It also provides background information about the outer London borough in which the five schools were located, and a pen portrait of each of the schools involved. It ends by describing the reason for our guiding mantra, *'we can if ... '.*

The 'Learning to Learn' project

The project grew out of a learning partnership between a group of primary schools, their local education authority (LEA), the outer London Borough of Redbridge and a higher education institution (HEI), the Institute of Education, University of London. The overall purpose of the project was to support, promote and share good practice in learning and teaching, so as to improve the quality of the learning experience for *all* young people and raise their levels of achievement. The emphasis on *all* the children was important because an inclusive approach to education for all was a guiding principle for the project. The project was underpinned by two fundamentals. First, that developing, changing and improving learning and teaching in the classroom is at the heart of school improvement. Secondly, that to do this children and teachers, along with the headteacher and other school staff and those who support them from outside, including parents, need to learn with and from one another. This belief was premised on our view that a focus on learning rather than on performance will enhance children's progress and achievement.

After much heart searching and debate, we decided to use the following question as our initial starting point:

Does the development of teachers' and children's metacognitive skills significantly enhance children's achievement in learning?

We began with this question because we were very aware that there is a growing amount of research evidence to show that, if children are taught to develop and understand their thinking strategies, then this can make a real difference to their learning in school and beyond. We knew that, as Stoll and colleagues (2003) argue:

Becoming skilled at metacognition requires focused teaching, lots of examples and a great deal of practice. When pupils have developed proficiency with monitoring their own learning and identifying what they need next, they are more able to transfer their learning to new settings and events, to have deeper understanding and to build the habits of mind that make them lifelong learners (p. 70).

We also knew that, to enable this to happen, teachers need to have a good understanding of how children learn, so as to be able to use this knowledge to try out and develop a broad repertoire of teaching strategies.

As will become clear in the chapters that follow, this question about metacognition, in other words – thinking about thinking – was the beginning of a long journey that led us along an exciting, challenging route with many different pathways and some dead ends! Very soon into the journey, we recognized that there was much more to learning than metacognition. Therefore, we broadened our horizons and focused on metalearning – learning about learning. In concentrating on the learning process, and the factors that can contribute to effective learning, we found ourselves exploring social, emotional, cognitive, neurological, psychological and physiological aspects of learning, and the practical implications of these in the classroom and across the school as a whole. The children had a central role to play in this process. Listening to children's views about themselves as learners, about their learning and about the things that teachers do that best supports their learning, was of fundamental importance to the project. So much so, that throughout the book, we have ensured that the children's story is described and told. We believed, as Jean Rudduck and colleagues (1996, p. 1) do, that:

what pupils say about teaching, learning and schooling is not only worth listening to, but provides an important – perhaps the most important – foundation for thinking about ways of improving schools.

In recognition of the fact that learning is a complex process, the project drew on a wide range of research and practice. We paid particular attention to the literature concerned with:

- effective learning (Watkins, 2000; Watkins et al., 2001; 2002)
- the development of metacognitive skills (McGuinness, 1999)
- formative assessment (Assessment Reform Group, 1999; Black and Wiliam, 1998)
- motivation (Dweck, 1986)
- accelerated learning (Smith and Call, 2000)
- multiple intelligence (Gardner, 1993; 1999)
- emotional intelligence (Goleman, 1996; 1998)
- learning and the brain (Greenfield, 1997; McNeil, 1999).

Preparations for the project began in 1999–2000 and then spanned two academic years, from September 2000 to July 2002. It combined support and pressure, in a planned way, at different, but complementary levels:

- within the schools
- between the schools
- between the schools and the LEA
- between the HEI, the LEA and the schools.

Chapter 2 describes how the project got started and what the schools, the LEA and the HEI did to make this happen.

The project was designed to ensure that the five schools that eventually became involved, took control of their own improvement processes. Although we were working on a 'project' together, the ultimate aim was to ensure that the learning and teaching practices, developed in the schools, would be sustained, developed and kept under regular review way beyond the life of the project. In other words, this was not simply another initiative or a one-off programme. Rather, it was a serious attempt to improve, change and embed learning and teaching in the schools now and in the future. There was also a commitment to disseminate good practice and lessons learned, not just within this 'networked community', but to a wider network of schools in the LEA in the long term. The writing of this book is part of that commitment.

There were a number of key elements that featured in this action research project. They included:

- a commitment to learning for all
- accepting oneself as a learner (both staff and children)
- rigorous 'critical friendships'
- high-quality professional development including dialogue between and across the schools about the nature of learning

- involving children in their own learning; in other words, viewing them as learning citizens involved in their own learning process
- exploring notions of intelligence and learning styles
- the need to be very specific about learning, so as to inform planning, learning intentions and short- and long-term targets
- quantitative and qualitative assessment to support learners and their learning
- supporting school self-evaluation.

To enable the schools to 'learn to learn' a wide range of strategies was used. These strategies included:

- combined in-service training sessions for teachers, support staff and governors across all five schools
- in-school staff development opportunities focused on learning and teaching
- inter-school visiting by teachers to observe and share practice
- a visit by teachers from all five schools to a Canadian school district
- feedback from regular developmental joint visits by the LEA Advisory Officer for special educational needs and the HEI partner
- the development of a 'critical friendship' network for the headteachers themselves.

The three partners (schools, LEA and HEI) in the project met on a regular basis throughout the two-year period. The LEA contributed the vital support of a management officer, Lisa Starr, who co-ordinated and effectively minuted all meetings, and distributed research papers and documentation. This enabled the process within the project to be clearly documented.

To monitor and evaluate the impact of the project, a range of qualitative (soft) and quantitative (hard) data was gathered at the beginning, during, and at the end of the project. These included:

- pupil, teacher and parent questionnaires
- systematic tracking over two years of the progress and achievement of a targeted cohort of children in each school (those who were in year 5 at the beginning of the project) using a wide range of measures including attainment data
- pupil, teacher and headteacher interviews by the LEA and HEI partners
- documentary evidence, for example, children's work and teachers' lesson plans
- regular joint LEA/HEI classroom observation in each school across the two years
- headteacher progress reports on changes in children's and teachers' behaviours over the two years.

The chapters that follow tell the story of our journey together and the final chapter draws out the important lessons that we learned. Without doubt we found that our learning partnership resulted in changes in the ways in which the children thought about themselves as learners and approached their learning. These changes led to improvements in motivation, behaviour, engagement in learning and learning outcomes. Similarly there were changes in teacher behaviours and attitudes in respect of their own learning, their understanding of children's learning and their teaching strategies. There were also changes in the behaviour and attitudes of the headteachers as their learning about learning developed over time.

Before embarking on the journey, however, we now turn to a description of the LEA context for the project and a pen portrait of the five schools.

The LEA context at the beginning of the project

At the turn of this century, the outer London Borough of Redbridge served a predominantly suburban area of northeast London with a population of approximately 235,000 inhabitants and a school population of about 43,000 children. Approximately 40 per cent of these children had English as an additional language and there were at least 50 different first languages spoken. Over 2,000 refugee children attended schools in the borough. Minority ethnic communities comprised just under half the total population which was much higher than the national average.

The proportion of Redbridge children with statements of special educational needs (SEN) was below the national figures at both primary and secondary levels. There were, at the time, just over 1,200 children who held a statement meeting their special educational needs, just over 600 of whom were attending mainstream schools.

The LEA maintained 51 primary schools (including nurseries), 17 secondary schools and five special schools. All of the secondary schools had their own sixth form. Some 56 per cent of pupils stayed on in their schools, which was more than twice the national average. Schools were popular both with Redbridge residents and with parents living in neighbouring boroughs.

The project evolved from discussions between the Chief Education Officer, the LEA Advisory Officer whose prime responsibility at the time was special educational needs, a serving primary headteacher and one of the Associate Directors of the International School Effectiveness and Improvement Centre (ISEIC) based at the Institute of Education. The LEA Advisory Officer, Melanie Foster, was committed to developing a network of schools in the borough to share learning and promote inclusion. She was committed to inclusion and she firmly believed that schools working in collaboration to pool expertise would be better placed to generate professional knowledge and skills in order to problem-solve, improve learning and teaching and raise achievement for *all*. The headteacher, Gareth Brooke-Williams, was committed to school improvement. He wanted to share the exciting practice that was developing in his school and to learn with and from others. The HEI partner, Barbara MacGilchrist, had a long track record in school improvement research and practice, and had already worked in partnership with the borough on a number of occasions.

The proposed project had the support of the senior management team within the LEA and of the Corporate Director of the Council. The LEA used Standards funding to help fund the project and during the project the LEA was also able to obtain sponsorship through the British Teachers' International Professional Development programme to fund an exchange visit to a Canadian School District. At the end of the project, funds were also made available by the National College for School Leadership (NCSL) through the Networked Learning Communities Programme (www.ncsl.org.uk/nlc) to enable some release time for one of the headteachers, Margaret Buttress, to begin to write up the research project for dissemination purposes.

A brief description of the schools

The five schools that volunteered to become involved in the project varied in terms of geographical location, ethnicity and size. They had the following characteristics when they joined the project:

- *Churchfields Junior School* was a large four-form entry school catering for 480 children. It served a community that was in the second highest socio-economic group in the borough. There were only a few children from minority ethnic backgrounds but between them they spoke approximately 25 different languages. The percentage of children on free school meals was below the national average. However, the percentage of children with special educational needs statements was above the national average. Baseline attainment on entry for the cohort group in the project was above the national average, but lower than pupils in the previous year. The cohort group was unusual as a high proportion of the pupils were summer born with over 50 per cent having had only seven terms in the infant school on the same site.
- *Highlands Primary School* was a large primary and nursery school with nearly 700 pupils. Over 34 languages were spoken by 84 per cent of the children, many of whom joined the school speaking little or no English. Refugees totalled 6 per cent of the school population. The school experienced high levels of pupil turnover and some characteristics of significant social deprivation. Induction of new children was a constant theme as was the challenge to maintain rigorous target setting processes in order to maximize progress and raise achievement. Baseline attainment upon entry was well below the national average. Low levels of pupil attendance and high levels of unauthorized absence were also a cause for concern. The number of children eligible for free school meals and with special educational needs (30 per cent) was above the national average. Management of the recruitment and turnover of staff was a priority.
- *Ilford Jewish Primary School* was a large voluntary aided two-form entry primary school. There were 528 children on roll, including a 26-place nursery. Five children spoke English as an additional language. The proportion of children on the

special educational needs register (26 per cent) was above the national average. Attainment on entry was average. The percentage of children on free school meals was well below the national average. During the period 1999–2002, the school experienced an 80 percent turnover of staff.

- *Oakdale Junior School* had 350 children aged between 7 and 11. Government statistics showed it to be a school very close to the national average in size, attainment on entry and percentages of SEN and children with English as an additional language. Sixty per cent of the children were from white UK heritage backgrounds and 18 per cent of the children were eligible for free school meals. It was the headteacher of this school who initiated discussions between the LEA and HEI partner about the project. Very sadly, early in the second year of the project he died and this book is dedicated to him. However, the school continued to flourish because the ethos and culture he had been so instrumental in developing, enabled the grief and loss felt by the whole-school community, to be sensitively managed.

- *Parkhill Junior School* was a large community school catering for 432 children. A quarter of the children were from white UK backgrounds and a quarter from white European backgrounds including a small number of refugee children. Another quarter were from Indian families. Other children represented a wide range of minority ethnic groups. Nearly half of the children spoke English as an additional language. The percentage of children entitled to free school meals was below average. Twenty per cent of the children in the school were identified as having special educational needs which was about the national average as was the percentage of children with statements. Children's levels of attainment were broadly average when starting at the school. In the two years prior to the project almost half the staff had left the school, mainly for promotions. Although they had been replaced, the school was finding it increasingly difficult to recruit qualified and experienced teachers.

Our guiding mantra – *'we can if ... '*

A guiding mantra for the project was a view held by all those involved that *'we can if ... '*. This positive view about learners, learning, teaching and achievement stemmed from the values and beliefs underpinning the project described at the beginning of this chapter. We all believed that it is possible for everyone – be they a child or an adult – to learn. As a result, 'yes, but ... ' was eliminated from our discussions. Instead, we embarked on our optimistic journey together determined to make a difference; determined to transform learning and teaching. The chapters that follow describe how we turned our *'we can if ... '* into a practical reality for children and teachers alike.

2

Getting started and keeping going

A journey of a thousand miles must begin with a single step. (Chinese proverb)

> **We can get started and keep going if we:**
>
> - take time to get to know one another and share concerns
> - take time to clarify the purposes of the journey (our learning intentions!)
> - begin to learn how to learn from each other
> - bring the rest of our travelling companions on board
> - collect baseline data
> - share 'highs and lows' along the route and support one another.

The 'round-robin' which dropped on the desks of all Redbridge primary schools was tantalizing. It invited us to participate in an action research project. It spoke of 'a wish to support and promote good practice ... and raise the achievement of all pupils, particularly those with special educational needs'. The project was 'rooted in sound academic research' and a belief in the 'major impact it may have on teaching and learning'. It was anticipated that schools opting into the scheme would develop and gain a further understanding of: brain-based learning, theories of multiple intelligence, emotional intelligence, formative assessment, the behaviours of an intelligent school and strategies for accelerated learning. All this sounded promising and, at that time almost radical – rather like focusing on children's needs again, instead of responding to another centralized initiative: 'If you would like your school to be involved in this project, please return the slip etc. ... '.

So it was, that just five rather tentative headteachers turned up to find out exactly what all this might involve ... and how our children and our schools might benefit. This inauspicious meeting was the start of a long uncharted journey we were to take together. It began with the need for us to get to know and trust one another.

Taking time to get to know one another and share concerns

We took time to get to know one another and share concerns by:

- meeting our travelling companions
- considering 'what's in it for me?'

Meeting our travelling companions

Immediately apparent from the first meeting of the five colleagues, was the broad sweep of the participating schools. Two primary and three junior schools drawn together from different geographical areas within the borough, reflected widely varying socio-economic profiles, levels of attainment, governing bodies, parent bodies, pupil needs and site constraints. How could purposeful and mutual benefits be achieved in such a conglomeration?!

As for the colleagues themselves, an equal range of skills and experience was apparent. Before this intriguing call to a new involvement, those of us in the group had only met intermittently, as professional needs occasioned. We now found ourselves deeply committed together, to a challenging exploration of new expanses. Some with confident, assertive and proactive leadership styles, encountered others with analytical or strategic skills, and yet others who were perhaps more sceptical. Accompanying deputy heads from some of the schools added another broad layer of experience and perspectives.

Considering 'what's in it for me?'

Whilst each of us had our own particular reasons for attending the meeting, everyone was keen to know, 'what's in it for me?' A priority was that attainment would continue to rise in our schools. From various rankings within the league tables, our schools were struggling to meet the demands of a national performance-driven culture. These concerns threatened the provision of a broad and balanced curriculum, and the development of the life skills and intelligences our future citizens so needed. Yet, paradoxically, we were responsible, and held accountable, for achieving those very performance targets whilst we all believed passionately in the development of lifelong learning skills for our children!

Additionally, there were school-specific motives in wondering, 'what's in it for me?' Each school community's profile, and prescribed list of issues to be addressed, were very different. Solutions, common but vital to the wide range of contemporary issues and challenges faced by many schools, were our aim.

Thus, at the outset, expectations of what might be in it for us were high, but doubts abounded. Would it make a real difference for children? Would the group dynamics, and the commitment to the time and reflection expected of us all, deliver sufficient answers to these questions? Were we adding to our workload, inasmuch as we would be doing most of the self-evaluative work ourselves? Would this be feasible on top of day-to-day management and strategic leadership? Would the project enable us to address some of the issues more effectively or creatively? Would it provide appropriate and differentiated professional development to deepen the breadth and quality of our own school's leadership?

As these questions and reservations surfaced, and were expressed, there was genuine concern about our ability to honour the time commitment entailed, over and above our daily workload. We had already realized that the commitments required were considerable. If we were to join the project, its demands would be unremitting, involving attendance at regular meetings, keeping records of progress, collecting data from parents, pupils and staff, evaluating our work in reports to be submitted termly and yearly, and disseminating outcomes with our colleagues. Nevertheless, stimulated and inspired by the refreshing thought of a more penetrating and intuitive approach to teaching and learning, and the quality outcomes it promised for our pupils, we began. This, in fact, was no 'new' initiative, no 'bolt-on' strategy; it was a simple but radical focus on pedagogy – what is taught and learned in the classroom. We sensed we were about to engage with the sentiments of Michael Fullan (1991, p. 117): 'Educational change depends on what teachers do and think – it's as simple and as complex as that'.

Taking time to clarify the purposes of the journey (our learning intentions!)

We took time to clarify the purposes of the journey (our learning intentions!) by:

- deciding our general direction
- clarifying aims and purposes for each school.

Deciding our general direction

Galvanized by Fullan's dichotomy, we considered how we could take this exciting agenda forward in our schools. We began a process of awareness-raising and enquiry around the subject matter. This included listening to overviews on the behaviours of an 'Intelligent School' (MacGilchrist et al., 1997) and a summary of accelerated learning principles from one of our headteacher colleagues, Gareth Brooke-Williams. In addition, we considered the potential role for information and communication technologies (ICT) in our learning, with a visiting consultant.

Despite the obvious moans and groans about workload/overload, we hung on! Our next step was to define the central theme for the borough's research programme. After much broad-ranging discussion, this was defined as: 'Does the development of teachers' and children's metacognitive skills significantly enhance children's achievement in learning?'

We had found this task very difficult. We spent many hours getting a shared understanding about what we meant by metacognition. However, for the sake of progress we chose to proceed, even though some of us were uneasy about the scope of the project and its precision! With the benefit of hindsight, we realized not long into the project that we should have focused on metalearning (learning about learning) rather than metacognition (thinking about thinking) from the outset, but that was where we were four years ago, and this is the account of our evolvement.

Clarifying aims and purposes for each school

Our next step was to translate our question into our own school settings, in order to prepare an individual school bid. This was to be our passport for inclusion in the project. Preparing a bid was, for many of us, a messy process, akin to wandering around in a theoretical fog! What was our working interpretation of metacognition and how was it to be translated and applied in our schools? Our discussions together, and our reflections back in our schools, still engendered some doubts and uncertainties and, somewhat disconcertingly, there seemed to be so much to include. A sifting process to extract and clarify our aims and purposes was now under way.

Several meetings included agenda items requiring us to share and feed back our thinking and emerging strands. Yet, hearing the individual contributions returned from other schools, almost compounded the difficulties – there was so much to consider, and the quality of others' ideas always felt 'better' than our own. Valid and potential ideas were tossed to and fro and duly analysed. For example, we considered:

- self-esteem
- broadening the concept of success
- sharing and celebrating achievement
- feedback
- effective leadership
- sharing knowledge with parents
- planning using visual, auditory and kinaesthetic (VAK) approaches
- improving learning through formative feedback
- enhancing the learning environment
- developing listening skills
- developing teaching styles to better serve different learning styles
- developing collaboration.

The first major hurdle was confronting us head-on. Concepts and objectives had to be clarified, as our equivocation was demotivating. Purposes, so difficult to define, were central to our success!

Gradually, we began to refine our focus and tease out success criteria and the intended outcomes of the project. We detailed the qualitative as well as the quantitative evidence that would inform our judgements by the end of the project. We were coaxed and cajoled by our mentors to peel back the layers of the onion, to be explicit about what we were looking for, and how we would know if we had achieved it. We recognized that the time we had spent seemingly 'lost' on our journey was time well spent as it ultimately enabled us to move forward. We were showing the first signs of developing as learners and of being critical friends.

Beginning to learn how to learn from each other

We began to learn how to learn from each other by:

- learning to trust one another
- learning to cope with support and pressure
- learning to learn with each other.

Learning to trust one another

Our first partnership meetings were spent getting to know each other – our institutions' strengths and the individual and group challenges we faced.

In the early stages, we learned to develop our trust in each other, respecting confidentiality, clarifying purposes and understanding. Yet, we also continued to be drawn by the need to move forward quickly, and to define our work in a more precise way than we were yet able to. This was the time when centralized initiatives were dominating schools' developments – literacy, numeracy, National Grid for Learning (NGfL), inclusion. The national imperative 'to deliver' was paramount and, of course, it was expected that our schools should be the 'delivery vehicles'! As headteachers we needed to drive the initiatives, and negotiate the best possible routes for our children. This was all required post-haste, yet we were now proposing to take on 'something else' over and above these imperatives'! We were still exercised by the precise nature of this 'something else' and grappled with the dilemma. Very gradually, however, through the skills of our mentors, we were confirmed in our desire to take the project forward in spite of the work involved. We were indeed committed to a 'wider' curriculum of lifelong learning for our children.

Our reflections were returning us to the notion of a learning culture rather than a performance culture – one that, as we were learning, would require the investment of time and deep thinking rather than quick-fix solutions. This was why we had all come into teaching in the first place!

As our confidence grew, we learned to challenge and encourage each other. We prevaricated at certain stages, waffled at others, but after a while we began to realize that each school was progressing at its own speed. Progress was not necessarily a tidy or regular process. Changes were effected in fits and starts. Hence, the language of our feedback became less aspirational, and more honest and reflective of where we were, rather than where we would like to have been. We learned to go easier on ourselves in this respect, but our mentors made sure we were still intellectually engaged with the deeper processes of school improvement.

The development of our professional honesty within our partnership, served to highlight that each individual had different strengths to contribute to the group. This reflected their own personal and professional skills, experience and the many achievements of staff in our schools. One member contributed great strategic vision, another was a charismatic leader and a creative thinker. Some of us felt almost inadequate at times! But, at different points, the skills of the quiet analyst or the excellent practitioner came to the fore, sharing the power and quality of the work that had been going on at school, leaving us all stunned! Our honesty also increased the quality and effectiveness of our mutual support. As progress inevitably slowed or regressed in a particular school, we were able to talk openly about it. Together, colleagues would help to put this dip into perspective, recalling progress and achievements that the school had made to date, reminding the downcast leader to hold fast to his/her identified leadership strengths, and aspirations for the school. We were learning to be really open and honest with other headteachers and with our mentors about our strengths and our weaknesses. For the first time we were experiencing the true benefits of 'critical friendship'.

Learning to cope with support and pressure

Our mentors expertly guided the rigours of theory and practice, challenge and debate. Time was given for slow thinking, and looking at how we would 'see' the tangible signs of our theoretical discussions, back at school. At first they would watch and listen as we coached each other. We shared examples of good practice in the classroom or school. But if we skimmed superficially or too confidently over the surface of our learning, they questioned us incisively: 'How has this improved the children's learning?' and 'How do you know?'. We were encouraged to reflect deeply around the processes we had used to effect our developments.

The administrator's role was equally vital in securing our continued progress. Usually a silent partner at our meetings, Lisa was nevertheless the one who kept us all on our toes, once we were back at school. Her gentle reminders that reports were required for approaching deadlines, and her endless patience in ensuring we would all be present at meetings, served to heighten our sense of inclusion, accountability and the rigour that was integral to the project. Her regular mailings would include not only notes from our meetings and copies of our reports, but also relevant articles, and details of books or courses which one member had discovered, and which Lisa would efficiently distribute for our benefit. Her facilitation served to cement our partnership, ensuring we communicated regularly and effectively – even if other pressures meant we were not always so inclined!

Learning to cope with feedback directly from each other, as well as from our mentors was a welcome challenge, but perhaps a less familiar experience within headship. None of us escaped the challenge. After one interview with our mentors, a colleague whose school was glowing from a recent Ofsted report and with future Beacon status assured, came out of the room exhausted by the drilling he'd experienced 'that was pin-down ... worse than any interview – where's the bar?!'

Further challenge and feedback occurred amongst ourselves as we shared our achievements either at our group meetings or during visits to one another's school. We were encouraged to be accountable to each other by making our feedback tangible or visible. 'So, how did that idea work for that child?' One carefully placed question from our mentors or peers could cause much reflection and sometimes pain!

Learning to learn with each other

Our partnership was gradually growing in strength and confidence, as we shared not just best practice, but looked beyond this, to share best process too. We had developed a collegiate dimension to our learning, developing our practice and understanding together, the sum of the parts being greater than the whole.

Such processes could not be expected to run without hitches though. Integral to each meeting was the hidden 'baggage': the body language, which signalled disagreement or despair because, 'I haven't even thought about "x"' or 'I can't do "y" yet, because we're losing half our staff in July!' or 'I don't agree with that', and, 'I'm not doing that!' At times we baulked, plainly feeling overburdened with day-to-day management issues, which deflected us from leadership, strategic and reflective thinking. So often, we came to school on Monday, intending to monitor teaching or developments, or to reflect, only to find by Friday that none of this had been possible, and the original 'to do' list was twice as long! It was as if one of us surfaced, and began to swim, sensing some progress on the journey, whilst another began to flail or drown. So we helped each other through the choppy waters and the crises, until we reached the next sandbank for a rest! Our shared mantra of 'we can if ... ' kept us together on the journey and soon the language of 'yes but ... ' and 'can't because ... ' disappeared from our vocabulary.

It had not been an easy journey thus far. We experienced our early difficulties at three levels. First, we were learning to work together as a new team, enrolled as team members and not as the leaders and decision-makers we were in our own schools. Secondly, each member brought personalized skills to the group, but as it was early days in our partnership and team-building, our individual roles had not yet clarified sufficiently for us to function as an effective team. Thirdly, we were engaging with a complex issue – trying to translate academic research into practical reality.

We experienced frustrations at some meetings as a result. Sometimes the excesses of our rhetoric, hampered the progress, clarity and the pace we expected of ourselves. One or two of us even expressed doubts about continuing, but we were to learn in due course, that action research is a journey, not a destination. It is about processes not ready-made packages. It is by definition, difficult to define at the outset, yet paradoxically, detailed clarification of purpose is central to success.

Discussion could also create diversion! Although carefully planned, some of our debates went off at tangents, which later proved to be fruitless. At first, we felt precious time had been lost, but we came to realize that through the process of getting lost together, we were simultaneously finding our way, clarifying our vision. In so doing we were developing a powerful shared language. A comprehensive understanding of our unwieldy subject matter, and its processes, had now emerged for us. We had clarified its scope and its nature, and over time we absorbed it into our teaching and learning. Formative assessment, raising self-esteem, creating a positive learning environment in which learning could flourish, taking children and staff outside the comfort zone, rigorous use of performance data to ensure progress, developing the emotional intelligence of pupils, the staff and the school itself ... we had understood the perspectives of academia, but at long last we were beginning to own it for ourselves and incorporate it into our school and classroom practice.

However, some of our tangents also proved to be creative. There were 'thinking outside the box' discussions which moved us forwards, so that we knew what our next practical steps would be. Gradually we learned to ease up with formalized agendas and 'go with the flow'. In fact, though we became more creative, and less task focused, we still left with our own action plans on each occasion. The greatest difficulty thereafter was ensuring the momentum was sustained back at school.

Thus, after our early days of soul searching, the group was fully committed to what lay ahead. Our project bids had been accepted, and now we were all 'ticket holders', ready to go! The group included the two mentors, five headteachers and, intermittently, three/four deputy heads, as often as they could be released. Some meetings in the early stages, were also attended by individual LEA advisers, or a corporate director. Now, however, it was time to move forward. We were confident of the core values we shared together, but we needed to share these thoughts, 'get real' with our staff and bring them on board.

Bringing the rest of our travelling companions on board

We brought the rest of our travelling companions on board by:

- understanding the difference in the staffing profiles of our schools
- working with the feelings of staff, – 'what's in it for them?'
- carefully planning the project launch.

Understanding the different staffing profiles of the schools

Our schools and their range of needs were very different. This influenced the way we wanted to launch our individual school projects. Recruitment was a shared concern. Its usual pitfalls, gaps in curricular expertise, pockets of inexperience, affected school continuity and progression, and condemned schools to repeated consolidation rather than school improvement. Yet even these issues soon diversified. Established staff, whilst considered a bonus in some schools, were perceived as energy consumers in others, because the focus was on teachers ... 'we can't do this because ... ' and not on children. Some leaders sought a more radical change of ethos for their school, whilst others wanted to tweak and build on achievements. Budgets were particularly tight for schools with high numbers of experienced staff, constraining investments for inservice provision. Conversely, schools experiencing the inconvenience of longer-term vacancies were for the moment more financially secure, and therefore wanted to be as bold and adventurous as circumstances would allow.

Despite these anomalies, we all desired and felt our staff deserved to benefit from quality input and time for reflection, such as we had learned from in our partnership group. We hoped staff would be convinced that this radical learning-centred approach was the alternative we had all been seeking to offset the pressures of performance.

Working with the feelings of staff, – 'what's in it for them?'

Like us, we felt staff would want to know 'what's in it for me?' How could this 'project' alleviate the day-to-day pressures of planning, pupil support and differentiation, classroom teaching, meeting pupils' needs, assessment, monitoring, initiative overload, and pressures of performance and accountability? This was potentially tricky to manage; indeed, it was potentially compromising, because we did not have the answers either. That is what we hoped our journey would unfold.

As an initial 'leadership' group of headteachers and deputy heads, we had benefited from much active discussion, the receipt of high-quality professional mentoring and the privilege of detailed reflections on the development of a learning culture. Meanwhile, staff in our schools were grappling so valiantly with the latest government initiatives in their classrooms. You may recognize the everyday story of teaching folk – implementing group reading here and plenaries there, getting to know their phonemes from their morphemes, managing large classes, providing differentiated support for many additional needs, whilst the class dynamics change weekly with the effects of pupil mobility, daily with the latest incident to be sorted, and hourly with the latest deadline to be met. Against this backdrop how could we convince our staff we were asking them not to work harder – just smarter?

Lacking answers or solutions at this stage, served only to highlight the dilemma. We knew how resigned teachers had become to providing their own professional development, by repeatedly undertaking the creativity or thought stimulation themselves. So often they had been subjected to 'death by flip charts', or didactic centralized training to kick-start the latest initiative! We rejected these approaches outright. Whatever the schools' starting points were to be, we were committed to the notion that our staff should feel valued as professionals, nurtured, fed, inspired, challenged and motivated, just as we had been.

Carefully planning the project launch

Much time and effort went into planning the launch of the project. We decided to bring the staff from all five schools together for a whole day so that we could all have a shared learning experience. The message we wanted to convey was that this was not just another initiative to be imposed on staff. Instead, the purpose of the day was to reawaken the beliefs and skills that staff held at the beginning of their careers by putting learning centre stage.

And so it was that, after investigation and sampling of providers, almost the entire staff (both teaching and support) from our five schools combined to receive one day's joint training on 'Accelerated Learning in Primary Schools' (ALPS) (Smith and Call, 2000). We approached the Director of Education and our individual governing bodies to request this additional joint training day, because in-service days in our schools had already been taken up by training for the Numeracy Strategy and pre-project School Improvement Plan (SIP) commitments. We hoped this would give the project a high-profile launch, and illustrate the commitments we were investing and expecting.

With nearly 200 staff present, the launch of our project at the end of May 2000 generated a sense of millennial promise, something exciting and full of resolution. We had fun and inspiration, we learned together, yet the serious professional messages for our teaching and support of children's learning were embedded. Ian Harris's energetic delivery of ALPS was the catalyst we had hoped for. Staff found the training information easily accessible, and the experience very valuable. It was a practical model that could be taken and transposed immediately into the classroom. It was also possible to approach the concepts on different entry levels, according to the needs of individuals and schools.

At the same time, the launch carried its risks. It coincided, unavoidably, with the end of the academic year. Several schools were about to experience significant staff turnover at the end of the summer term – up to 13 staff in one instance, after a long period of stability. Some of us were concerned that we might lose the impact of our initiative before it had even begun. We considered a September launch, but that would have delayed the start of the project, and we needed to be up and running with baseline questionnaires completed by July 2000. We were left with little choice other than to continue. As our mantra was always *'we can if ... '*, it was simply decided to change our mindset! Instead, we viewed this as an opportunity: to induct the new staff appointed to.date; to encourage current applications from newly qualified teachers (NQTs) and managers as we were offering a strong commitment to continuing professional development (CPD); to raise the morale of staff remaining; and to signal loudly and clearly, the future potential within our schools.

Slowly, yet noticeably, our staffrooms, variously run down by leavers, summer heat and the usual end-of-year routines, moved up a gear, even at this late stage of the term. There was a palpable sense of curiosity, looking forward to 'something'. Even one or two teaching 'London leavers', sensing they were going to miss out, expressed their regret at having to go now. Professional dialogue was taking place, in some instances for the first time, as staff were challenged or inspired to opinions, for or against accelerated learning techniques. Books were being purchased and photocopied articles were being read.

Collecting baseline data

We collected baseline data by:

- gathering together the end-of-year test results for the project cohort
- using questionnaires to survey children's, teachers' and parents' perceptions about learning.

Gathering test data

Although all of the schools decided that 'Learning to Learn' was to be a whole-school project, for the purposes of our action research we decided to track progress and achievements in learning over the two years for a particular cohort of pupils. We chose the children who would come to the end of Key Stage 2 at the end of the project in 2002. This would enable us to identify the 'value added' for this cohort over the lifetime of the project, and to compare their progress with other schools in the borough. To do this we gathered a range of baseline test data on the cohort.

Using questionnaires

We also wanted to gather some qualitative data from the cohort, their teachers and their parents. In the summer of 2000, therefore, we surveyed our focus cohort to discover the baseline perceptions that existed around and about their learning. It was important for us to understand the children's views about learning, their learning environment, their response to challenge and difficulty and their perceptions of themselves as learners. Teachers' perceptions of both their own and children's learning were equally important to understand, as were the perceptions of parents. These surveys, provided and analysed by the Institute of Education's International School Effectiveness and Improvement Centre, helped to inform our future planning.

As expected, the questionnaires raised a number of issues and sensitivities. It was feared turnover within the pupil cohort could have an impact upon the results – in either direction. Significant staff turnover, it was felt, might skew the teachers' survey. Moreover, would those beset by tiredness at the end of the year reflect negative perceptions, which might be unjust, into the survey? We tried to reduce the potential variables with the pupil survey, by ensuring the questionnaires were administered consistently, by one member of staff. In the event, we reminded ourselves that this was simply a baseline survey, reflecting where we were at that particular moment. Whatever perceptions were held, they were, by definition, valid. At this stage we decided to heed all these concerns whilst not being sidetracked from our aim. We pressed on and looked forwards, rather than questioning or attempting to dilute any information arising from the surveys.

Sharing 'highs' and 'lows' along the route and supporting one another

We shared 'highs' and 'lows' along the route and supported one another by:

- having some early successes
- coping with a great loss
- facing up to difficulties experienced en route
- making tangible progress and growing in confidence.

Having some early successes

During the course of the summer and autumn terms, classroom practice was 'licensed' to include water, brain gym, brain breaks and music. Like the earlier leadership group, staff began to take their first tentative but practical steps with children in the classroom. With the first school year of the project now under way, a range of early developments were noted by schools during the first term. There was already a developing interest in the principles of accelerated learning, with a positive impact on teachers' and teaching assistants' behaviours. It was patchy of course, but the processes were being modelled by a few willing and high-quality practitioners who were making the connections very quickly in their classrooms. Teachers began to suggest changes themselves and then to initiate them. They sought feedback from children to inform their teaching. Some schools noted the favourable impact on children's learning and behaviour management. Children in one school began working collaboratively, sharing, discussing and learning with partners, for the first time. Another school began to share information about pupils' progress more proactively with parents. Focused teacher–pupil dialogue, and sharing marking levels honestly with pupils developed elsewhere, but it was by no means plain sailing. Five 'real' schools had generated some short-term successes but we were also experiencing our share of difficulties and pain.

Coping with a great loss

Our dear headteacher colleague, Gareth Brooke-Williams, became suddenly and seriously ill at the end of our first year, and tragically died in November 2001. His comradeship, good humour and professionalism, his aspirations and determination were an integral part of his visionary leadership, both within the school and the borough. He had been a driving force in establishing the project and building our team. His school had just received an excellent Ofsted report and, unbeknown to him, would later be awarded Beacon status. His death was an incalculable loss to his school, to the borough and to the project.

The greatest professional tribute that we could offer would be to ensure that the project continued to drive forward and achieve the successes he would have wished.

However, the implications of this wish were keenly felt within Gareth's school. At such a time of grief and loss within the school community, could the progress made be sustained through a change of leadership? These were testing times for the school and the acting headteacher.

Facing up to difficulties experienced en route

It was not easy getting started. It involved uncertainties, encouraging staff to take risks, and feel confident about making mistakes in front of each other and in front of the children. Whilst this might have been broadly acceptable to a NQT 'learning the trade', it raised many issues for experienced staff, many of whom were already very good or excellent Ofsted 'graduates'. What would happen for instance if we 'let go' of our usual practices and behaviour management routines, and involved the children more in feeding back their perceptions on the management and teaching of their learning? Simple-sounding challenges were beset with complexities and deep-rooted issues for staff, whatever their level or range of experience. Sometimes it was difficult for school-based staff and the headteacher partnership group to recognize the good work they were actually doing. However, as the going got tough, we constantly reminded ourselves that it was understandable to feel threatened. We were working outside our comfort zone, and this showed we were learning.

Recruitment and retention of teachers was another major issue for us. These difficulties affected the consistent implementation of accelerated learning practices, as we had anticipated. Progress, whilst good in some areas of the schools was in others, patchy, lacking continuity and understanding of the purpose and, sometimes, commitment to the cause.

Significant staff turnover, which coincided with the new school year, meant that, in some cases, developments were barely recognizable as schools directed their initial efforts towards the induction training and support of staff before they could begin to move forward.

Another challenge was that some staff reflected different perceptions from the headteachers as project implementation got under way. School leaders advised class teachers to 'start small', taking an agreed area such as the display of learning maps and working it gradually into practice. Then the plan was that staff were encouraged to share quality outcomes, learning from each other. The reality for teachers, however, was that they started big. In their enthusiasm, they wanted to try everything immediately, and there were subsequent reports of feeling overwhelmed and reverting quickly to smaller and more manageable steps.

Within the headteacher partnership group, we also realized that we were moving quickly beyond the practical experiences of accelerated learning, to consider much deeper issues. We were involved in a learning process not a 'package' of ideas to be implemented. Paying attention to the literature of school improvement, meta-learning and metacognition, we became aware that there were neither any 'quick fixes', nor were there many practical examples of building capacity in schools that we could learn from. Again we found ourselves at the cutting edge, learning about our learning as a school, and trying to translate this into practical reality. What did all this look like in our schools?

Making tangible progress and growing in confidence

Partnership within our leadership group was now developing, and we were beginning to work more effectively as a team. Through a combination of support and pressure from our mentors, we developed a spirit of mutual trust, recognizing, and learning from, the strengths contributed by each participant. We received regular focused visits from our mentors, who also ensured that we attended meetings and submitted the required evaluations. One such evaluation involved the headteachers writing a mid-project progress report. The focus of the report was the identification of changes in the behaviours of children and staff. The reports we presented to one another demonstrated the progress that had been made across our schools:

> The focus of the project was in Y5, but it became a whole-school learning experience. In the course of the year there were continuous developments phased in slowly through an action plan. However, it took five terms before everything clicked into place. Since then it has been uplifting to see how much change has actually taken place.

> 'We can if ... ' attitudes have finally prevailed, after the tortuous years of 'we can't because ... ' this has been the greatest step forward for the school. The development of a whole-school shared language for school improvement,

focused on teaching and learning and aspiration is evolving as a result.

The atmosphere in the school and the practice of staff for the start of term was markedly different from previous years.

The most exciting developments have been the children's growing awareness of their own preferred learning styles ... staff are now much more aware of the need to vary teaching styles to ensure that various groups gain greater access to the curriculum.

The physical environment has been addressed. Water, sound systems and CDs are available in all classrooms. Displays in the classrooms, including learning maps, are related to visual cueing for the knowledge/concepts being taught. Codes of behaviour and values that are being focused on are displayed. Teachers are trialling different classroom layouts to suit differing teaching styles.

Planning identifies key questions for evaluation. Teachers are focusing on developing a balance of visual, auditory and kinaesthetic activities, and being more specific about learning intentions and plenary questions.

The curriculum has not been compromised – there is evidence of all National Curriculum subjects and other discreet teaching – we are trying to create a learning community, and not a school pursuing high SAT results. The project can be used to enhance preparation for the tests.

When talking to the children about the changes they used the words 'fun' and 'enjoyment' about school, and felt staff were available to listen.

Our reports reflected our growing confidence in pursuit of school improvement and radical change. This meant that whilst one school pursued ALPS approaches more exclusively, others began to 'cherry-pick' from a more eclectic mix of methods and approaches, gathered in the borough and from national and international research and practice.

We recognized that although we were not all pursuing exactly the same path, we were all moving forward in a similar direction, and sharing many of the same processes and inherent difficulties we were unearthing on the way. The added bonus was that there were corresponding improvements in national test results too. It was great to have come this far and to see what had been achieved on our journey of learning about learning. We embarked on the second year of the project with renewed enthusiasm and determination.

In the chapters that follow we describe in detail the range of practical strategies we deployed across the two years.

Conclusion

We conclude by:

- ▪ reviewing what we did
- ▪ reflecting on what we learned.

Reviewing what we did

We:

- formed a network group of headteachers
- clarified our project focus thus far, as being the impact of metacognition on children's progress
- defined each school's project focus
- learned about the profiles of participating schools
- planned a grand launch for the project
- gathered baseline data in order to inform our action plans and our evaluations of the success of the project.

Reflecting on what we learned

We learned:
- the importance of clear purpose when defining the research focus
- that time spent carefully considering the manageabilities and sensitivities of workload pressures for class teachers is a good investment for the success of the project
- that investing in high-quality training for *all* staff reaps a rich harvest of learning.

By the end of the first year of the project we had also learned a great deal about the factors that need to be taken into account to enable schools to collaborate with one another effectively. We identified twelve:

Commitment Each headteacher needs to be committed to working collaboratively with other schools so that 'what's in it for me?' becomes 'what's in it for us?' Learning may be different for each school, but collective learning enhances the singular lessons learned. Also, it is important that each headteacher is intellectually engaged, and personally involved with the group's process of enquiry and research, in order to 'drive' the learning processes that are unleashed during the enquiry.

Confidence and conviction Each headteacher needs to come to the partnership with a degree of confidence about themselves as leaders and about their schools. This involves personal and professional convictions that 'we can make a difference if … '. A sign of a successful partnership is that personal and group confidence grow and grow.

Trust and respect Learning to trust and be open with one another, and to value the contribution that each person has to make, are essential ingredients of a successful partnership. This involves skills of active listening, incisive questioning, collegiate support, and the ability to work effectively both as a leader and a follower within a group. It also requires deeper reflections that recognize potential, as well as need, in the personal strengths and weaknesses of both self and others.

Shared values and beliefs The partnership needs to be underpinned by a shared set of values and beliefs. For us these concerned our commitment to inclusive education for *all* in the context of the provision of a broad and balanced curriculum. Our guiding mantra was *'we can if ... '*.

Knowledge about one another No two schools are the same, so learning about one another's context is very important. With this shared knowledge and understanding the group can support one another in implementing ideas and developing strategies to bring others on board.

Knowledge creation and transfer Working together to problem solve, to generate new ideas, to try them out, to review and evaluate the learning and then to disseminate and spread what works, ensures that the group, as David Hargreaves (2003) puts it, 'learns to do things differently in order to do them better' (p. 27).

Clarity of purpose Agreement about shared aims and purposes of any joint project whilst not easy to achieve is essential to enable the group to have a clear focus and sense of direction.

Robust working practices Agreement about the respective roles and responsibilities of each member of the group is important, as is the provision of some administrative support. The establishment of agreed ways of working and keeping to them from the outset enable a group to stay together and function effectively. This requires much discipline on behalf of all those involved. It requires a determination not to be distracted by crisis management and to guard the diary and learn to say no. Careful planning, good communication, timetabled meetings in advance at which attendance is expected, are all useful strategies for keeping the group together, maintaining momentum and enabling colleagues to stay on task.

Risk-taking and working beyond the 'comfort' zone If transformation of practices is the aim then there will inevitably be an element of risk taking by members of the group. Colleagues need to be prepared to 'think outside the box'. They need to experience a degree of discomfort, as this is a sign that 'deep' as opposed to 'shallow' learning is taking place.

Supportive challenge Constructive feedback, critical friendship and sharing what worked (and what did not) enable the partners to learn with and from one another. The role of external partners is integral to this process and can help to ensure a degree of objectivity across the partnership.

Rigorous data-gathering and evaluation Two questions in particular need to guide the partnership: 'Have we made a difference?' and 'How do we know?' To be able to answer these questions requires an agreement about the evidence to be gathered at the outset, during and at the end of a project and who will do this and how. It is only through systematic data-gathering that a group of schools can assess the value that working together has added. Such an approach combines assessment for learning with a summative evaluation at certain points in time.

Sustainability Michael Fullan (2004) argues that sustainability 'requires continuous improvement, adaption and collective problem-solving in the face of complex challenges that keep arising' (p. 8). Long-term improvement takes time, energy and a willingness to cope with peaks and troughs along the way. A recognition of these challenges can bind the group together and, when necessary, help to re-energize and refocus efforts in the collective determination to make a difference to learners, be they children or adults.

3

Developing our teaching practice to enhance pupils' learning

In times of change, learners will inherit the earth, whilst the learned will find themselves beautifully equipped to deal with a world that no longer exists. (Hoffer)

We can develop our teaching practice to enhance pupils' learning if we:
- **encourage thinking skills and learning skills**
- **develop the 'language of learning' in classrooms**
- **stimulate the learning brain**
- **develop emotional intelligence.**

Encouraging thinking skills and learning skills

We encouraged thinking skills and learning skills by:

- moving towards a learning orientation
- identifying the changes to be made in classroom practice.

The changes that occurred within our classrooms were informed by two fundamentals. First, as teachers, we re-committed ourselves to the belief that we should focus primarily on learning as opposed to performance. We resolved to do so with confidence and commitment not least, because professional self-esteem had been severely dented during latter years. Secondly, we became convinced that a concentration on learning would better equip our pupils with lifelong learning skills, and the knowledge and skills of a broader and more balanced curriculum. Superficially, these fundamentals may sound like a pretty easy subscription for teachers and schools to make. However, the reality was a little more daring. If, as teachers, we felt a performance orientation was not working in the best and wider learning interests of our pupils, then it was beholden upon us professionally, following careful evaluations, to make the appropriate changes to the curriculum, and the ethos within our schools. This effectively questioned our compliance with national pre-scription, the notion of teaching to 'one-size fits all' strategies, unrealistic targets and higher test results. A simple but renewed emphasis on learning, actually meant taking some complex, calculated professional risks!

That being said however, we needed to stand back, and evaluate for ourselves, the profession's learning points through the dark days of prescription. It was vital to ensure that we were not compromising the real achievements made during the pro-tracted national debate. Implicitly within our schools rather than explicitly within league tables, these achievements had led to standards, achievement and progress being defined more rigorously and explicitly for the benefit of individual pupils. With all this in mind we began to focus more and more on learning.

Moving towards a learning orientation

An overview of the discussions which clarified our thinking regarding a perfor-mance versus learning orientation was helpfully illustrated in Chris Watkins's com-parative model (Watkins et al., 2001, p. 2). See Figure 3.1.

'Learning orientation' *Concern for improving one's competence*	'Performance orientation' *Concern for proving one's competence*
• Belief that effort leads to success • Belief in one's ability to improve and learn • Preference for challenging tasks • Derives satisfaction from personal success at difficult tasks • Uses self-instructions when engaged in task	• Belief that ability leads to success • Concern to be judged as able, concern to perform • Satisfaction from doing better than others • Emphasis on normative standards, competi-tion and public evaluation • Helplessness: evaluate self negatively when task is difficult

Figure 3.1 Chris Watkins's comparative model
Source: Watkins et al., 2001, p. 2.

We recognized of course that we were not dealing with an either/or. There is a continuum between learning and performance orientations and what we wanted to do was to redress the current imbalance between the two. We knew only too well that children have to learn to deal with competitive situations when their perfor-mance is under scrutiny. But, our firm belief was that they could face up to such challenges so much more successfully if they developed the characteristics of a per-son with a learning orientation. To turn the bullet points in the left-hand column in Figure 3.1 into a practical reality for children, we thought long and hard about the changes we needed to make to current practice in the classroom.

Identifying the changes to be made in classroom practice

At the beginning of our project, the borough's defined focus was metacognition, thinking about thinking. This included the metacognitive processes of 'planning monitoring, reflecting upon and self-regulating one's own learning' (Gipps and MacGilchrist, 1999).

As we have already indicated, we soon realized that these processes had but a part to play in the much wider process of metalearning. Learning about learning included reflecting and 'making sense of one's experience of learning'. It was laden with the subjective emotions and approaches we bring to our learning, the 'goals, feelings, social relations and context of learning' (Watkins et al., 2001, p. 1). Therefore, the challenge for our practitioners was to create the classroom context in which our learners could develop a more extensive learning disposition, no matter what their predilection. The schools defined the scope and range of this intent in their project bids, and these duly informed the changes we sought to make in our practice:

Raising achievement of *all* children by increasing their understanding of how they learn, and adapting teaching styles to facilitate and energize this process.

Raising achievement and attainment of *all* pupils through sharing with them the analysis of their preferred learning styles; establishing their individual intelligence profiles; sharing the knowledge with parents; planning teaching and learning activities with specific reference to VAK preferences; ways to improve learning through formative feedback.

To further develop a positive learning environment and climate for *all* members of the school community.

To develop teacher skills in planning a range of classroom interventions that respond to the needs of a range of styles.

To raise achievement through heightening children's self-esteem.

So how did we effect these changes to rediscover the fresh taste of learning within our schools? Many of our strategies detailed below, whilst familiar to teachers, may of course be used superficially or in isolation. However, carefully 'cherry-picked' by our schools, these individual strategies were ingredients for a much larger and juicier recipe – our fruit cocktail for successful learning!

It is important to stress a health warning here. This collection of ideas is not a 'package', and we are by no means purporting this to be 'the way' for other schools to follow. We developed these practical approaches through our own lengthy processes of school self-evaluation and reflection. Our schools followed what is detailed below to a lesser or greater extent, according to individual needs. What was common between us, however, was that whatever strategies we used, they were connected to the 'big picture' – to the values and beliefs underpinning our project. The purpose of each strategy was ultimately to achieve our inclusion and lifelong learning agenda. We were determined to ensure that all our children had access to high-quality learning experiences that would have long-term benefits.

Developing the 'language of learning' in our classrooms

We developed the 'language of learning' in our classrooms by:

- hearing the language of learning
- understanding the language of learning
- speaking the language of learning
- seeing the language of learning.

In acquiring any new language, a student needs to progress through certain stages before becoming proficient in its use. So it was both for our staff and children, for all of us were learners together. Our wish to develop a 'common language' of learning, referred to in Chapter 2, presupposed that if 'the language' was to be meaningful, it first needed to be heard. After some immersion in hearing the language, we believed increased levels of confidence would encourage the second phase of speaking it to and with others. A fuller understanding could then emerge in the third stage as the conversants began to communicate with each other, understanding the nuances and its richness.

However, Chris Watkins's model illustrates just how 'process rich' this language is. Therefore to reach a full understanding, the semantics needed careful but precise translation in order to be articulated into our classroom practice. As our project unfolded, it meant we needed to be quite deliberate about sharing our understanding, and clarifying any misconceptions that might occur.

Hearing the language of learning

In order to hear the language of learning, we considered how we could 'hear' it at the point of entry to the research project. We looked at teachers' practice, school policies and curriculum planning. We 'listened' for any correspondence between current practice and the active learning we were seeking. In order to 'hear it' we had to know the language was based in practicalities, so that we could progress to speak about tangible classroom practice.

We were able to pinpoint current 'learning-friendly' practice within our school policies, SIPs and classrooms. There were good things going on but they needed to be connected more explicitly with our 'big picture'. So, we began to identify our learning points and the amendments that needed to be made to curriculum and lesson planning.

Over time, as we were able to listen more acutely for the language of learning, it led several schools to conduct in-depth reviews of the quality of their long-, medium- and short-term planning, in order to provide a curriculum honed for lifelong learning. A return to topic approaches and blocking units of work were features that ensured learning was given an appropriate context and was more holistic. Literacy sessions were reviewed to create greater links between literacy and the rest of the curriculum. The skills developed were seen as a valuable and essential means of communication throughout life learning, and not as a discreet area of learning for one hour a day. Time spent on the speaking and listening components of the National Curriculum was increased, enabling children to make the essential progress needed to become confident communicators. This was also planned for systematically, in schemes of work. Extra time was allocated for extended and independent writing to ensure pupils had opportunities to develop creative writing skills, and could draft, improve and complete pieces of work to their own personal satisfaction.

Such initiatives were much longer-term outcomes in our quest to develop a learning-orientated curriculum, but to begin with we started with very simple measures. We began in this way for two reasons. First, we wanted to make the project work manageable and accessible for everyone to sign up to. Secondly, we assumed that by taking small steps, it ensured everyone knew what they were supposed to be doing!

Teachers were asked to prepare a display to share with pupils (and parents), which reflected medium-term plans. The purpose of this was to enable pupils to share in the language of learning, and begin to hear it in a systematic way. Rather like a jigsaw, it showed an entire picture of the term's planned learning but, where necessary, there could also be a focus on separate pieces – chunks of knowledge or skills to be acquired. The children's awareness that all these little pieces could come together to make a significantly larger whole, encouraged their commitment to and ownership of the purpose for each lesson or piece of learning, especially if difficulties were encountered. This 'big picture', provided a visual illustration of the interconnectedness of the planned learning, and the incremental development of knowledge and skills. Teachers began to discuss the content and the context of this learning with their pupils, so that they too could 'hear' about its wholeness rather than its disparate skills or subjects. The connection of this learning to wider life experiences also meant pupils 'heard' about its relevance to everyday life. This listening promoted a purpose and pupils' enthusiasm for, and commitment to, learning as an end in itself.

Our schools displayed these 'big pictures' as three-dimensional mobiles, or in two-dimensional format on display boards, charts or pieces of paper. Older pupils responded well to mind maps. Younger children enjoyed the information displayed in many different ways, such as a train, to enhance the notion of a learning journey. The term's contents or skills, within each area of the curriculum, were represented in words, or pictorially, in each separate carriage. In a nursery, it was presented as a flower, with each of the areas of experience shown within a petal, and made accessible to the children through pictures and photographs. Parents engaged with this as they came in and out of the nursery, and it helped them to see the wholeness of the child's curriculum, as well as the development of their knowledge and skills through play. These are just some practical ideas for the reader, but how it is presented is really not as important as the learning intention behind it.

Children and teachers referred to the display to reflect on the purpose or progress of individual lessons against the whole. Children commented:

> The big picture has pictures that relate to our subject, this helps us understand what we're learning. By seeing what we are learning we can prepare and get more information on what we are learning. It gives us an idea of what we will be learning about during the school term.

> The big picture is of use for a majority of children and me as when I look at it' and read it through it helps me to understand what we are going to learn and it gives us a head start. Moreover if somebody else does not understand anything they have an opportunity to ask questions which helps us to learn.

Early skills of time management developed as pupils were able to articulate that, 'we can't do this yet, but by the end of this lesson we will be able to ... and by the end of this term it will mean we can ... '. They also used the big picture retrospectively, to recognize achievements and progress. 'At the beginning of term I didn't know how to do a forward roll correctly, but I've learned these skills, so now I can!' The big picture display was a powerful tool to encourage a new dialogue of metalearning and metacognition.

Simple as this process may sound, the early implementation phase was, of course, trickier. Actually sharing the big picture with children and parents was difficult for some staff. Some felt they might be opening up their past practice to criticism and this added to the feeling of unease about the project. For such staff it was important to proceed slowly and carefully, and start with strategies they could accept such as displaying learning intentions for individual lessons. As this new practice became embedded in everyday classroom practice, the children helped to keep the momentum going by making such comments as 'you've forgotten the learning objective!' This in turn encouraged staff to begin to open up the 'big picture' more and more.

There were others who were ready to have a go at the 'big picture' straight away. At first they found it challenging to engage with 'the language of learning' and to 'hear' it sufficiently well to impart it. 'Just what should we display for children in a "big picture" display? What should be included/left out? What level of detail was required? Would it be too complicated? Should every subject be represented? Should we focus on the knowledge or the skills to be developed, or both? What about differentiation, and what messages were we sending about inclusion, if some of the children may not be covering some of the knowledge?'

Careful thought and discussion took place in planning and staff meetings. In the end, staff were simply encouraged to have a go at presenting a year-group format, so that the planning and effort involved was shared and the outcome standardized. There was no right or wrong way. Teachers were just encouraged to present their big picture in an attractive and appealing way for reference by the children. Thereafter, some teachers shared the outcomes by visiting each other's classrooms, and gradually learned different child-friendly ways to present this important overview of planned learning. Initial concerns did not last long, meaning new staff were seamlessly inducted into this approach thereafter. We had begun 'to hear the language of learning'.

Understanding the language of learning

After first hearing the language of learning, the next stage was to understand it, through constant immersion in its rich and process-laden vocabulary. Understanding the language would later enable us to speak it.

Thus 'learning-teachers' helped 'learning-pupils' to understand that each one of them had their own profile and identity as a learner. They began to explore the notion that a better understanding of individual approaches to learning would help pupils to learn better, and teachers to teach better. Thus, plenary sessions not only evaluated the curricular learning of knowledge and skills that had taken place but they also evaluated developing skills of metalearning, through the simplest questions: 'what are the things that helped you to learn today?', or 'did anything happen to stop you from learning?' or 'how do you learn best?' or, 'what kind of support is helpful to you when you are working?' The information returned was akin to a lottery windfall!

Recognizing the challenge to adapt classroom practice to meet these identified learning preferences, teachers included visual, auditory and kinaesthetic stimuli into their weekly planning. They ensured activities and interactions, which were compatible with these approaches, by introducing appropriate pictures, sound or movement. Visual, auditory and kinaesthetic planning raised the importance of such provision, and subject leaders monitored its implementation, in order to maximize the school's provision and the individual's capacity for learning. This use of other sensory dimensions to learning, helped to improve the learner's concentration or facilitated the learning. Effectively this meant that much of what teachers would recognize as basic good practice was already pursued, but with a revised layer of understanding: 'Aha! That is why it works!'

Early years practitioners continued to douse children in first-hand experience, with renewed vigour, increasingly empowered to resist national or even school-based imperatives. These, we realized, had effectively served to block crucial early developments in the language of learning. Mathematics materials encouraged concrete and tactile approaches. Creative writing was stimulated through banks of resources, such as music, photos, pictures, artefacts, music and recorded sounds. History was rooted in artefacts and use of primary sources wherever possible. Geography was enhanced by field trips to bring the subject matter to life. In their long-term planning, teachers and subject co-ordinators gave considerable thought to the development of appropriate resources, in order to provide a classroom and a curriculum enriched with opportunities for visual, auditory and kinaesthetic cues. The focus, therefore, was not only on what was to be learned, but how.

Teachers also considered their own learning preferences, to understand how these might influence their teaching style. For example, how much they moved in class or travelled around, their proximity and practical help might appeal to kinaesthetic learners; their gestures and the objects they showed might appeal to visual learners; the variety of homework they set to suit the different learning styles; the information imparted, with a range of 'telling it' for auditory learners, 'reading it' for visual learners, or perhaps introducing it through a task for kinaesthetic learners.

Increasingly aware of pupils' learning preferences, we did not try to pursue exclusive approaches aimed at enhancing a particular learning style. Rather, we ensured that the three sensory channels were integrated into our teaching, understanding that we seldom use just one channel for our learning.

All staff learned to use the abundance of information returned to them through their knowledge of the learning styles of individual pupils. The observations of support staff were particularly helpful to teachers in enhancing provision, developing better understanding and, therefore, meeting the needs of the children. Kinaesthetic pupils tend to move about, fidget, wriggle or tap. Some were provided with stress balls to manipulate as the teacher talked, or even allowed to doodle, if it helped to sustain their listening skills. Others, who may in the past have seemed inattentive or insubordinate as they looked out of the window or away from the teacher, were now recognized as auditory learners, and not necessarily challenged to 'look at me' any more – except to check understanding.

Speaking the language of learning

Our learning communities, increasingly exposed to the language of learning, now began to use it for themselves. The more it was used, the more proficiently it was expressed by teachers and pupils alike. Big pictures, which featured within our classrooms, were joined by other systematically introduced initiatives.

For example, all lessons had focused objectives and success criteria which were shared explicitly with the children in the manner suggested by Shirley Clarke (2001): 'We are learning to … ' (WALT) and, 'What I'm looking for' (WILF). Learning was broken down into chunks, and explained within the wider context of the longer-term plans and the real world. To reinforce intent, objectives were displayed visually, in each lesson, for the benefit of children and adults who may be working with them. Learning intentions were sometimes broken down again, into group objectives for differentiated or guided work, appearing on tables for group-specific reference. In some cases learning intentions were sent home to parents to assist more focused discussion. 'What did you learn today?' rather than, 'What did you do?' meant that the language of learning was beginning to have an impact in the home as well. Such approaches helped us to engage more effectively in a learning-specific dialogue with parents, and to evaluate progress.

Key words connected to learning were displayed within the classroom, so that pupils were able to access the routes to widen their vocabulary, building it appropriately into their work, or discourse. For children developing English as an additional language, such words or key phrases provided vital scaffolds for their learning, in addition to the modelling of English provided by their teachers or some of their peers. Amazingly, as our language of learning became tangible, we noted how pupils learning English as an additional language, efficiently incorporated more abstract reflective and process speech into their everyday vocabulary.

We also engaged pupils in daily evaluations and reflections on how they were learning – how they learned best, what they found difficult, how they overcame difficulty, what or who helped or hindered them in their learning? We borrowed Shirley Clarke's list of self-evaluation questions (2001, p. 41) for children – such as 'what really made you think/did you find difficult while you were learning to ... ?' – and with low threat and no-blame discussions, through mechanisms such as plenary sessions, circle time or guided groups, ensured that teachers were presented with valuable information to inform future planning and future teaching for learning. In fact, pupils became so empowered that supply teachers were challenged occasionally if they had not provided opportunities for the usual explicit learning dialogue. This involved the giving and receiving of feedback that pupils found so helpful and quickly became accustomed to.

Staff were careful to ensure the language they and the pupils used was always affirmative. Classrooms were redefined either as 'no put-down zones', or 'put-up zones'. These were referenced in class codes of conduct, which children signed up to, and were displayed prominently as you entered the room. Peer pressure mechanisms described below were particularly effective in helping children to self-regulate their behaviour. In practice, for any group of children working together, it was used as follows. If positive encouragement or a compliment was given by one individual towards another/others in the group, the speaker was rewarded by a simultaneous 'thumbs-up' from within the group. If a speaker used derogatory terms about his/her own work or self, the group showed a 'thumbs down', to raise awareness of the self-deprecation being practised. On the other hand, if one member of the group insulted the work or traits of another, the group simultaneously 'clawed' their hands towards the perpetrator. Nothing was said, but feedback to the recipient was powerful and startlingly effective. The children felt very positive about these strategies:

> I feel that the no put-down zones have been very effective at stopping put-downs in the classroom. The claw is very good at making people know they are putting somebody down or upsetting them and that they should stop. One example of when no put-down zones have worked well is in the classroom when a child puts their hand up to answer a question and gets the question wrong, the person will not be laughed at.

> If someone does something bad, you can show them the sign and it makes me feel happy that they know how I feel.

> It makes us safe.

Teachers also helped pupils to develop a different mindset towards the challenges they experienced whilst working. As a task became difficult and perseverance waned, staff encouraged the learners working outside their comfort zone. 'You're finding that hard? Wow! That's really great, keep going now, because it means you are just about to learn something new! We can celebrate in a minute!' Later, opportunities for metalearning and metacognitive reflection followed with the class. 'Fantastic! How did you learn that? What did you say to yourself to keep yourself going? Who helped you and how? Which bit did you find difficult? Why do you think that was? What have you learned about the way you learn, that you will be able to apply next time you find something difficult?'

In strategies learned from neurolinguistic programming (NLP), language used by staff presupposed success at all times, and permitted no reference to failure. Language was affirmative, not conditional. 'When [not if] you swim that first width today, we will all cheer as you reach the other side, and you can show your certificate to the headteacher when you get back to school!' Staff at local swimming baths unknowingly confirmed the success of such strategies, when they volunteered amazement and admiration for children's positive determination and their sense of shared success and mutual encouragement.

Some staff did an NLP diploma and were asked to reflect on how they had been putting the training into practice. A nursery teacher had this to say:

> We have focused on using positive language when giving instructions to children. We have reinforced good behaviour using praise and have tried to eliminate use of words like 'naughty', 'good' etc. When reprimanding children we have used language like 'I don't like it when' or 'It makes me feel sad when you snatch things from your friends.' In this we aim to make children feel positive about themselves. We encourage children to develop confidence by doing as much as they can for themselves, e.g. pouring drinks, putting on coats. We have used music for tidy up time and this has proved successful.
>
> Children have responded well. They enjoy doing things for themselves and develop self-esteem through their achievements. The use of positive language encourages good behaviour.

As part of the language for learning, children were encouraged to visualize success, and how it would feel, through direct appeals to their senses. 'What will you see/hear/smell/taste? What will you be doing? What will you be wearing? Who will be there? What are they doing?' The teachers' language evoked both the proximity and the reality of success waiting to be grasped.

Such visualization allowed children to manage their fears and anxieties over aspects of their learning, whilst in the security of the safe setting. It was useful in

many settings where emotions were aroused, and particularly useful in test preparation or mathematics. 'What worries you when you come to take a test? When
does this happen? When does it start? How does it start? How do you feel? What do
you see/hear/smell there?' The same type of questions applied to positive experiences provided the teacher with the ammunition to promote pupils' relaxation
exercises, in the face of anxiety. This was a practical tool to freeze-frame declared
fears and literally reduce them in the mind's eye. For example, sensory anxieties
experienced on entry to a test room were explored, then 'maximized', as on a computer screen. Then pupils were trained to 'minimize' the picture into a corner, and
substitute their own maximized vision of relaxed learning.

Success was also presupposed within the 'magic circle', an imaginary place for children to place their emotional props, and take with them as they faced their challenge.
A tool to manage peer pressure, tests, bullying, 'hard maths', public speaking – its uses
were endless. 'What do you need with you to help you to succeed?' Visualizing/
smelling/hearing the chosen components, the child, group or class physically placed
them in the magic circle, before finally stepping inside it him/herself to 'feel' the success. As seen with ace tennis stars or football players, these visualizing techniques
were powerful tools on the road to success, but for our learners it also developed the
language of emotional intelligence. As one child described:

> I remember when I felt a bit down and unconfident in maths. When (my
> teacher) saw how I felt, she came over to me and said to follow her, so I did.
> She told me to put my hands to my chest and take out the bad and good feel-
> ings about maths. I did this. She also said my hands were cups, holding my
> emotions for maths. I spilt my good emotions for maths in the bad one. 'Don't
> do that!' She (my teacher) burst into a fit of giggles. We laughed for ages, then
> I did as I was told, and put both of them back into my body. I was learning to
> live with difficulty. It really worked and boosted my confidence in maths.

Children were also encouraged to talk through their learning processes to aid understanding:

> Pole-bridging is a deliberate attempt to connect-up internally our own under-
> standing using the appropriate language. (Smith and Call, 2000, p. 199)

In our classrooms teachers helped to facilitate the 'aha!' factor. They encouraged pupils
to talk through and describe what they were doing. Their use and manipulation of
appropriate language strengthened neural pathways. Talking through what they were
doing helped children to make stronger connections and embed the new knowledge.

Seeing the language of learning

The processes described above were enhanced by the teachers' use of display. This
enabled pupils to see and read the language of learning which was becoming famil-

iar to them. Over time, both the content and the quality of these displays raised issues for further consideration within our schools. For instance, some developed teacher-generated 'learning resource displays' to provide information and reference with provision of key words, or learning points. Others felt it was important to hold fast to the wider purpose for display – provision of a comfortable and attractive learning environment, which displayed and valued each child's best effort, no matter how small, in order to enhance self-esteem. A third approach, perhaps seen more generally within our schools, was a blend of these two extremes.

One headteacher summarized the approach in her school: 'Classroom display was felt to have a mixture of informative displays and children's work in the classrooms. A list of "must haves" was drawn up and staff were monitored in class for these. They included displays of key words connected to literacy, maths and topic; a world map on display with key locations being identified; display of class rules, water rules, whole-school behaviour and playground rules and bilingual signs.'

The compromise described above was as likely to reflect metalearning processes, as to display the child's end product: 'How well do you think these writers have worked together to assess the character of Tracy Beaker?' From initial class discussions or group brainstorms on the qualities of a particular character, the display may also reflect the children's resultant writing, the teacher's framework and their joint evaluative questions or paired assessments, manifesting active plenary processes, and evaluations and reflections within metacognitive and metalearning realms.

Some of these classroom 'process' displays were, however, more temporary in nature, and therefore did not necessarily reflect usual display standards. An example might be group feedback to an individual on the enabling role played in task-work. Children's group reflections on a large sheet of sugar paper on what they knew about the mathematics topic of the week was another example of 'work in progress'. These displays were left pinned up for all to see and read. At the end of the week each group shared with the rest of the class the learning that had taken place. Later, these became useful revision tools. However, this needed some careful thought because of the potential impact on qualitative display standards expected. Purposes needed to be clarified, and understood by all staff, so that standards/expectations were maintained. More particularly, for some, the enhancement of self-esteem was a priority, so children needed to know where their work was displayed, if it was moved outside the class, whilst learning focused or didactic display remained within it.

Stimulating the learning brain

We stimulated the learning brain by:

- understanding basic physiology
- brain food
- brain training
- activating the senses to support learning.

Understanding basic physiology

Daniel Goleman's work on emotional intelligence (1996; 1998), the ALPS training received and NLP diplomas gained, meant some school staffs were equipped with an understanding of the basic physiology of the brain and the way that biological and environmental factors impinge upon successful learning. Teachers shared this information with the children, so that they too understood factors of brain processing, given certain circumstances. Together, teachers and pupils recognized that if they had come into class stressed, tired or anxious, it was unlikely that effective learning would take place. For some children, exhibiting extreme circumstances or needs, such understanding helped to open new channels of communication, in terms of effective anger management. Together, we could discuss what was happening physiologically, why they had lost control of their behaviour, how they could regain control of the situation, and suggest ways in which they could dispel their own anger.

Teachers also helped pupils to recognize that the everyday difficulties they experienced as they were doing their work were, in fact, positive. 'I can't do this' did not mean you were stuck, it meant you were about to learn something new. We explored with the children how they might develop the connections and make that learning happen for themselves, without recourse to a teacher, perhaps by consulting a partner, or by asking questions to enable their own learning, or by consulting posters around the room. Gradually, as these strategies took effect, we began to realize that our encouragement of independent and resourceful learners was freeing up teachers to teach.

Brain food

We encouraged our pupils to understand the need for appropriate brain sustenance in a variety of ways. Bringing water into the class ensured their brains would be well hydrated and therefore in the optimum physical condition for learning. Some schools had drinking water plumbed into each room, others provided water dispensers and others simply asked the children to bring bottles in each day. Each school had its own way of implementing the practicalities. Classroom organization concerns centred on the possibility that children may abuse this facility by increased visits to the toilet, or by spilling their drinks on their work. Various contingencies were set up to avoid the pitfalls, such as keeping bottles in an accessible area away from desks, storing bottles in plastic boxes on the tables and so on.

Water is now a much more common and accessible element within many classrooms around the country, so schools may be generally aware of some of the reservations and potential doubts that can be expressed when introducing it. Suffice it to say, we had the same thoughts, but at the end of the day our concerns were unfounded. Children did not take endless trips to the toilet, or abuse the privilege, and where any problems arose, they were easily ironed out, in the better interests of well-hydrated brains!

The developing issue arising from this successful initiative, was to pursue more rigorously, the children's wider needs for a balanced brain-enriching diet. To this end, some schools began running popular healthy-food tuck shops at playtimes, to support children who may not have had a nutritious breakfast. Others reviewed the content of school dinners to eradicate E numbers, thereby seeking to avoid the onset of lunchtime hyperactivity, whilst simultaneously working with parents to encourage healthy packed lunches. Others pursued their commitments as a designated 'Healthy School'.

Brain training

Many children with significant additional needs attended our schools. Aside from a high proportion of pupils who spoke English as an additional language and many others with SEN, there were also significant minorities who were variously traumatized. Some children were victims of unfortunate or shocking circumstances. Asylum-seekers, those torn between two parents, those subjected to aggression or abuse, needed sensitive support for their learning. For these children, the emotional burdens they carried into school each morning effectively blocked their ability to learn effectively.

Brain training was integral to our commitment to inclusion. Whilst we may have been all but powerless to change the 'givens' just described, it was incumbent upon us to facilitate the progress of all our children, so that they were not being excluded from their entitlement to learning, an entitlement which might serve to prevent their ultimate disaffection. In order to develop, or for others to sustain, a more receptive state for learning, we considered various ways that might address these significant concerns regarding our pupils' concentration and application.

Our mantra was 'we can if ... '. Having exploited all the other possibilities, as far as we were able to, with 'social worker' hats on, we resolved to try a different problem-solving approach. We began to think through a series of brain exercises and school-based actions, which would help to promote a relaxed state for learning. This we provided for through school-specific packages of brain gym, brain breaks, the use of music and the organization of school routines.

Brain gym Brain gym exercise is for 'waking up the mind/body system, and bringing it to learning readiness. It activates full mind/body function through simple integrative movements, which focus on specific aspects of sensory activation and facilitates integration of function across the body mid-line' (Hannaford, 1995, p. 112). Not only does such cross-lateral exercise increase concentration, it also 'produces increased neuro-trophins (natural neural growth factors) and a greater number of connections among neurons' (p. 112).

Our understanding was enhanced by attendance at courses and by the works of Dennison and Dennison (1994) and Hannaford (1995). Initially, brain gym was built explicitly into our lessons. Information was cascaded to teachers, and then to pupils, who were taught how to go about it and what purpose each exercise served. Carla Hannaford's book, *Smart Moves* is of great practical help here. At a later stage, these exercises became an integral part of lessons in the classes that were using them with understanding. They were woven seamlessly by teachers into literacy or numeracy, to help children to refocus on the next stage of the lesson. With further encouragement from their teachers, pupils began to use them individually, as they worked and felt their concentration wane. They even remembered to use them during statutory tests, as a vehicle to diffuse stress, assist memory and aid full concentration.

A good deal was achieved, and though we are aware that a great deal more remains to be done, we became increasingly convinced of the effectiveness of brain gym. As a group of schools we produced a video to support our own practice and to disseminate our work to other schools in the borough. When we look at it now we realize how our learning about, and understanding of, brain gym has moved on. Some schools would like to build it more systematically into their practice, through, for example, schemes of work or Individual Education Plans (IEPs). We now know that we need to exploit opportunities for regular use of cross-lateral movements presented within the curriculum – PE, dance, music – to name but a few. For instance, a teaching assistant in one school noticed that the hard work and preparation she and year 2 children had put into an Indian stick dance presentation, was matched by significant developments in the spelling abilities of some participants with significant special educational needs. Moreover, the wider evidence in brain gym literature is compelling. So too is the response from children:

Brain gym has helped me calm down.

I like doing brain gym when we shout because it makes me feel better.

Brain gym helps quite a lot for me because it pushes away the last work and stores it and gets me ready for the next work. Brain gym is also fun and gets me going!

Brain breaks In order to refocus pupils' energies as concentration waned, teachers used brain breaks as another tool. Here the intention was to benefit from a break in concentration in order to refocus on learning, or the task, with renewed energy. Brain breaks were introduced through short activities or games, perhaps by inducing therapeutic laughter, or by hearing a piece of music. Teachers also encouraged pupils to work with 'carpet partners', so that information could be discussed and shared, providing another opportunity for interlude, whilst also consolidating the learning. At other times, a brain break required pupils to walk around perhaps collecting information. It was intended to have energizing or relaxing purposes, with appropriately paced or concentrated activities, enabling 'brain-refreshed' pupils to refocus on their learning.

Activating the senses to support learning

Attention to bricks and mortar ensured important attractive physical qualities in the learning environment, and created the ambience for learning. Development of the learning environment was a priority in our schools. However, we also wished to appeal more directly to the sensory dimensions to enhance learning. This we did through stimulating visual, aural and olfactory senses as detailed below.

Improving the physical environment Developing a comfortable environment, conducive to learning was a long-term programme for all our schools. Remodelling and capital-building projects, had allowed considerable rationalization and reorganization of space. This set the stage for a comfortable well-organized learning environment and improved curricular provision. More structured, purposeful and attractive learning environments evolved through the additions of libraries, ICT facilities, group or resources rooms, first aid and activity rooms and so on. Furniture was similarly upgraded and standardized by some, to make classrooms equal in quality provision. Complete redecoration and carpeting helped to raise the quality of internal teaching and learning environments. The impact of these qualitative developments improved general standards of classroom organization and display significantly, and served to make school-based statements about the standards expected. Upgraded staff facilities provided pleasant and practical environments for professional use, and helped staff to feel valued equally with children. Simple things like the provision of a dishwasher made all the difference for some.

Music – aural stimulation There is a body of research, which indicates that music can significantly enhance learning concentration and performance. Therefore, we decided to introduce music into our classrooms, to see if we could use it as a tool to create the atmosphere of relaxed awareness, so important for learning. It was used to enhance performance in certain tasks, to invigorate, or create a particular mood and to demarcate time or activities. It was used as a stimulus, or mood maintainer, as the children worked at their creative writing or art. It invigorated children, perhaps at the start of a mathematics lesson, to ensure their brains were alert. It accompanied brain breaks and brain gym. It calmed children when, perhaps after a windy lunchtime, gentle mood music played them into the classroom after the lunch break. It was also attached to activities to stimulate a response without any teacher input. For example, a busy piece of music played at tidy-up time meant children just knew what was required, and the time allocated to do it.

Some staff are still working on including a musical dimension regularly in their lessons, and have found it a more difficult thing to do. Although they were provided with tape recorders and CDs they felt it was wrong to play music if they wanted the room to be quiet and peaceful. Others felt it 'hyped' the children up when they had been calm, and others simply forgot. In these instances alternative strategies are being tried such as building music stimulation into planning twice a week and encouraging staff to invest time in talking to the children about it.

Smell – olfactory stimulation Classrooms were made as pleasant as possible by use of incense sticks, pot pourris and plants. Some of the displays in the public areas of the school included olfactory stimulation. Similarly, staffrooms and the headteachers' rooms were made pleasant places to work in and go to.

Developing children's emotional intelligence

We developed children's emotional intelligence by:

- using a wide range of strategies.

"Emotional intelligence" refers to the capacity for recognising our own feelings and those of others, for motivating ourselves, and for managing emotions well in ourselves and in our relationships. (Goleman, 1998, p. 317)

Daniel Goleman identifies five basic emotional and social competencies that are an essential part of emotional intelligence:

- self-awareness
- self-regulation
- motivation
- empathy
- social skills (p. 318).

In many respects, these competencies reflect two of the intelligences identified by Howard Gardner (1999): intrapersonal – the intelligence of self-knowledge; and interpersonal – the intelligence of social understanding.

Within and between our schools a diverse range of intrapersonal needs and interpersonal relationships was manifest. To some extent socio-economic status and cultural or religious norms perhaps influenced this, but the potential debilitating effect of these needs on children's learning could not be ignored.

At one end of the scale the manifestations included egocentricity, domination of peers, awareness of sexuality. Some exhibited disrespectful, confrontational and attention-seeking behaviour with peers and staff. They were well versed in the use of put-downs in order to gain control or manipulate others, and thereby gain status or precedence. At the other end of the scale were more passive individuals, introverted, submissive to or excluded from 'popular' groups, intimidated by stares or personal comments. They were withdrawn, often seeking invisibility in class, and generally exhibiting all the withering signs of low self-esteem.

This complex range of individual emotions and classroom and playground dynamics needed to be managed by teachers and support staff, to ensure inclusion and effective learning for all. We used many strategies, which would encourage reflective, resilient and self-motivated learners.

Using a wide range of strategies

In our efforts to enhance children's self-esteem, and their awareness of citizenship, we cherry-picked a variety of approaches. We paid attention to the work of those concerned with neuro-linguistic 'programming', behaviour management (Rogers, (1997; 2002) 'Tribes' (Gibbs, 1995) and 'Circle Time' (Mosley, 1996).

Many of the following strategies are well used by schools, but perhaps in isolation. We tried to make them a coherent whole, by building them with their attendant vocabulary into the 'big picture' – the learning language that was being used in the classroom. These strategies were not used in isolation. Together, they provided rich and varied opportunities to explore rights and responsibilities, and the expressive language needed to develop emotional intelligence. They furthered our aim of inclusive education for all.

School codes of conduct School codes of conduct detailed fundamental community rights and responsibilities of our citizens: the way we expected them to behave towards others, and their entitlement to be similarly respected whilst they were at school as indicated in the example in Figure 3.2 for children in years 5 and 6.

The Code of Conduct – Years 5 and 6...

At .... School we have duties and rights.

We have a duty to:
- treat each other with politeness and respect
- call each other by our own names
- help each other and work and play together
- listen to what people have to say
- share with others when it is time to share
- care for each other and for our school
- respect each other's property
- be honest and truthful
- trust each other and be responsible

We have a right to:
- be treated with politeness and respect
- be called by our own names
- expect help in working and playing together
- be listened to
- expect others to share with us when it is time to share
- work in a school where people care
- have our property treated with respect
- expect honesty and truthfulness
- be trusted and given responsibility.

Figure 3.2 The code of conduct for years 5 and 6

Class codes Class codes interpreted the school's community code into more detailed practice, looking closely at ground rules. The tenets were always worded positively to encourage positive behaviours. They were also carefully worded to pre-suppose success, 'we will' rather than 'we will try to', as exemplified in 'Our Community Agreement' by one class shown in Figure 3.3.

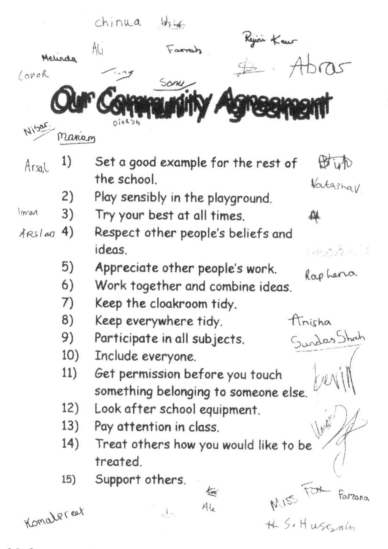

1) Set a good example for the rest of the school.
2) Play sensibly in the playground.
3) Try your best at all times.
4) Respect other people's beliefs and ideas.
5) Appreciate other people's work.
6) Work together and combine ideas.
7) Keep the cloakroom tidy.
8) Keep everywhere tidy.
9) Participate in all subjects.
10) Include everyone.
11) Get permission before you touch something belonging to someone else.
12) Look after school equipment.
13) Pay attention in class.
14) Treat others how you would like to be treated.
15) Support others.

Figure 3.3 Our community agreement

A chain of consequence A chain of consequence detailed clearly, for pupils and parents, the certainty rather than the severity of action to be taken in the event of anti-social behaviour. It ensured that children and their parents were clear about what steps would be taken and when. Children learned that their actions had an impact on others for which they may be called to account. Figure 3.4 provides an example.

CHAIN OF CONSEQUENCE

It is important to note that Initial or "one off" offences are treated totally separately from **the Chain of Consequence** and are not recorded. Most incidents are dealt with in this way.

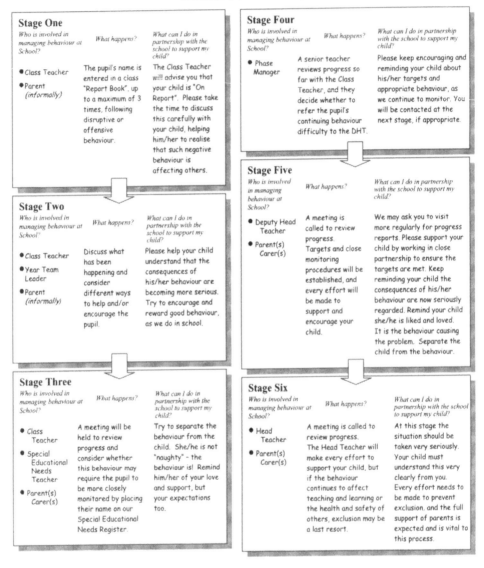

Stage One

Who is involved in managing behaviour at School?

What happens?

What can I do in partnership with the school to support my child?

- Class Teacher
- Parent (informally)

The pupil's name is entered in a class "Report Book", up to a maximum of 3 times, following disruptive or offensive behaviour.

The Class Teacher will advise you that your child is "On Report". Please take the time to discuss this carefully with your child, helping him/her to realise that such negative behaviour is affecting others.

Stage Two

Who is involved in managing behaviour at School?

What happens?

What can I do in partnership with the school to support my child?

- Class Teacher
- Year Team Leader
- Parent (informally)

Discuss what has been happening and consider different ways to help and/or encourage the pupil.

Please help your child understand that the consequences of his/her behaviour are becoming more serious. Try to encourage and reward good behaviour, as we do in school.

Stage Three

Who is involved in managing behaviour at School?

What happens?

What can I do in partnership with the school to support my child?

- Class Teacher
- Special Educational Needs Teacher
- Parent(s) Carer(s)

A meeting will be held to review progress and consider whether this behaviour may require the pupil to be more closely monitored by placing their name on our Special Educational Needs Register.

Try to separate the behaviour from the child. She/he is not "naughty" - the behaviour is! Remind him/her of your love and support, but your expectations too.

Stage Four

Who is involved in managing behaviour at School?

What happens?

What can I do in partnership with the school to support my child?

- Phase Manager

A senior teacher reviews progress so far with the Class Teacher, and they decide whether to refer the pupil's continuing behaviour difficulty to the DHT.

Please keep encouraging and reminding your child about his/her targets and appropriate behaviour, as we continue to monitor. You will be contacted at the next stage, if appropriate.

Stage Five

Who is involved in managing behaviour at School?

What happens?

What can I do in partnership with the school to support my child?

- Deputy Head Teacher
- Parent(s) Carer(s)

A meeting is called to review progress. Targets and close monitoring procedures will be established, and every effort will be made to support and encourage your child.

We may ask you to visit more regularly for progress reports. Please support your child by working in close partnership to ensure the targets are met. Keep reminding your child the consequences of his/her behaviour are now seriously regarded. Remind your child she/he is liked and loved. It is the behaviour causing the problem. Separate the child from the behaviour.

Stage Six

Who is involved in managing behaviour at School?

What happens?

What can I do in partnership with the school to support my child?

- Head Teacher
- Parent(s) Carer(s)

A meeting is called to review progress. The Head Teacher will make every effort to support your child, but if the behaviour continues to affect teaching and learning or the health and safety of others, exclusion may be a last resort.

At this stage the situation should be taken very seriously. Your child must understand this very clearly from you. Every effort needs to be made to prevent exclusion, and the full support of parents is expected and is vital to this process.

Figure 3.4 Chain of consequence

Prides When staff from the five schools visited schools in Thunder Bay, Canada, they were introduced to 'Tribes' developed by Jeanne Gibbs (1995). Although they were not very keen on the use of the word 'Tribe', our staff were very impressed with the positive impact the processes involved had on the behaviour and emotional development of the children.

Tribes is a democratic group process, not just a curriculum or set of coopera-
tive activities. A 'process' is a sequence of events that leads to achievement of
an outcome. The outcome of the Tribes process is to develop a positive environment that promotes human growth and learning. (Gibbs, 1995, p. 21)

One of our schools drew on the ideas of Jeanne Gibbs and introduced 'Prides'. Children worked in collaborative groups, over the course of a year. Throughout the
process, they learned 'to use specific collaborative skills, and to reflect both on the
interaction and the learning that is taking place' (Gibbs, 1995, p. 21). Community
agreements (see, for example, Figure 3.3) formed the basis for developing a learning
community and sustaining a positive classroom environment. These were centred on:

- attentive listening
- appreciation
- no put-downs
- the right to pass (for example, to be a silent observer from time to time)
- mutual respect.

Having involved the children in wording the agreements, the teacher asked them
to help each other to remember them at all times, and transferred the responsibility to the Prides to maintain them. Groups were defined by a process of careful
observation and determined by identifying and understanding the particular skills
each child brought to the group. Working through different activities and curriculum tasks, the children learned to evaluate the encouraging contributions they and
others had made in order to move their learning forward. A system of long-term
membership assured mutual support mechanisms within each small group and
within the classroom. The collaborative skills that developed the learning community are shown in Figure 3.5.

The children valued Prides for a wide range of reasons and they proved to be very
successful:

After becoming a member of my Pride we decided on our roles, we worked
together and analysed each other's abilities and weaknesses. I think S is a
peacemaker because she never fights or argues. In this Pride I also realised that
T is very persuasive and enthusiastic (when he's not moaning), and a motiva-
tor. He may get bored sitting there for hours doing his work, and I don't blame
him, but that's because he's kinaesthetic. He's one of the best arts and crafts
people in our Pride. A like S are the peacemakers, but I'm not.

The way our group get along is because of S and A who are very patient with
T But I'm beginning to learn how I can cope with him, and that's something
I'm learning in my group, to not get annoyed with people like T.

The teachers also valued Prides, as described by one of them in Chapter 8 (see pp.
149–51).

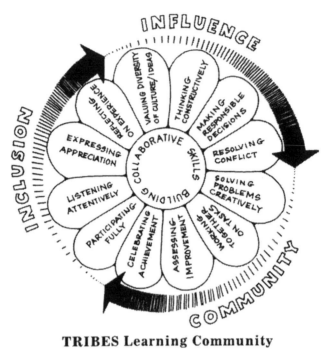

TRIBES Learning Community

Figure 3.5 Tribes learning community
Source: Gibbs, 1995, p. 158.

Put-up zones As we described earlier, put-up zones proved to be a powerful mechanism against negative peer pressure, and the culture of diffidence, which can quickly be perpetuated by a small or 'cool' minority. How they worked in practice was described on pages 37–8. The feedback from the children emphasized the importance of this strategy:

> In the past I always gave put-downs and now I know what it means, so I keep it to myself.

> I feel very happy being a learner in my class because I can put my hand up to answer the questions and if my answer is wrong no-one gives me put-downs, everyone gives put-ups. I feel very happy when no one gives put-downs because if they don't give me put-downs I won't be shy to answer a question in the class even if it is wrong.

School councils Several of our schools' teachers attended training with the pupils to facilitate the inception or development of school councils. One school, for example, established a school council through elections. Each class had a suggestion box and the elected members of the council had discussions with their class before each meeting. Representatives were responsible for collecting and presenting ideas to the council, and they had a budget to administer. Through their vocal force, the LEA refurbished a set of toilets and a 'healthy-eating' tuck shop was introduced. Whilst obvious vehicles for the citizenship curriculum, our schools also saw school councils in the broader context of developing emotional literacy.

Circle time Many staff received input from Jenny Mosley (1996), and used this in their work with the children. It complemented very well the skills that we were trying to develop. In one of our schools, for example, circle time was seen as an important development which supported the personal, social and health education programme and the citizenship curriculum as well as children's academic progress. The school was fortunate in having an experienced member of staff, trained in New Zealand, who knew all about circle time. She trained the whole staff and worked with individual class teachers where there were difficulties. On one occasion, when the LEA and the HEI mentors were on a joint visit to the school, they witnessed the whole of year 6 (120 children!) having circle time all together in the hall. All the children sat listening, waiting for a turn and contributing with confidence. All the teachers observed what was happening. They were learners too and were modelling working as a group for the children. This contributed to the development of an ethos of everyone working in the same direction with shared expectations. This circle time was just before the children were due to sit their national tests. What was so moving was the way the children felt able to express their anxieties (and there were many) in a 'safe' environment and how they received in turn the understanding, support and encouragement from others. Without doubt, this opportunity enabled the children to face the ordeal of national tests with greater confidence and assurance.

Coaching As a result of taking an accredited course on coaching for her own interest, one of the headteachers transferred what she had learned into practice in her own school. She modelled coaching behaviour in assembly. For example, if a child was misbehaving, rather than getting into a confrontational situation with 250 other children (and staff) watching, she placed responsibility for subsequent action on the child. She gave him or her a choice:

> What you've just done is inappropriate behaviour. Now, you have a choice. You can stay where you are, you can come and sit by me or (if the behaviour was really bad) you can leave the room.

After a pause she would ask:

> Have you made a choice? Please tell us what you intend to do!

Invariably the child chose to stay put. The strategy diffused and calmed the situation quickly. It was a 'win–win' for both parties. It was another way the school found to implement their 'no put-down' policy.

Behaviour management Positive approaches to behaviour management had long been a feature within a majority of the project schools. One, however, experienced significant and long-standing difficulties with pupils' attitudes, pre-dating its first

Ofsted inspection. Its present headteacher was trying to effect radical change within the school. However, serious issues of recruitment and retention compounded this situation, and ultimately led to the school's placement in 'Special Measures', at the end of its second inspection which was right at the end of the project. The moral was that the strategies we used required consistency, continuity and commitment of staff, which, given the very high levels of staff turnover in this instance, was difficult to secure. What is pleasing however, is that in March 2004, the school was given a clean bill of health, and wholesome praise by Ofsted. With a new headteacher continuing the work begun, it came out of 'Special Measures' six months earlier than would normally be expected which was a remarkable achievement.

Despite less strenuous circumstances, others also experienced their share of difficulties and challenge. Though effective behaviour management featured within the schools, the potential for very different profiles existed simultaneously. Many 'frustrated' pupils, unsettled, traumatized, or 'angry' pupils, were prone to bouts of anti-social behaviour. Staff continually reviewed strategies and policies to suit the pastoral needs of individual pupils. As one year 4 pupil put it:

> The teacher helps me to control my anger, which helps me learn.

Resources were directed towards areas of greater concern to combat pockets of poor behaviour that existed within cohorts or 'power groups'. Social skills groups were run by SEN support staff; a lunchtime 'Play Club' was run by one special needs co-ordinator to aid children's self-management of their behaviour and voluntary 'cooling down'. Behaviour targets were set up for specific pupils in one year 3 cohort where there was a predominance of boys. Monitored by a teaching assistant offering equal measures of tender loving care (TLC) and encouragement, the impact was stunning. Training for midday assistants (MDAs) in behaviour management helped needs to be recognized, understood and more effectively managed. Designated staff such as play leaders and a co-ordinator for the outdoor learning environment developed playground environments and the quality of play.

The use of this wide range of strategies helped to generate respectful, confident and empowered learners who listened to and valued each other's contributions. Some developed sufficient emotional maturity to overlook certain peer foibles perhaps 'because he is a kinaesthetic learner and he needs to ... '. Children became confident about their rights and responsibilities as school citizens, and aware of the role they played in developing the school community for their mutual benefit. Equally, these empowered citizens became armed with a degree of emotional maturity that some teachers may find threatening. Aware of their entitlement, pupils challenged supply staff who were not following these approaches, and involving pupils. Our staff learned from their pupils, and the children took their role very seriously.

Conclusion

We conclude by:

- reviewing what we did
- reflecting on what we learned.

Reviewing what we did

We:

- identified metalearning-friendly practice in our school policies
- developed a language of learning by starting 'big picture' displays in our class-rooms to show the interconnectedness of the term's learning
- made learning intentions and success criteria specific to our pupils
- built VAK into weekly planning to ensure it had a high profile in our lessons
- provided water and healthy brain foods
- established brain gym
- enhanced the learning environment
- provided music
- cherry-picked a range of practical strategies that supported the development of emotional intelligence.

Reflecting on what we learned

We learned:

- the importance of prioritizing learning as well as performance
- that a shared language of learning emerged as pupils and teachers learned from each other
- that development of self-esteem was the most vital prerequisite for effective learning
- that the strategies we cherry-picked needed to become a coherent whole in order to develop emotional intelligence
- the importance of managing the recruitment and retention of staff.

The different ways in which we developed our teaching practice to develop pupils' learning taught us a great deal . Most of these strategies will be familiar ones. However, given appropriate staffing levels, they worked effectively because they contributed to our overall vision by opening up the learning dialogue. Teachers and children listened to each other in a spirit of mutual respect. Teachers taught learners, but learners also taught teachers.

We know only too well that it takes years to build and consolidate these practices into our schools in ways that ensure consistency and continuity, particularly in the face of high staff turnover and new centralized initiatives. The sad experience of one school shows we are by no means intending to tell a 'happy ever after' story. We are all still wrestling with the implications of the strategic and operational issues involved in developing a learning orientation in our schools. Though we have made significant progress, the road that stretches ahead is still a very long one, and we are still finding our way. To a large degree we are unable to circumnavigate the pot-holes, which may send us off-course or cause us to crash!

Our greatest challenge proved to be the pressures on teachers' class-time, and the varying degrees of courage and willingness to step outside the comfort zone, that existed within all the schools. Such was the pressure on teachers to 'deliver' units of knowledge that they still felt forced to feed children with performance-related programmes of work, often before they were ready for their next meal! The enriched diet of learning which we were introducing required time for the chefs to hone their skills, and for the gastronomes to develop a palate for these new tastes! It proved difficult for some teachers to loosen the curriculum constraints of strategies and performance expectations, which had been imposed upon them, and insert a more 'open' enquiry and dialogue for learning. It was also difficult for other teachers to 'let go' and manage behaviour with a different mindset. A good deal of 'un-learning' for teachers needed to be facilitated, and that will be the subject of more detail in the next chapter.

4

Supporting teachers as learners and researchers

Teachers' learning and pupils' learning are inextricably linked. (MacGilchrist et al., 2004, p. 92)

> **We can support teachers as learners and researchers if we:**
> - develop teachers as learners
> - coach managers in the skills of leadership for learning
> - provide induction programmes for newly recruited staff and NQTs
> - invest in high-quality training opportunities for all
> - embed support and development within our school improvement plans.

During the two-year project, we established a network of headteachers and teachers, supported by teaching assistants and administrative staff, committed to the principle of changing and improving learning and teaching in the classroom. We were starting to build a learning community, which could generate support and sustain professional learning. However, it was important to cater for and nurture these needs, so that the learning community could continue to grow and build capacity. Developing adults as learners was central to this process.

Developing teachers as learners

We developed teachers as learners by:

- developing their metalearning
- paying attention to the practicalities involved
- being clear about the purposes of our in-service provision.

Developing the metalearning of teachers

A key element of the work we were undertaking was developing recognition of ourselves as teacher-learners. This meant we needed to understand more about learning processes for pupils and professionals. These were brimful with metalearning potential: what could we learn about our teaching and professional learning as we worked with children who were simultaneously learning about their own learning?

We aimed to foster teachers' active intellectual engagement with learning about learning. Professional learning was far more than the simple acquisition of facts, the reading of books, implementation of strategies or a pedagogical formula. It involved careful and incisive questioning and a quest for thorough understanding. It required the learner to make connections between existing and new information and subsequently develop the ability to make use of this newly processed information in the classroom. It involved the development of personal and social skills and was dependent in many respects upon the feelings, motivation and self-confidence of the person concerned. Such learning often functioned outside the comfort zone in an arena of challenge. In other words, the characteristics inherent in children's learning were equally applicable to our own professional learning.

We were firmly of the belief that teachers are also lifelong learners, requiring continued training and support. The practicalities and the challenges of providing such support and opportunities for development needed careful thought, however, as we describe in the next section.

Paying attention to the practicalities involved

As in every walk of life, the enthusiastic and committed worked alongside the reluctant and disaffected. The challenge therefore, was to engage *all* our teachers as learners by trying to meet their varied needs. We wanted to develop understanding of how children learn, and factors that affected this process. This we tried to facilitate through the provision of high-quality professional development and support. We were also keen that the 'believers' should intermingle with the 'sceptics'. This was not because we were seeking their immediate conversion, but because we were hopeful that in sharing knowledge and practice, asking questions and airing doubts, connections could be made which would further individual professional development and corporate school 'intelligence'.

Working in partnership, our five schools were sustaining at any one time a large number of teaching staff and learning support staff between them. We were all firmly committed to the notion of whole-school as well as networked approaches in the implementation of the project. This, we felt, would help communal development and the acquisition and understanding of what we meant by the language of learning. It would also enable us to share challenges, achievements and classroom practice. Yet, based on these numbers, the first simple problem we encountered was that there were no quality venues that could accommodate us all, within our limited resources.

Immediately, we had to make some hard decisions and compromises, beginning with our project launch on 'Accelerated Learning'. Present were staff who directly supported children from our five schools – class teachers, support teachers, teaching assistants, learning support assistants. We wanted to include administrative staff too, but this was prohibited by the sheer weight of numbers. Even so, we trawled conference centres, theatres, secondary, primary and civic halls for a large but quality venue. Our criteria were that it had to be comfortable, attractive, relaxed and informal, and could provide adequately for culinary and dietary needs. Ideally we wanted to be away from a school setting, to aid reflection and maximize enjoyment. We were insistent that we should set the stage for the comfortable learning of our staff just as they did for their pupils. In the end we came full circle and arrived at the borough's Teachers' Centre, where most of our criteria were met, and everyone at least felt 'at home'.

Later on we questioned and revisited the original purposes we had assigned to the inclusion of all staff in all training opportunities. There were too many things that militated against the consistent inclusion of teaching assistants (TAs) and learning support assistants (LSAs) to make it viable. Much as we wanted them included in training opportunities, their after-school commitments, job descriptions, our depleted budgets, differing ethos and the conflicting demands of school-based priorities and curriculum reviews meant, to our regret, that we were unable consistently to sustain their inclusion. At the time, we compromised with an understanding that once in-service became school-based and more finely tuned to individual establishment's needs, schools would make their own decisions about who attended.

Being clear about the purposes of our in-service provision

However, as time went by, the continuing issues of prohibitive costs, staff turnover, induction, recruitment and retention forced us to think yet again. We knew these issues were there to stay, and recognized that we needed to think much more creatively about the purposes of our in-service provision as a whole. Four principles emerged for us:

1 *Providing quality in-service.* First, we wanted to provide quality in-service that 'fed' and nourished professional appetites. After all we were effectively training brain surgeons who were to work on children's minds! In-service delivered by text, without engagement or thinking, and death by flip charts was not for us! We wanted staff to feel valued and nurtured, and to be equipped with the appropriate instruments, tools and knowledge of their trade. It required the provision of high-quality trainers, who would help us to reflect creatively on our practice.

2 *Providing quality time.* We wanted to build in more quality time for staff to reflect on their practice. Snatched opportunities during workshops or staff meetings did not provide enough time for in-depth reflections, which would help us to make connections, generate new knowledge and promote excellence in our learning and teaching.

3 *Encouraging teachers and others as learners and researchers.* We wanted to encourage teachers as learners and researchers. We were excited about the part we could play as classroom practitioners at the cutting edge, translating brain research, for example, into classroom practice. Dominated for too long by government edicts, here was the opportunity for educational professionals to take the initiative, show creativity, professionalism and strengths in rigorous school self-evaluation, whilst at the same time revitalizing teaching into a learning profession.

4 *Providing differentiated professional development opportunities.* The need for differentiated in-service became apparent. Initially this stemmed from our early discussions about the practicalities of including teaching assistants. However, high teacher turnover, a feature of our region, meant there was a constant need for the induction of new staff into our learning-centred ethos. Certain areas of training also required 'action replays' as an initiative waned or the connections to develop classroom practice had not yet been made.

To enable these principles to be translated into practice we recognized the need to support those staff who were responsible for managing the process.

Coaching managers in the skills of leadership for learning

We coached managers in the skills of leadership for learning by:

- strengthening the importance of 'middle' managers
- providing 'in-house' professional development for managers.

Strengthening the importance of 'middle' managers

As a group of headteachers we were united in our view that despite national initiatives, middle managers were still an underrated force in the march for school improvement. Crucial to the development of our schools, they were appointed to lead subjects or year-group teams, often with little relevant or quality training to support them in their curricular or management tasks. Hence there were great variations not only in the performance of middle managers but also in the achievements and successes of their teamwork. With this in mind, the recent introduction of the National College for School Leadership's 'Leading from the Middle' course has been a welcome development.

We had sampled from the usual variety of external course providers, but often these focused exclusively on essential management skills in isolation from their application to curriculum management. Frequently, learning points and any valuable connections made, were quickly swallowed up on return to the daily hurly-burly that is school. We were conscious that opportunities we set aside for course feedback were also insufficient, given the constraints of time. Alternatively, if individual staff development was secured, it was often followed by promotion 'up and away' before effecting desired improvements 'at home'.

There was therefore a real quandary for our schools, which we felt many others probably shared. Investing money for continuing professional development was at best effecting limited individual staff development, but the consequences of teacher turnover meant it was not necessarily effecting significant whole-school improvement as it should. Our team leaders were the staff routinely responsible for managing school improvement and policy implementation at the chalk face. Yet, whilst in the throes of co-ordinating planning processes, subject leadership, monitoring and class teaching, they had precious little quality time for in-depth reflection. Thinking time to engage with and scrutinize such issues was effectively limited to weekly management meetings. This forced us to use time for CPD more creatively.

Providing 'in-house' professional development for managers

We took pride in developing the skills of our 'home-grown' managers who had arrived at our schools as NQTs. We wished to retain their talents, aware of their quality as well as their potential. Experienced managers worked alongside newly appointed ones, creating a whole spectrum of training needs. It was important to respond creatively and individually in support of our managers' professional development to build capacity. Hence, with these diverse needs in mind, and budgets limited by the usual constraints, we began to consider different ways to induct and train our managers in-house, with the additional hope that we might also retain their expertise.

One school reasoned that monies invested in courses might instead be spent on supply cover, releasing staff to fulfil a variety of school improvement functions through investigative workshops. Such an idea may be a contentious issue for some, but it was felt that time for detailed reflection would have high yields for children's learning. The usual risks and potential pitfalls of taking class teachers out of situ were discussed, but it was concluded that potential advantages outweighed any predictable disadvantages. The school ensured cover-staff were familiar to the school and the children, and allocated specifically planned tasks or areas for which the cover teacher was responsible. This scheme was not managed with low expectations of class performance.

In this way, therefore, managers participated in day-release in-house workshops, perhaps in key stage teams or small phases. Led in rotating groups by members of the leadership team, a specific agenda, task and time line focused an investigation, which ran through the entire school or was phase specific. Continuity and progression were highlighted through scrutiny of children's work, curriculum review, assessment, aspects of SIPs, analysis of performance data and policy implementation. Managers explored their roles and responsibilities in developing focus areas. Simultaneous coaching in management skills and techniques ran alongside these processes. These opportunities provided quality time for vital and extended reflection on our curriculum for learning. All staff learned together in inverse proportions – senior managers kept abreast of operational issues – feedback which informed the leadership and management of whole-school planning. Equally, middle managers developed strategic skills, widening their managerial experience and whole-school perspectives. Interpersonal skills were honed and the best qualities of 'assertive', proactive and distributed leadership were fostered and encouraged. Management training and school improvement were simultaneous and definite outcomes.

Issues under review created the inevitable challenges and, as the going got tough, the opportunities for professional metalearning were ever present. This principle applied equally within workshops, middle management or staff meetings. As staff were moved quite deliberately outside the comfort zone and into areas of challenge in the quest for school improvement, there was reassurance in the language of learning they now shared, which helped to defuse professional frustrations: 'I know this is challenging and causing concern and anxiety for some, but let's remember we are finding this difficult or contentious because we are learning something new ... .'

With their middle managers the school leadership team explored not only what needed to be done and why, but also how such situations could be managed. 'What issues are these actions likely to raise for your team? How will you manage these? How will you support staff if they feel challenged by these proposals? How will you motivate your team? How will you make sure this is implemented in your year group?' Working through such issues proved an invaluable learning curve for many. It helped the leadership team to pitch the support appropriately and proceed at an appropriate pace, surging forward or backtracking to meet perceived needs. As the headteacher reflected:

> The dialogue surrounding this process highlighted for me just how far we as a staff had come along the route of school improvement. I found that for what felt like the first time, I could really enter into a genuine and open debate with the whole staff, knowing that whilst some were significantly challenged, they were finally open about their concerns, and able to express them warts and all! Yet the discussion was now pupil rather than teacher focused! More enabling and 'we can if ... ', rather than disabling and energy consuming, 'we can't because ... '. Staff were accepting of the challenging principles and acknowledging the ultimate benefits! Feedback from staff was a developmental and professional dialogue, not simply the negative or blocking mechanisms of the past. We were really learning together!

In another school CPD was a particular focus within the school improvement plan. There had been a 40 per cent turnover of teaching staff and it had become increasingly necessary to provide differentiated in-service opportunities. This enabled the varying needs of staff to be met and at the same time enabled new co-ordinators to work with smaller groups of staff, in order to build up their own confidence as middle managers.

In yet another of our schools, with a more stable staffing situation, monitoring by middle managers entered a new phase which in turn provided rich CPD opportunities both for them and for the staff with whom they worked. The four year-group leaders were released for two hours a week specifically to monitor their year groups for various developments including 'Learning to Learn'. The headteacher monitored specifically for 'Learning to Learn' initiatives. Feedback was instant with targets, where needed, set for the following week. This was important because as more and more 'Learning to Learn' initiatives come on board as well as other LEA and government initiatives, it would have been easy, under pressure to forget the former and concentrate on the latter. The weekly check took five minutes with the help of a checklist (see Figure 4.1).

Monitoring classroom display for 'Learning to Learn'

Class..........................
Date...........................
Return visit.................

	On display	Comment
Class rules		
Guided reading		
Water use rules		
Dual language signs		
Behaviour guidelines – playground rules, toilet rules, dining hall rules		
Positive affirmation posters		
Learning outcomes headings and outcome DAILY LESSON OBJECTIVES WEEKLY LESSON OBJECTIVES		
World map with countries/or cities identified or Lego Len and relevant newspaper articles		
Word banks		
Planning with all columns filled in including VAK		
Playground rota/hall timetable/ICT timetable		
TAPE RECORDER in use		
General information board – currents topic		
FLIP CHART in use		
Explanations/prompts on show		
DISPLAYS Key questions/lesson objectives as titles		

Figure 4.1 Monitoring classroom display for 'Learning to Learn'

Problems could be dealt with by the year-group leader and no teacher had to go on with something whilst struggling and being unsure. Also, instant feedback was given to staff. This process provided:

- instant challenge
- gentle coercing of the unsure
- a focus on pupil learning
- dialogue between teachers, year-group leaders and children
- a structured opportunity for moving forward together
- distributed leadership – year-group leaders reported to the deputy head half-termly and then the deputy head reported termly to the headteacher

Providing induction programmes for newly recruited staff and NQTs

We provided induction programmes for newly recruited staff and NQTs by:

- being clear about the rationale for our induction programmes
- facing challenges and our 'ups and downs'
- maintaining momentum and embedding practice.

Alongside the development of our middle managers there was an ongoing need to provide induction programmes for new staff and NQTs. This section summarizes the perspective gained over two years of reflection and learning on the recruitment, retention and induction of new staff. There is no particular chronology of action points to recount, although certain induction tools were developed and these are summarized for the reader later in the section. It reflects some of the tussles and bittersweet processes in which we were engaged, illustrating that change and school improvement are not tidy or regular processes. Rather, like climbing a mountain, there are peaks to be scaled and troughs to be wary of. Periods of inclement weather can cause setbacks at any time!

Being clear about the rationale for our induction programmes

In the past, induction served to familiarize new staff with policies, priorities and school organization. Now, however, it was an essential part of developing our schools' capacity for improvement, and imbued with much greater significance. Induction was the vehicle that would both encapsulate and perpetuate our revised approaches to learning. It needed to raise awareness of the ways we taught for learning, and help new staff to see, acquire and share the rationale for the metalearning practices that had been developed. It was a tall order to distil such learning, but as one headteacher commented: 'Our schools will never be the same again! There's no going back now'!'

We had to find a way to 'bottle' what we had learned, yet without giving it a trendy designer label. It was a *process* not a product and we were wary of defining it as a commodity, perhaps making it appear too weak or strong, too fizzy or frothy. Yet at the same time we had to identify 'it' for the consumers and the soon-to-be practitioners to sample. We needed to find ways to engage our newly appointed teacher-learners, encourage their development in teaching for learning, and welcome their own ideas, so that we could all continue enriched on our learning journey.

Induction was vital for external reasons too. Teacher turnover in the London region had escalated dramatically, and continued incessantly. Thus an annual depressing and demotivating recruitment jamboree left schools and pupils subject to 'chance', akin to jackpot winners – or losers.

Many of our teacher-leavers migrated simply because they wanted to settle down and were financially unable to sustain expensive London rents or set up mortgages. Others sought to widen their experience in a different school setting. Our carefully groomed 'learning-teachers' were now a very attractive, saleable 'commodity', ripe for such promotions. Our first tranche of 'Learning to Learn' teachers were beginning to move on, and we had to work even harder to sustain the progress we had made, against a backdrop of teacher shortages. On the whole, we chose to do this by recruiting newly qualified staff rather than covering with expensive long-term, supply staff. Some of our recruits were on the Graduate Teacher Programme, and others were overseas-trained. But, by far the majority of our staff-joiners were NQTs, with as many as 15 being recruited by one school over a two-year period. Their recruitment was a deliberate ploy, for three reasons.

First, we had emboldened ourselves to be risk-taking schools in order to develop our learning and teaching. We knew NQTs had a great deal to offer, and might wish to 'train-up' in their first school for a few years, if they received professional development appropriate for their needs. These few early years, we reasoned, may help to provide a little more continuity, whereas supply staff were highly likely to be moving on at a much earlier stage, so the vacancy would recur. Yet such a tactic was laden with significant risks, which were not to be discounted. A loss of established experience substituted with, as yet unproven, newly qualified skills, might also be a destabilizing force for school development, classroom practice, behaviour and whole-school management.

Secondly, this tactic was deliberate because last-minute resignations meant schools needed to 'carry' a vacancy for at least a term, as experienced quality staff could rarely be recruited after resignation deadlines. By recruiting NQTs the vacancy was filled promptly with enthusiastic practitioners, who could be trained immediately into teaching for learning. Yet again the risks were significant. It entailed commitments to set aside financial resources to ensure provision of the appropriate training opportunities. It also entailed recruiting the 'right' candidate no matter how desperate we were, and having the nerve to hang on, sometimes until the last minute, until she/he arrived!

Thirdly, we felt that it would be beneficial to recruit and train staff who would be encouraged from the outset to think 'outside the box' and share the risk-taking to enhance learning in their classrooms. In this way teachers could become more creative but rigorous practitioners, maximizing pupils' progress. The children could reap the rewards of such creativity and have the means to accelerate their own learning. The school could generate further capacity from its heavy commitment to staff training. The risks were that staff could become overwhelmed by the demands they perceived were expected of them, and this could be off-putting or unnerving at the start of a career, and become a demotivating force within a staffroom. Sensitive support, which recognized progress and achievements, and allowed mistakes and learning to take place, in the context of a supportive environment, were vital to the success of our strategy.

Facing challenges and our 'ups and downs'

We knew the management of our CPD strategy was high risk. Seeking high levels of motivation and enthusiasm from our staff joiners, we needed to provide a professionally enriching environment in return. Beyond that, the way was unclear, because we were rather at the mercy of the 'unknowns' and 'any other factors' which may arise as a consequence.

In the event, we reaped a harvest of additional unexpected consequences, some unwelcome others pleasing and rewarding. Unfortunately, it meant our plan had its share of casualties. Three schools needed to restructure internally, following bereavement as well as the long-term illnesses of senior managers within the leadership group. Another endured protracted frustrations, through a gruelling period of staff turnover and the challenges of recruitment, retention and long-term sickness. It was hurtful as Ofsted delivered the inevitable 'snapshot' judgement, despite acknowledging some hard-earned progress:

> High staff turnover and absence have made it very difficult to implement plans for improvement, particularly in relation to improving standards of work and the quality of teaching and learning ... However, where staffing has been stable, improvement has been good. (2002, ref. 102847)

Others, who had experienced some gains in the recruitment lottery, had also benefited from longer-term developments. Ofsted's judgement on one of these schools was that:

> It has had a great turnover of teaching staff since the last inspection, with many teachers moving on for promotion. About a third of staff are new to the school in the past year. The very good management systems in place and the well-organised induction programmes for new and newly qualified staff have ensured that these teachers have quickly settled into the [school's] way and have become valuable members of the team. The comprehensive programme of lesson observations by the headteacher and the deputy ensure that weaknesses in teaching are

quickly identified and the necessary support given. (2001, ref. 102813)

Another inspection judged that:

> The school currently has seven newly qualified teachers on its staff, which, at the moment, creates some imbalance in the range of experience that staff provide. However, there is an excellent induction system of support and professional development for newly qualified teachers which helps them settle into the school and extend their professional skills. (2002, ref. 131013)

What was particularly pleasing in these reports, all published during the life of the project, was recognition for the high-quality teaching and learning which had developed. This progressed soundly for most of the schools, but due to recruitment and retention issues, was more tentative for others. Even so, we all shared the joys and celebrated the professional expertise and exemplary practice that had developed, when one school was asked to take Beacon status for creativity and thinking skills. Another was credited with two Advanced Skills Teachers (ASTs), and between us we boasted several leading teachers for literacy and numeracy. The exemplary skills of these teachers were shared not only within our schools and our network now, but were modelled and shared within other schools in both the primary and secondary sectors.

Maintaining momentum and embedding practice

The diverse circumstances in our schools and the judgements made of them, illustrated that in order to uphold teaching for learning, we needed to seek different ways to 'ring-fence' school-based developments, and sustain the developments in children's learning. Our children quite rightly had high expectations of their teachers. By now they were sufficiently empowered to voice their concerns if staff did not follow learning-based approaches. We wanted to secure the commitment of all new staff, whatever their levels of expertise or experience. Sustainability was clearly conditional upon the development and maintenance of systematic in-house induction programmes. 'Teaching for learning', needed to be fiercely guarded, saved and seamlessly transferred, rather than lost with leavers like just another initiative. Hence, despite budget restrictions and inordinate amounts of time spent on recruitment, we made every effort to vary our induction provision through, for example:

- *An annual staff handbook* – the school's 'who's-who?' and 'what's what?' covered curriculum information, organizational issues, tips for NQTs and so on.
- A *'Learning to Learn' handbook* followed, as we developed our classroom practice. It provided staff with practical checklists, articles, bibliography, brain gym exercises, music for moods, to provide continuity and information about the features and requirements of our learning classrooms.
- *Demonstration lessons.* These provided opportunities for new staff to see our established teachers at work with the children, demonstrating particular strengths and techniques in their classroom practice. In this way they could observe the prac-

ticalities and the effectiveness of Prides, circle time, class councils and no put-down zones in action. Later, they could begin to implement them in their own classes, ably assisted of course, by classes full of our own enthused and experienced 'teacher-pupils!' Furthermore, such opportunities provided early indications of the standards of teaching expected in the schools. Any staff, from NQTs to ASTs, modelled the good practice. Everyone had some area of expertise to offer, and this sharing was actively encouraged, gratefully received and effective in its outcome.

- **Embellished teamwork.** Deputy heads were variously assigned to manage subject leaders, which enabled support for co-ordinators to implement the school's vision and needs in their area. Their management offered support and guidance of more experienced co-ordinators and mentoring for newer, less experienced co-ordinators. Curriculum teams were established in some schools covering a range that included literacy, numeracy, topic and inclusion. As well as sharing the load in our large primary schools, it gave aspiring managers opportunities to be actively involved and to receive training opportunities in curriculum 'shadow' management.
- **Specialist co-ordinators.** They were employed not only to raise standards of provision, but also to work alongside teachers as internal consultants, providing support and feedback to staff joiners on their teaching and the development of subject knowledge. This covered areas such as neuro-linguistic programming, music, PE, science, literacy and special educational needs.
- **Employment of additional staff.** Within the usual budget constraints, this was done not only to enable co-ordinators to monitor and develop standards, but also to provide valuable feedback and professional development for new teachers.
- **Focused regular feedback on classroom practice.** The schools devised ways of doing this tailored to their own circumstances. Though the agenda was primarily one of school improvement, opportunities for professional development were built alongside, to encourage engagement with the development points. For example, one term's monitoring and target setting, was followed by another term's support with opportunities to observe practitioners. This simultaneously raised standards of teaching and aided professional development.

Investing in high-quality training opportunities for all

We invested in high-quality training opportunities for all by:

> seeking a range of provision
> ensuring feedback for learning
> exploiting opportunities for professional development.

Our induction programmes formed one part of our overall strategy for CPD. Provision of high quality training for *all* our staff was of great importance to us, and was, we believed the key to effecting the changes we desired. We hoped that learning about learning would enable staff to make connections that would enhance their teaching and support of our pupils. Moreover, quality provision was a practical manifestation of the value we attached to our staff. We wanted to set the state for relaxed learning for our staff in a comfortable and stimulating setting – as they did for their pupils.

Seeking a range of provision

The providers were many and varied, as were the partakers that attended. Sometimes, because of budget constraints or the nature of the provision, just one school representative attended. On other occasions, particularly in all-through primaries it was felt that key stage or phase representation was important to cascade information, thus enabling development of whole-school perspectives, or applications of an issue such as brain gym or creative writing.

Some of our professional development opportunities required more substantial commitments and entailed long-distance travel, long-term training, diplomas, participation in the borough literacy forum, or voluntary commitments to complete reflective assignments. However, the opportunities to complement school improvement with individual professional development were always ensured.

Advantage was taken of national programmes. For example, one headteacher secured a Research Associateship at the National College for School Leadership and some staff went on the college's National Professional Qualification for Headship (NPQH) and the Leadership Programme for Serving Headteachers (LPSH).

In some instances provision was whole or part grant funded, although supply costs were additional. On other occasions our schools worked in creative partnership and shared the high costs administered by some providers. Thereby, whole-staff access was secured to training that had previously been financially prohibitive for individual schools.

Sometimes expensive four-day courses were costed across two financial years whilst closely delivered across the perimeters of two academic years – in the summer and autumn terms. This proved to be an effective additional tool, to support the induction of new staff.

Ensuring feedback for learning

Because our language of learning was now explicit and shared by all, it was much easier to provide a variety of opportunities for feedback. Lengthy explanations of rationale were unnecessary – we could concentrate on technique and craft and the simple 'tricks of the trade' which we had gleaned. The parlance of our shared language had taken a while to become established, but once understood, it helped us to surge forward quickly. Thus professional development was contributing more effectively to facilitate improvements in learning and teaching.

Opportunities to feed back learning assumed many different guises:

• A high-profile 'Learning to Learn' display board was maintained in the staffroom by one deputy head. Articles or creative summaries she thoughtfully prepared were wont to disappear – a minor irritation, but one that was secretly interpreted very positively by the leadership group!

- A focus of the week was displayed within another school, and these ideas were collated into a book. Here, a particular epithet or 'Learning to Learn' prompt was the essence of the week's assemblies and featured as a high priority in classroom practice. It proved a practical way of ensuring issues raised did not wane.

- Pre-school briefing meetings on those dark or dull days were quickly energized with a newly acquired brain gym exercise, for everyone, now smiling, to take away, and develop with their class. This was also an opportune time to 'drip feed' and share many individual achievements and provide positive feedback.

- Music to calm or energize and motivating treats after a long hard day, became features of many staff meetings, reminding us of the powerful impact this could have for teachers' as well as pupils' learning.

- Pre-school daily briefing meetings were held in roving classroom venues, allowing staff to 'see' and 'hear' general principles of how 'Learning to Learn' classrooms had been set up, or to look at a particular display focus or an aspect of classroom organization.

- Staff who had attended courses were often asked to participate in staff meetings, and contribute proactively, or in specific ways to reflective workshops.

Our approach to CPD paid off. Teachers' learning and children's learning began to go hand in hand as the following comments from staff, when reviewing the project in July 2002, illustrates:

I am much more conscious of children as different kinds of learners. I look with greater awareness for a range of approaches and differentiated tasks.

... freed me up to do my own style of teaching ... all seem to be working towards the same goal and celebrating the success.

The children are positive and self-assured.

The children have an expectation to be fully involved in the whole lesson. They want to learn, to communicate and participate.

The children are focused on what they are doing.

The focus on targets for lessons has helped them to a satisfactory outcome e.g. WILF.

The initiative is being taken away from teacher-led activities.

... more displays of a 'working' nature rather than double mounted 'end products'.

The children are keen to be treated as partners in their own learning.

I have felt unlocked as a classroom teacher – the National Curriculum was so prescriptive that it could dampen down teacher initiative and creativity. Having always had a deep commitment to creativity and the importance of the arts, I have so enjoyed incorporating these things into the children's learning once again. I appreciate the move away from simply viewing the children as a 'level' and towards a holistic view of the individual.

Exploiting opportunities for professional development

With the help of the LEA and our mentors we made the most of a wide range of external opportunities for professional development.

The Teachers' International Professional Development Programme (TIPD) This scheme, administered and funded by the Department for Education and Skills in liaison with the British Council, provided opportunities for LEA co-ordinated study visits and school determined bids. It provided chances to look at models of world class practice and to engage and share in transatlantic professional dialogue. 'TIPD provides an opportunity for teachers to act as reflective practitioners, engaged in critical dialogue over the skills sets and methodology for enhancing classroom performance and school improvement' (http://www.centralbureau.org.uk/tipd/).

The LEA submitted an application to focus on thinking skills. The bid was successful and staff from each school and the LEA mentor visited Lakeshead District School Board, Thunder Bay, Canada, in February 2001. The potential of this experience was summed up in the aspirations of one member of staff:

> The opportunity to develop professional capabilities through visiting another country, would not only enhance my own classroom practice and knowledge, but would lead to the whole school benefiting from a host of new ideas and understanding ... These exciting new developments for our school would become an integral part of our teaching and learning policy, central to the philosophy and ethos of our school, and standards in our everyday classrooms. Therefore our children would have the necessary tools to become lifelong, successful and confident thinkers and learners.

The visit was enormously successful and personally and professionally enriching. The staff came back enthused and this enthusiasm was infectious. The introduction of 'Prides', described earlier, was just one of the tangible benefits disseminated to staff and pupils alike.

Dissemination opportunities Dissemination of our learning to others provided rich professional development opportunities locally, nationally and internationally. During the project, the LEA began to establish what has become the country's largest learning network of schools within the National College for School Leadership's learning network programme. As part of this initiative, the group was invited to provide feedback on our work to other headteachers within the borough. Halfway through the project, the Institute's International School Effectiveness and Improvement Centre invited us to run a session on the project at a school improvement conference. Later, through the NCSL's Research Associateship scheme, we were given the opportunity to disseminate our 'Learning to Learn' project with practitioners from across the country. In turn, the conference enabled us to learn from the practice-based research projects in which others were engaged.

At the end of the project, with the help of our HEI mentor, we submitted a bid to give a symposium on our 'Learning to Learn' project at the International Congress for School Effectiveness and Improvement (ICSEI) to be held in Sydney, Australia, in January 2003. Our bid was successful and seeing our project named in the list of symposiums was somewhat daunting but also exciting. The journey to Australia was made possible with support from the NCSL, Redbridge Business Education Partnership and our governing bodies. The headteachers of three of our schools were accompanied by our two mentors. Together, we wrote a paper for distribution at the conference (MacGilchrist et al., 2003) and shared the presentation at the symposium. The symposium and our paper attracted much interest and as a result there have been information exchanges with academics and practitioners, and visits to some of the schools. The conference also provided an opportunity for the headteachers to engage with researchers from around the world and to learn with and from them.

Embedding support and development within our school improvement plans

We embedded support and development within our school improvement plans by:

- building 'Learning to Learn' strategically into our plans
- translating 'Learning to Learn' into practical actions.

Building 'Learning to Learn' strategically into our plans

Staff and governors in our five schools developed clear ownership of the ways in which their schools were moving forward through involvement in formulating the SIP, the main vehicle for school improvement. Coincidentally and quite independently of the others, each school had felt the need to rewrite or revise the content or the format of their SIP to make it more 'Learning to Learn' friendly. For one school, this meant that 'futures thinking' was portrayed on a digestible one-sheet overview of strategic issues, which was then broken down into specific curricular objectives for achievement by the school.

Another school started similarly, and ended with three separated levels of planning. At the first level, were strategic aims. At the second level, aims were translated into the leadership group's plans, ensuring that a clear programme of work and individual direction existed for the two deputies working in partnership. At a third level, the plan was interpreted into subject leaders' plans and individual tasks for implementation. Thus a detailed working document for each layer of school management, enabled the continued development of standards and greater accountability for school improvement. It proved an invaluable tool for governors who tuned their monitoring visits ever closer to the specifics within the SIP, and for parents who evaluated school performance from the strategic summary.

A plan which combined the post-Ofsted Action Plan and the SIP and linked it totally to 'Learning to Learn', was written by a third school. It detailed initiatives term by term, and proved a very important vehicle in getting established staff on board – they supported the need for change, as they understood the reasoning behind 'Learning to Learn'. It had an overview sheet and curriculum postholders had their targets linked with individual performance management targets. Some were school-wide whereas others were much more individual and represented an area for development for a particular teacher. The governors also had a development plan which was linked to 'Learning to Learn'.

Translating 'Learning to Learn' into practical actions

Through our SIPs we were able to:

- employ consultants to contribute to professional development in specific ways, in order to develop whole-school initiatives and realize our strategic plans. These ranged from NLP consultants to playleaders.
- enhance specialist provision for children, either through subject expertise, support for talented and able, or through variations on booster groups or setting. This ensured children were getting the support to progress their learning.
- facilitate developments in distributed leadership by clarifying line management of the processes for school improvement. This ensured consistency in standards and provision. In one school this meant two deputy heads each had responsibility for a phase or team, and a group of subject leaders. Termly meetings between the deputy heads and phase and subject leaders reviewed standards, teaching and learning, progress against the SIP and set targets for development. With subject leaders, they audited their area of the curriculum. Standards and progression were monitored in three ways – through observation and collection of planning, work samples and discussion with pupils. Curriculum teams were established for literacy, numeracy and topic, to share the load and further delegate many practical tasks within a large primary school.

Such approaches ensured our staff were clear about responsibilities and reporting structures, and that accountability for high standards and pupil progress were applied at every level.

Conclusion

We conclude by:

- reviewing what we did
- reflecting on what we learned.

Reviewing what we did

We:

- provided in-house training to develop metalearning managers
- developed 'Learning to Learn' induction programmes
- took calculated risks in order to develop the schools' capacities (for example, when recruiting staff)
- developed learning-focused school improvement plans.

Reflecting on what we learned

We learned that:

- teachers are still learners and researchers, requiring and deserving quality and continuing professional development
- teaching assistants need to be included in as many training opportunities as possible
- the challenges of recruitment and retention can undermine pupil progress and school development.

In our efforts to develop teachers and others as learners and researchers we also learned that:

- there is no 'one size fits all' approach to professional development
- CPD opportunities need to be built on a shared set of values and beliefs about learners and their learning
- simply relying on LEA and nationally prescribed in-service provision is not the answer to school improvement. Such provision has a role to play but it is only one part of a much wider strategic approach to changing practice in the classroom
- however good external provision may be, it has to complement and be integrated with a planned approach to in-school professional development opportunities.

This chapter has concentrated on teachers' learning and the learning of other adults in a support role for children. We now turn, in the next chapter, to the strategies we used to provide leadership for learning.

5

Providing leadership
for learning

Leadership for learning isn't a destination with fixed coordinates on a compass, but a journey with plenty of detours and even some dead ends. (Stoll et al., 2003, p. 103).

> **We can provide leadership for learning if:**
> - **headteachers model total commitment**
> - **leadership is distributed across the school**
> - **deputy heads become the 'levers' of school improvement**
> - **middle managers and teams become leaders of learning and learning leaders**
> - **leadership roles are developed amongst other members of staff**
> - **children become leaders of learning.**

The more we researched and understood about metalearning the greater were the connections made. Initially focused on pupil learning, we soon realized that the metalearning principles and meta-perceptions we were applying to the children were equally applicable to ourselves as leaders and managers of our classrooms and schools.

Our organizational and professional metalearning were taking place at several levels. First, on an individual basis pupils and professionals were reflecting and developing their own particular skills and competencies. Secondly, recognition of each individual's skills was enhancing teamwork and outcomes – both in the classroom and across the whole school. Thirdly, the quality of our organizational and strategic learning was enriching whole-school 'intelligence'. We were showing the characteristics of the 'Intelligent School' (MacGilchrist et al., 1997; 2004).

Headteachers model total commitment

Headteachers modelled total commitment by:

- thinking radically and pursuing the transformation of learning and teaching
- regaining the initiative

- getting and keeping staff on board
- practising joined-up thinking.

The role of the headteachers in the leadership of learning was pivotal in as much as it involved a fundamental commitment to create a learning community. Our mentors made it very clear to us from the outset, that the headteachers' leadership of cultural change within the schools, and direct involvement, would be conditional to success. The headteachers worked together initially to consider the implications of all this in some depth. If they were not to fall at the first hurdle, they had to be emotionally and professionally prepared for the challenges that lay ahead. It was important for the headteachers to be resilient and overcome their own professional feelings of 'we can't because'. The barriers to our learning had to be removed. For example, 'we haven't got the money; we haven't got the staff; the governors won't like it; you can't find the time'. We were all offenders in turn! We learned to challenge and to help each other to change perceptions. Running as a distinctive thread throughout was our strapline 'we can if ... '. Every time there was a temptation to feel or think 'we can't because ... ', the view was challenged, the needs of the children prioritized, and the mindset changed. Later, this was passed on to staff and through to pupils. It engendered thinking 'outside the box' and positive language that presupposed success. With barriers and preconceptions removed, ways were then found to do what had seemed impossible at first. Every challenge or difficulty was viewed as an opportunity.

Thinking radically and pursuing the transformation of learning and teaching

Our maxim challenged us to think radically and to pursue school transformation. We were determined to transform learning and teaching in our schools. Tentative at first, but increasingly confident, we sought new or different ways to prove the value we knew we were adding to pupils' learning. We were not just seeking to prove value added in a performance context, but value in terms of life skills, citizenship, emotional intelligence, commitment and progress – value in its widest sense. In 2000, league tables did not have the capacity or the inclination to reflect this. We determined to try and make this value explicit through our own school self-evaluation processes.

Government initiatives were also subsumed into schools' agendas. The five headteachers became more confident to question and think through the benefits of participation in the latest tactic purported to raise standards. We focused firmly on what we believed we had to do in our schools and, as far as possible, rejected peripheral intrusions. In practice, therefore, at the child's level, whilst many schools cancelled afternoon playtimes to create more time for curriculum 'delivery', some within the group restored it, believing children's needs for brain breaks and fresh air were fundamental ingredients for effective learning. At curricular level, dedicated literacy sessions were revised and restructured, curriculum breadth was sustained and developed – all against the tide, at the time.

This new-found confidence arose from increasing conviction that what we were doing was right for our children and their learning. It even helped on the rocky road to inspection. At the national level, the drive for inclusion was breaking news during the project. Inevitably, yet another whole-school audit was the suggested way forward. One school, approaching inspection was initially concerned that the school might be penalized for not doing 'what was required'. Yet one look in the newly published index for inclusion folder (Centre for Studies on Inclusive Education, 2000) convinced the headteacher that the school's 'Learning to Learn' practice ensured the school manifested very good practice in relation to requirements. The onset of school self-evaluation within the Office for Standards in Education inspection handbook (Ofsted, 1999) was another example of the same principle. The schools found that they had reflected so deeply about their schools and had supporting evidence, that they experienced a far more 'natural' approach to inspection.

Regaining the initiative

Thus it was, as headteachers, we felt we had regained the initiative for our schools. It had not happened this way since the onset of the National Curriculum, and it was truly liberating. This was, after all, 'our' initiative. We did not have to do it, we chose to do it, simply because we wanted to improve children's achievement and learning. It was a process not a package. It was a lot of work but staff, too, were invigorated and committed. A powerful, fertile and transforming energy had injected creativity, motivation and enthusiasm into our schools. There was a mounting tide of: 'Is it alright if I ... ? I'm concerned about ... could we ... ?'

We proceeded at a pace, but more importantly at our own pace – to meet the individual needs of our learning communities. Some schools had well-established staff, others a raft of NQTs; some were recognized as high attainers whilst others were causing concern; some schools had well-developed resources and learning environments, others did not; some schools had the supportive governing bodies others wished for. Thus, headteachers chose their school's starting points and with staff became the designers and owners of their own school's transformation. We learned in a most powerful way that we can transform our schools ... if we are simply allowed to lead and manage from a basis of what we know and understand and continue to learn about children's learning, pedagogy and school leadership. 'We can if ... ' underpinned it all. It drove our inclusive education agenda.

Getting and keeping staff on board

Responsibility for securing support and encouragement for staff through the uncertainties and sensitivities of research-based learning, also sat with the headteachers. After all, pupils were to be asked to provide feedback on professionals' teaching styles. This could be perturbing, even for the most highly organized, self-confident and well-planned teachers. Those trained into the structures of Primary Strategies, those highly respected in their field or deemed to be highly experienced and successful were all potentially vulnerable to the different perceptions of their pupils. Yet for others, who relished the challenge, it was exciting. Thus there were creative – but diverse – forces at work. The headteachers tried to keep everyone on board, manage the spectrum of needs and celebrate the achievements.

Practising joined-up thinking

Joined-up thinking was also essential to plot the strategic and operational connections to be made in terms of whole-school learning. Policies needed revision and new systems were required to ensure that lessons learned were implemented and traced through into classroom practice. The metalearning practice that was developed was interpreted into revised SIPs, and interpreted into bedrock policies such as those concerned with learning and teaching, and monitoring and assessment.

It was the process of joined-up thinking that encouraged the headteachers to acquire the discipline of weighting more of their 'quality' time towards leadership. An area that we knew required the greatest concentration and professional focus, it was always found wanting! To build capacity in their schools required long-term strategies rather than short-term tactics. That in itself required quality thinking time.

Towards the end of the two-year project, the group evaluated their work in the context of the work of John Gray and colleagues (1999). We discussed and reflected upon the three different approaches to school improvement we had used that were identified by John Gray and his team when studying school improvement in 12 secondary schools. Yes, we had certainly used short-term superficial 'tactics' such as our booster groups to improve the percentage of children achieving level 4 and above in literacy and numeracy. Yes, we had taken a strategic approach to improvement. We had our SIPs and we had paid careful attention to the refinement and development of whole-school policies. But, most importantly, yes, we had been concentrating on capacity-building. In other words, we had gone beyond incremental approaches to change and were focusing our efforts on changing and improving learning and teaching in classrooms. This was the only approach John Gray and his colleagues found that led to capacity-building and sustained improvement over time. With the benefit of hindsight and in this reflective context, the headteachers really realized the quality of the outcomes of their increased focus on leadership for learning. Two 'everyday' anecdotes illustrate this process in action.

The first example involved the challenge of staff recruitment in London schools at a time of severe teacher shortage. As described in earlier chapters, two project schools had experienced two years of significant staff turnover, with a consequent loss of curriculum as well as teaching expertise. It was potentially a destabilizing force, at a time of national teacher shortage. In one school the leadership team focused on this challenge in leadership meetings, in order to assess, plan for and manage the situation. Continuity for pupils was essential, and the governing body and parents needed to feel the situation was being well managed. Raising and maintaining morale and valuing the contributions of remaining staff were also vital to develop and sustain a positive ethos of 'we can if ... '. Finally, despite it all, it was naturally 'expected' that school improvement and standards would continue to rise!

You will not be surprised to discover there was no magic formula for success! Initially, the headteacher and deputy weighted their time towards the day-to-day organization and management, to ensure the school and its systems continued to run smoothly. Simultaneously, they selectively recruited and – crucially – waited, to appoint 'the right' staff to take the school forward. It involved risk, holding fast to the strategic vision, maintaining continuity for the pupils with the best long-term supply staff. Sometimes the 'right' teachers, including a second deputy head were recruited after several re-advertisements. Finally it involved a decision to recruit 15 NQTs over a two-year period. A dearth of quality applicants for experienced posts was the catalyst for a decision to 'grow your own'. As described in the previous chapter, staff joiners then received carefully planned induction programmes to support both them, and a raft of new mentors. There were highs and significant lows. However, ultimately this three-year plan was responsible for a complete and positive turnaround in the school's development. Carefully crafted professional development opportunities encouraged the growth of future managers and leaders within the school. They in turn then inducted and trained others into the meta-learning approaches that increased the school's capacity for improvement.

The second example of the headteachers' role in capacity-building involved revision and clarification of their own roles in a wider process of curriculum enrichment and integration. With hindsight, the catalyst for this was the onset of the Literacy and Numeracy Strategies. Despite the fact that Redbridge schools received superb LEA support in literacy, the five headteachers felt increasingly deskilled by the onset of both the strategies. Initially, because they did not have sustained experience of class-teaching the two developing national strategies, it was challenging to know how to lead and support the concerns our class teachers articulated. Subject leaders appeared well equipped with 'the knowledge' of how to tweak for improvement, but that was only part of a bigger picture. The headteachers were keenly aware of the need to provide support for the planning, guidance and leadership of revisions. The Literacy Strategy, in particular, did not suit the needs of all our pupils. Yet, the detailed level of knowledge required for such a task seemed, in the early stages, a daunting barrier to those outside the classroom. The heads grappled more widely to redefine both their roles, and those of their managers. The objective was 'taming' the strategies, subsuming them into a broader and more balanced curriculum to ensure real 'ownership' rather than delivery of a 'containerized' curriculum, the importance of which Geoff Southworth, responsible for research at the NCSL, reminded us in a lecture some of us attended at the Institute of Education.

However, as the rather predictable learning outcomes emerged from the strategies, they served only to affirm the headteachers' earlier commitment to a broad and balanced curriculum that developed lifelong learning skills. Thus, after defining the core 'life-values' to be imparted, the headteachers asked staff to consider how literacy and numeracy skills could be integrated into a wider curriculum that was more relevant and contextual for our learners. The process of maximizing pupil achievement and the development of accountability was also a main focus. In retrospect, it is now clear that we were managing the yet-to-be-published sentiments of *Excellence and Enjoyment* (DfES, 2003).

Work began with leadership and curriculum teams. The detailed knowledge and expertise of classroom practitioners needed to be merged with the strategic perspective of senior managers, to reconcile any jarring curriculum factors. The challenge was to balance the demands of core curriculum attainment alongside progress and the need for a wider set of life-skills and competencies. The outcome needed to incorporate flexible curricular approaches alongside rigorous assessments of pupil progress. Ironically, our core values served to emphasize the risk entailed. Would we really be able to prove that in prioritizing learning over performance both areas would be enhanced? The emerging role for the headteachers was to scrutinize available evidence and make sure evidence could be made available. This was in order to 'measure' the effectiveness of the curriculum that was being provided to ensure that learners made good progress.

Developing patterns of leadership throughout the school became another feature of the headteachers' role. During the project the headteachers noted changes in their leadership styles. Most attended LPSH during this period and identified shifts that had occurred in the use of previously dominant styles. We shared together our strategies for putting into practice what was being promoted in the school improvement literature – namely, 'distributed leadership'.

Leadership is distributed across the school

We distributed leadership across the school by:

- coaching and training
- using a range of approaches
- providing differentiated professional development.

Leadership in the schools did become more distributed. A much bandied-about phrase, simple delegation and management this was not! Distributed leadership developed from a process of coaching, training and empowering staff.

Coaching and training

At that time in Redbridge, we were fortunate that an LEA adviser and headteacher duo were providing generic management training, based on Coverdale (www.coverdale.co.uk) approaches. Participating staff found this opportunity most beneficial. In practice however, once back at school, they expressed how quickly newly learned skills became displaced or subsumed by day-to-day realities. It was clear that school systems and structures needed to be adapted to nurture these skills that were yet in their infancy. Headteachers tried to find individual ways for our leadership teams to coach and develop their managers and future leaders, and to enhance opportunities for development and consolidation of these generic skills.

Thus, one school decided to limit attendance at external courses for middle managers! Once trained up and armed with sufficient subject knowledge via LEA or external providers, ways were developed that enabled them to practise their management skills 'on the job!' The school facilitated the development of generic management skills, and applied them in different ways to effect school improvement. Thus, whilst staff meetings might focus on a policy issue, middle management meetings that followed would involve the metalearning and management dimensions, such as understanding the big picture and the way this impacted on school improvement. As described in Chapter 4, managers were asked to consider: 'How are we going to implement this challenging issue in our teams? How will you support staff when you encounter difficulties? How will you ensure your team is implementing this policy? How will you know if it's working?'

Using a range of approaches

The approaches were different in the schools but had several shared outcomes. First, we developed much higher expectations of all our postholders. Secondly, we found staff keen to join our learning schools even in times of stringent teacher shortages! Thirdly, we took risks that we might not have taken in the past, recruiting less-experienced managers, because we had confidence in our abilities to train them. Fourthly, we retained staff longer because they enjoyed working in the schools. They were highly motivated, aware of how much they were learning. Above all, their work with the deputy heads helped them to realize they could make a difference within their year group. Our managers displayed high levels of professional responsibility. Inevitably, there was a flip side of course, but it served only to indicate the success of our strategies. Our staff became highly desirable to others! Our emergent leaders and managers had the generic skills and professional confidence to move on to headship, advisory work, AST posts, and leading literacy and numeracy posts both in and beyond the schools. Interestingly, some gained promotion when returning to their home counties – places where it was historically difficult to gain even mainscale posts, because a surfeit of teachers was already resident in the locality.

Providing differentiated professional development

Finally headteachers were firmly committed to the professional development of staff. It was there for *all*. Professional development opportunities gradually became more differentiated and flexible according to the needs of the professional consumer. The range of opportunity was varied, and the following gives but a sample:

Induction briefings were held for new staff or NQTs.

Teaching assistants participated in 'Learning to Learn' staff meetings.

The administrative data manager honed her skills alongside an LEA adviser.

Year-group working parties revised schemes of work for curriculum 2000.

Literacy and numeracy teams shared in the delegation of tasks without the burden of responsibility, and enabled staff to shadow co-ordinators.

Teachers modelled techniques for others in bespoke ways.

Deputies and headteachers worked with subject and year-group leaders setting targets and developing their managerial awareness.

Coaching was built into a three-week cycle of middle management meetings.

The permutations were as wide as the range, with the trainers learning alongside the trained. The overarching principle was that headteachers encouraged managers to wrestle with the challenges, come up with solutions, communicate them and act upon them, whilst keeping the leadership team informed. Their role was 'pivotal'. This ensured those spinning plates remained airborne!

Paying attention to the leadership roles of particular groups of staff, helped us to think through how best to distribute leadership roles and responsibilities in our large schools. An obvious focus group was the role of deputies, often described as the 'go-between' between the headteacher and staff. We preferred to see them as 'levers' of school improvement.

Deputy heads become the 'levers' of school improvement

Deputy heads became the 'levers' of school improvement by:

- resolving tensions and challenges
- taking a strategic role
- working with staff 'on the ground' to turn plans into action

and by being

- a 'troubleshooter'
- a realist
- well organized
- versatile
- an extra pair of eyes and ears.

The role and work of the deputy heads was also central to the success of the work being undertaken. If headteachers' roles were defined above as 'pivotal' then the function of deputy heads was perhaps akin to that of a 'lever' of school improvement. They forged the powerful links between the strategic and operational levels.

Their metaphorical leverage helped to create, mould, mediate, promote and define curricular and management issues requiring whole-school creativity and interpretation. With clear views of the strategic direction of the school, yet firmly rooted in the classroom, their skills exerted curricular or collegiate pressure to create movement – at any level – above or below them. Their ability to work fluidly as leaders or members of strategic and operational teams was an example of this plurality.

Resolving tensions and challenges

For the deputy head working at the strategic level with the headteacher, thinking 'outside the box' was an essential prerequisite on the basis that, 'if you always do what you've always done, you'll always get what you've always got!' However, challenges – of professional and perceptual diversity – could beset work at this level. The quality of working relationships enjoyed between deputy heads and headteachers was one factor in the equation. Deputies' professional competencies, confidence and intellectual capacities was another. Thirdly, the leadership styles, organization and competencies of the headteachers themselves compounded any potential difficulties. It was complex terrain to navigate – full of meta-perceptions and position power. What could a deputy head do if a headteacher moved a school too quickly or too slowly? What if the two disagreed or were not mutually supportive and understanding of each other? What if staff were not on board? What if the head was not leading to meet the needs and sensitivities of staff? How could a new second deputy be inducted to lead others in such a powerful process after it had started? Conversely, what could a headteacher or deputy head do if one or the other was not connecting the learning, in order to support the development of whole-school processes? The heads and deputies knew, of course, that neither could exist without the other if the school was to move forward. In each school, relationships worked differently, but all had one thing in common. Dependent on the size of the school, the two (or three) had to work 'as one'. The predicament below illustrates some of the dilemmas and difficulties that had to be resolved when the project was under way.

One of the paradoxes during the project was that in developing a learning culture, the schools needed to enquire, discover and try things out, just like any learner would. Schools had to get lost in order to find the way! There were risks attached, because learners need to make mistakes in order to learn. Conversely, however, staff were looking for clear direction from their leadership teams. Teachers used every precious moment to 'deliver' the 'required' curriculum within the class. The curriculum, the school day, teaching and support staff – all were suffering the effects of centrally imposed initiative overload. The system was stretched to the limits, there really was no slack left. Yet, to add insult to injury, the schools needed to make more time to investigate and immerse themselves in a whole set of challenging issues. Working outside the comfort zone, staff needed to define the ethos of 'our' school curriculum, and refine its weighting and contents in order to progress towards a 'learning curriculum'.

The leadership teams were supremely aware of their responsibilities to lead staff through this conundrum. So, whilst a cup of coffee on the table might have looked a luxury to the careworn class teacher on the journey past the headteacher's office, inside, senior managers were wrestling hard to assimilate the learning that had been articulated by staff. Initiatives tried and tested in the classrooms needed to be monitored and evaluated. Working together, headteachers and deputies tried to connect the learning, returning later to staff having refined, connected and woven it into school systems and policies. It was akin to navigating through fogs, hazards and rough seas, whilst also changing speed, temperature and direction en route. Each leadership team focused in different ways on what they were trying to achieve, and worked creatively to make it manageable for staff – without getting distracted by minutiae or barriers to whole-school learning such as 'we can't because … '.

Taking a strategic role

As an example of a working model to explore these issues, one large school's leadership team comprised two deputy heads and the headteacher. Each deputy had line management of particular year groups, specific subjects areas and teams. Working in tandem with the headteacher to monitor the implementation of the SIP, whole-school learning was constantly reviewed. Each member of the leadership team brought different skills and perspectives to the discussions. Potential solutions to address whole-school issues were sifted and sorted, revisited and revised. Then they were scrutinized for durability, practicality and workload, until an appropriate solution could be drafted to present to staff. In this way connections were made that:

- secured the pace and quality of whole-school learning
- saved time for the overburdened classteacher
- decreased bureaucracy for staff
- kept staff regularly informed of changes and 'policies in progress'
- reassured staff particularly as we became 'lost' in our learning – before we found our way again
- ensured the effective day-to-day management and organization of new initiatives
- ensured in-service training (INSET) was specific and relevant to classroom practice, differentiated and responsive to the needs of teachers.

Working with staff 'on the ground' to turn plans into action

Working at the next level, the deputy heads showed particular diligence in operational mode. Here, they focused on turning plans into practical realities, working closely with subject leaders and curriculum or year-group teams. Termly targets were set and reviewed with subject leaders to keep the learning moving forward.

'New knowledge' was translated into the curriculum, schemes of work, and through to classroom practice. With year-group leaders, it was a similar process. One model used successfully was to have a three-week cycle of middle management meetings. In the first week a main item was tabled at a full meeting and all team members developed an understanding of the big picture. However, over the second and third weeks, the deputies worked in rotation with individual team leaders they line managed. Therefore, in week two, a team leader might have the opportunity to clarify what needed to be done with the deputy head, and give detailed consideration as to how to manage implementation with the year-group team. Alternatively the team leader could talk through any potential barriers to implementing the plan with the expertise and support of the deputy available on tap. It was an open agenda and a bespoke coaching session for the individual team leader who might be a newly-appointed manager. During the third week there was time to implement the action, collect relevant information or samples from year-group colleagues, reflect or monitor, as the task required. In week four the whole team met again either to look at the learning points gleaned and to share best practice, or to move on to a new topic and begin the round again.

Being a 'troubleshooter'

Another role for the deputy heads was that of troubleshooters. New initiatives and systems tend to have their pitfalls, and require tweaking. The deputies listened and learned about what was going well and what still needed development. Sometimes it meant the leadership team going back to the drawing board. At other times, it involved empowering staff to let go of what had gone before. Thus, for example, through the involvement of the deputies in planning meetings, teachers were encouraged to plan creatively for cross-curricular integration. This was not a comfortable process for many. Many teachers found it hard to let go of familiar structures, and venture out into the unknown. The strategies had encouraged teachers to behave with compliance and to be the deliverers of 'containerized' learning using particular teaching methods. Conversely, our leadership teams were encouraging creative thinking, originality, involvement, engagement, and listening to and learning from our pupils. Staff found it hard, and at times unpalatable. Frankly, some deputies were – and secretly still are – conscious of the private groans that preceded their attendance at weekly year-group planning meetings. Thinking through connections between design and technology and literacy, music and science and VAK-ing the planning took time – and, frustratingly, lengthened planning meetings. One school tried to address this issue by holding a series of year-group curriculum workshops that met during the school day, whilst revising Curriculum 2000. Continuity for the children, and the school's budget, dictated the frequency, scope and duration of such exercises. However, it was felt that periods of quality time for detailed reflections were vital for teachers. The process bore particularly productive fruits for integration and blocking of schemes of work during the revision of Curriculum 2000.

Being a realist

Deputies also needed to be pragmatists and realists. Manageability for class teachers' workload was a top priority. However, this realism needed a hard edge as well as a softer centre. Tempering workload had to be set against the urgent need to progress the quality of learning for pupils, staff, the school and the community. Sometimes extra meetings or longer meetings were required, and deputies gently encouraged and tried to offset time in lieu for staff. At other times deputies were wise and advised the head or each other that enough was enough. Their sensitivity, care and day-to-day knowledge of colleagues' needs helped to regulate the speed and direction of the schools' work.

Being well organized

Our deputies were also superb organizers – leading the interpretation of initiatives into the realities of inflexible school timetables, and moulding the curriculum to meet the needs of the pupils it served. In schools where teamwork was at its best, they were adept at finding ways to fit square pegs into round holes. For example, when the creative process was under way in a leadership team meeting of three, one deputy had particular skills in interpreting why an idea would or would not work in practice. She could quickly interpret what the initiative would look like on the timetable, who it would affect, the knock-on effects for support staff, which venue would be the best and which staff would need to know what. Spotting the fallout a mile away, she saved the team hours of fruitless planning with an apparently good idea that might ultimately go nowhere in practice. The other deputy had in-depth knowledge of the curriculum and an excellent understanding of the Literacy Strategy. With such complementary skills and abilities working within the leadership team, the quality of teamwork and the outcomes for children's learning were boundless.

Being versatile

The deputies were also visionaries, exemplars and researchers. Some within the group were class teachers during the project. Through trial and error they were able to pilot what at the time were new ideas, such as the use of water, music and brain gym in class. They knew the pitfalls. They helped to overcome the obstacles on the way.

Yet modelling was not the only way. Others provided different types of focused support. Some deputies had carefully researched and read about brain-based learning. Their knowledge became a point of reference for staff, as well as the much needed benign and ever-present 'irritant'. If, for example, the purpose of brain gym was confused with brain breaks, it was clarified to refocus staff efforts in this area. If an area such as 'big pictures' or didactic-displays waned, staff were reminded why they were doing it and how it helped children's learning. If chill-outs in the staffroom became 'we can't because ... ' it was connected to children's self-esteem and professional well-being, and gently corrected. There was no sense of failure – simply feedback that connected theory and practice.

Whatever their role however, they were well respected by colleagues for their versatility as practitioners and for their willingness to model or induct staff in practical strategies for enhancing the effectiveness of learning and teaching. In this way they spearheaded the implementation of major changes in practice from brain gym and music to literacy and behaviour management.

Being an extra pair of eyes and ears

Finally, in the very best sense of the word, deputies were 'spies' for learning. They listened and looked and were adept at picking up positive 'vibes'. They identified what was going well, and found different ways to share successes with colleagues so that we could celebrate achievements en route. For example, one deputy used part of the 10-minute morning briefing meeting. Every week the meeting was located in a different class to see how 'big pictures' had been implemented through the school. Later the focus changed to brain gym to refresh the memories of experienced staff and induct new ones.

Deputies' listening ears were also sensitive to areas that required development, resolution or closure. It might be an area for induction, training, policy clarification, cover, or release. Alternatively it might be an area for improvement identified through official monitoring procedures. Spotting the need for 'TLC' or support for staff was another domain. Our successful deputies displayed high levels of emotional intelligence and were responsive to organizational nuances, which in turn helped the school to support the learning teacher or pupil.

We now turn to middle managers and the role they played in leadership for learning.

Middle managers and teams become leaders of learning and learning leaders

Middle managers and teams became leaders of learning and learning leaders through, for example:

- curriculum management teams
- the assessment coordinator and the inclusion team.

If leadership was to be successfully distributed it was clear that our schools required emotionally intelligent leaders of learning, as well learning leaders, in order to build capacity. We spent some time thinking how best to provide training for this purpose and for this group of staff. The five headteachers questioned the quality and purpose of external training. At that time we felt pressured to implement national agendas, which focused training on subject knowledge. Insufficient opportunities existed to develop generic management skills. So, we decided to trial school-based training. What follows are some examples of this work in progress.

Curriculum management teams

In one school, management meetings ran in parallel with staff meetings. The subject matter was the same, but management meetings focused on the *how* of leading policy implementation. There were three areas of focus:

- management
- metalearning
- curriculum.

Learning to hone management skills Within each focus, there were three levels of managerial learning:

- development of individual management skills
- leadership and management of a year-group team
- membership of a middle management team.

Our staff learned and honed their management skills working on projects and challenges that were firmly rooted in the schools' contexts. It ensured extended opportunities for management in practice, rather than a short focus on a detached case study. Supported to think holistically, managers developed organizational and curricular connections, to ensure continuity and progression. In turn, their support or direction for team members, kept all staff informed of updates or changes. Effectively we were training staff in the skills required for deputy headship. The learning 'curve' was vertical for some, but it was experience based, so staff learned quickly and were highly motivated. Management meetings generated high-quality discussions with high-quality outcomes.

Metalearning in teamwork At one level, middle managers honed their management skills. At a much deeper level, they developed the links between management and metalearning. The challenge for managers was to articulate organizational learning in digestible chunks for staff consumption. Getting 'lost whilst learning' was hard. Overburdened class teachers already had enough to contend with. For teachers not yet engaged with the learning, it could be very unsettling. A blanket of fog sometimes descended around work in progress: 'I don't understand! Can somebody please tell me what am I supposed to be going?' The inherent danger was that, seeking order, the teacher did not ask questions to further learning, and instead, decided to go it alone. Thus, learning became incidental or fragmented, rather than a coherent whole. Therefore, it was incumbent upon leadership and middle management teams to work together, focusing firmly on compass directions in the eye of the storm. Managers helped to clarify what we were trying to achieve and where we wanted to be. Purposes were repeatedly made explicit, calm maintained and a climate of trust and *'we can if … '* preserved. Without the benefit of such directional beacons, school-weary travellers and initiatives were doomed to sink.

A prerequisite for success was that managers themselves felt confident and secure when cast adrift and 'lost in learning'. Engaging with, connecting and articulating the learning to others, was a vital skill for new managers to learn. This higher-order skill was at the core of all middle management training. It necessitated support for newly appointed managers who found it a challenging mindset to adopt.

Middle managers helped to translate each school's understanding of metalearning into the practicalities of a learning-focused curriculum. Knowledge gained from classroom or year-group pilots was augmented to form a whole-school perspective. The five schools developed a range of cherry-picked strategies for the teaching of learning, but there were inherent difficulties with progression to iron out on the way.

For example, one school investigated whether a focus on emotional intelligence and learning styles could be interpreted in Reception and Nursery classes – where additionally most of the children were also beginners in learning English. The Foundation Stage co-ordinator led staff to make the termly big picture a visually accessible learning tool for early years pupils. Age-specific enquiry was repeated for other areas such as making learning intentions explicit and the development of our collaborative Prides groups with young pupils. The curriculum management team (CMT) also worked with trainee educational psychologists in order to define and assess the progressive skills of self-efficacy, so that staff and pupils knew the skills and competencies to be developed in these areas. Completion of the task would see such skills then woven into schemes of work. Middle managers encouraged staff to 'see' the big picture and develop their understanding of the challenges of policy interpretation for particular phases or cohorts.

Developing the curriculum Middle managers led the implementation of curriculum revisions. A constant focus on literacy led to gradual but radical revision of the Literacy Strategy that was at the epicentre during this two-year period. One CMT, trying to address depressed standards in writing, developed three different age-appropriate models to provide dedicated literacy sessions across the primary range. Led by a deputy head and an advanced skills teacher, opportunities for speaking and listening increased, through participation in debates, presentations and so on. The unsuitability of the hour for young children meant it was cut into strips with portions delivered across the day. Alongside this, opportunities for children to write independently and more regularly were developed. Immersion in text to develop reading for writing, and scaffolding to support the writing process were inbuilt. Targeted guided writing became a daily feature that began to impact favourably on standards. In time however, despite the progress made, feedback from the CMT on the challenges of time management in implementing such a structure, effected further change. To complement the demands of a wider and richer curriculum, and the need to work with more flexibility and creativity, marking and feedback systems were allocated more time for response to inform focused target teaching. This snapshot across two years perhaps gives some idea of the quality and depth of analysis, soul-searching, the processes of piloting and evaluation, and the amount of time invested by managers in focused discussion. Needless to say, the work is still in progress!

The assessment co-ordinator and the inclusion team

Inclusion was the rationale underpinning the whole project. Our mentors encouraged detailed evaluations of pupils' progress. We looked at the incidence of underachievement. Then we asked ourselves the awkward questions. Why had this occurred? What was learning like for this child? How did she/he feel about school-based learning? Had we been reflecting his/her learning style in our teaching? Did we have the highest expectations for this child? How would we share underachievement with the pupil so as not to demoralize him/her further? How would we share this with the whole parent body? Were there any patterns of underachievement? How would the school manage this information? Was the SIP addressing the issues? There was much to unpack and many internal obstacles and anxieties to overcome, in order to develop systems to address these difficult questions.

One school used their whole-school data as a starting point to identify areas of underachievement throughout the school. The assessment co-ordinator led a detailed scrutiny with the inclusion team that comprised teachers for SEN, English as an additional language (EAL) and more able pupils. Staff discussed what was known about each individual. From this, a register of underachievement was drawn up. Then, members of the inclusion team visited every child listed, to draw up a profile of his/her self perception as a learner. After reporting back to the team, the children's needs were 'banded' by the team to define the type of support needed and match it to the skills the staff could provide. Thereafter, an intensive programme of support was put into place to close the gap in the child's learning. After three months the school sought evaluations of progress made to ascertain if a third of a level progress had been secured in English, mathematics and science.

The high levels of leadership and evaluation undertaken by this team, ensured its focal role in whole-school planning. For a large school with high levels of mobility to manage, it formed the crucial link between a faceless database and the detailed understanding of every child's individual needs. It helped to ensure that every child was 'known', her needs understood, and his progress entitled.

As well an enabling our middle managers to develop as leaders and learners, we also focused on other staff who could take leadership responsibility. We offer just some examples of what we did.

Leadership roles are developed amongst other members of staff

We developed leadership roles amongst other members of staff, for example:

- the data manager
- the office manager
- teaching assistants
- consultants
- governors.

The data manager

The duration of the project marked the period in which our schools 'got connected'! However, 'baby-Broadband's' arrival quickly highlighted the new parenting skills to be developed. The work above could not have even begun without the support skills of various staff. One school administrator with fantastic ICT skills was quickly 'redesignated' as a data manager in the making. The long-awaited capacity to generate and manage our *own* information seemed an apocalyptic development, but such a glut of information meant it was difficult at first to know where or even how to start.

After the databases were up and running, data was scrutinized drawing out whole-school issues. However, our mentors had other thoughts. Throwing us in at the deep end, they challenged us to take a bottom-up rather than a top-down model. They asked us to justify the progress – or lack of it – of individual pupils selected at random. What had caused this to occur? How were the issues being addressed? Were the school's organization and systems sufficiently supportive of this child's progress? The inclusion team's processes described above, dovetail here. However, the role of the data manager was to provide the initial information to be analysed, and to draw up the register of underachievement to be addressed. Her assistance in the development of ICT systems to monitor the complexities of mobility, EAL, SEN and gender was also crucial, such was the size and scope of the task. Working closely with the headteacher and the assessment co-ordinator, various profiles were developed. A whole-school profile was the leadership team's tool. The curriculum management team used a year-group profile. Class teachers used a class profile (see pages 128–9). These documents helped us to get a big picture, to track the progress of pupils, groups and cohorts, so that we could use the data formatively and, for the first time, preventatively. It helped to inform deployment of staff, and secure timetables that worked more flexibly and in more focused ways to enhance children's learning. The ability of the data manager to inform discussions on progress with the rigours of evidence added a powerful new dimension to discussions on school self-evaluation. For us the data manager's contributions were a vital link in the process of children's learning!

The office manager

Another invaluable contribution to the learning community was that of the office manager. In one school she regularly attended weekly 'whole-school planning meetings' with the leadership team and the data manager. The office manager helped in the processes of joined-up thinking. Her initiative to deal with the tasks arising from meetings, lifted huge administrative burdens off the leadership team and class teachers. The agendas would include such items as co-ordinating a whole-school week sheet, developing or tweaking systems, pupil attendance, ongoing issues such as school meals, caretakers, lettings, contracts, letters to send out, budget monitoring and so on. The net result was teachers were freed up to teach and prioritize children's learning. The leadership team was freed up for strategic thinking time. The invaluable skills of the office manager were another vital link in a complex chain of school improvement!

Teaching assistants

Throughout the project our teaching assistants, were involved in a cross-section of the training for metalearning. Working alongside teachers, TAs became co-leaders of the class-based initiatives that enriched children's learning. As the project work developed, some TAs became increasingly involved through attendance at weekly planning meetings. Thus support offered to children became even more finely tuned to learning needs. Fully cognizant of the initiatives introduced in our classrooms, our TAs perpetuated the language of learning in their work with children. Their perceptions enhanced the processes of formative assessment, through their individual or group contacts with children, their liaison with teachers, and their understanding of the language of learning.

However, this co-leadership developed in other ways too. The range of skills possessed by our teaching assistants offered great capacity for enriched learning and teaching. It was to pupils' immense benefit that these competencies came increasingly to the fore. Willing to work flexibly, teaching assistants became leaders in their own right, teaching to or using their talents. One presented her counselling qualifications in support of year 3 pupils struggling to self-regulate their behaviour through the lunch hour. Another TA proffered an Indian dancing club for Key Stage 1 pupils with special educational needs. Incorporating lots of brain gym, we all noted with pleasure corresponding improvements in participants' spelling over time. Yet another loved project-focused work and, with consummate skill, organized school fetes or charity events from beginning to end, involving and motivating children, and leading the whole staff to participate in all sorts of fun. Another group patiently catalogued library stock onto the computer, to upgrade facilities for borrowers. Another tallied and co-ordinated numerous responses to a wide-ranging school improvement plan consultation process. Dedicated first aid and TLC through the lunchtime was calmly and reliably provided by yet another, whilst two in partnership unfailingly loaded and unloaded staffroom dishwashers – and cajoled and organized staff – to ensure continuing health and welfare from sparkling coffee cups. Each of these wide-ranging and individual talents was a priceless contribution to school improvement and learning, and illustrates the scope of distributed leadership.

The willingness of teaching assistants to lead projects or initiatives according to individual strengths impacted favourably on teachers' workload. The range of learning opportunities for pupils was enriched, as were the opportunities for individualized approaches. Advocates for children, TAs also made connections that encouraged children's self-esteem and enabled individual children to be noticed and individually valued within a large school. Their contributions vastly enriched organizational joined-up thinking, and helped to perpetuate the positive ethos, and thus the overall intelligences of our schools.

Consultants

Beyond the teaching establishment employed by the schools, a variety of consultants led developments that enriched staff and pupils' learning.

Neurolinguistic programming practitioners worked in three schools. Their leadership focused staff and pupils on the importance of positive and 'can-do' language use, raised awareness of the different perceptions that may be present in any one situation, and encouraged use of visualization techniques, so vital in the development of pupils' self-esteem.

A special educational needs consultant with great expertise in the development of literacy skills, provided detailed assessments of children's reading and writing. These assessments were invaluable in the development of focused classroom programmes, honed differentiation to improve support, and the development of greater independence for all those learning to manage specific learning difficulties.

Co-ordinators for gifted and talented (GaT) pupils enhanced the quality of 'learning outside the comfort zone' for more able pupils. A wide range of intelligences was supported. Talented gymnasts and writers, musicians and mathematicians, athletes and artists benefited from a variety of extra-curricular opportunities. In class work, direct support from the GaT co-ordinator or indirect facilitation through liaison with the class teacher ensured challenging differentiation for able pupils.

A grant-funded children's yoga consultant, who worked in two schools, enabled those who were challenged by the need to listen, concentrate and relax, to receive dedicated time and carefully paced yet sustained training in essential skills.

Governors

Leadership from and within the five governing bodies was interpreted individually. Each governing body faced distinct challenges and opportunities expressed within the school's school improvement plan. The skills and competencies represented within the membership also ensured each group possessed individual attributes, its own informal code of conduct and ethos. Broadly speaking, governing bodies welcomed either the project's creativity and wider learning opportunities or, post-Ofsted, supported the sustained focus on excellence and school improvement.

Corporately, interest and support for the initiatives were diverse. Some governing bodies listened, learned and enquired about brain-based learning from school-based training and briefings. Some governors attended staff INSET. Others were less sure – perhaps feeling 'If it ain't broke don't try and fix it!'

Whatever the perspective however, we found that the usual processes of critical friendship became more sharply focused. Such was the intensity of the schools' emphasis on learning in headteachers' reports and ensuing discussions, that governors' meetings were drawn in as yet another piece of the metalearning jigsaw.

Some governing bodies therefore connected to a much deeper understanding of their strategic function and their capacity to influence and monitor the implementation of the school improvement plan. Working with headteachers, they articulated their own 'big picture'. This helped them to 'see' the processes of school improvement interpreted through from strategic decision-making to practical reality.

In one of the schools, the school improvement plan document format was layered to reflect the connections between each tier, so that link governors and the governing body could monitor implementation in a more informed way, during their termly scheduled visits. The tiers were:

- a mission statement connected to lifelong learning
- aims of the school
- overview of focus areas to be developed (published to parents)
- key priorities for both curriculum development and for the leadership team (overview for governors and published to parents)
- breakdown of priorities (detailed tool for governors to monitor implementation)
- curriculum co-ordinators' action plans and success criteria (provided detail for school's own self-evaluation processes)
- record of reviews and evaluations.

The governing body used the layers of information to develop their monitoring programme and the role of link governors.

Coupled with this, a ring-binder file was developed for each governor to ensure key documents were readily to hand when required. An example of the contents page is included in Figure 5.1.

By connecting resources to ways of working, governors refined awareness of their strategic role. Knowing *how* to go about it heightened the quality of critical friendship. The challenge was real and insightful. The governing bodies became more self-evaluative, reflected on their corporate metalearning, took time to review their ways of working and their collective effectiveness in completion of their duties. One governing body built in two review meetings each year. The first was a summer term meeting of chairs of committees with the governing body chair, vice-chair and

CONTENTS

SECTION 1 – Information

Governors' Annual Calendar (included meetings, committees and termly monitoring schedule)
List of Governors
Staffing List
Management Structure
Term Dates
Committees and Working Parties
Plan of the School

SECTION 2 – Key Documents

School Prospectus
Governors' Report to Parents
School Improvement Plan Summary
Governing Body Terms of Reference
Ofsted Action Plan
Committees' Terms of Reference

SECTION 3 – Selection of Governors' Policies

Monitoring
Complaints
Uniform
Leave of Absence
Appointment of Staff
Health and Safety
Home–School Agreement
Attendance
Pay Policy
Performance Management Procedure

SECTION 4 – Meetings

Business Meeting – Agenda and Minutes
Head Teacher's Report
Monitoring Reports
Other Documents or Reports
Local Authority Items
Personnel Committee – Agenda and Minutes
Finance Committee – Agenda and Minutes
Premises Committee – Agenda and Minutes

Figure 5.1 Governors' pack

headteacher. The purpose was to reflect on the learning from the current academic year and subsequently draw up the annual calendar of termly meetings and visits to be made by governors. The second meeting was for the whole governing body. The purpose was to review committee structures, and evaluate their effectiveness in relation to monitoring the implementation of the school improvement plan. This enhanced connections between school improvement and governing body committee and meeting structures. It also ensured that patterns of leadership and expertise within the governing body could be reviewed to ensure that both were well distributed.

Last, but by no means least, we extended our development of distributed leadership to the children themselves.

Children become leaders of learning

Children became leaders of learning by:

- leading their own learning
- leading the learning of peers, parents and siblings
- leading the learning of teachers and governors.

A consequence of Ofsted's focus on class teaching over the last few years, was that learning was firmly relegated into second place. The implication – and the presumption – was that 'power-teaching' enabled effective learning. Our mentors encouraged us to think through and challenge this assumption in our schools, as we began to articulate our thoughts about learning in our discussions.

At first, we found it difficult to bring learning to the fore, and to differentiate it from teaching, but we soon realized in this rare instance, that a quick-fix solution and a richly abundant, but free, resource was to hand. The children were our teachers! By listening to their voice, and letting them lead our learning, we could subsequently wrap our teaching around pupils' needs, in order to take individual and whole-school learning forward.

However, although this was a free resource, the children's tutelage came with conditions attached. The challenge for our schools, was that the listening had to be 'real', not tokenistic. This meant that we had to engage proactively with what the children said, whether we liked what they said or not. If they had formed particular perceptions about the conditions for, and quality of, learning and teaching in our schools, then these were the areas in which we had to manage and effect change. The more staff listened, the more they learned from the children as leaders of learning.

Children led their own learning

As our children benefited from opportunities to reflect on their needs as learners, they communicated ways in which they could further their own learning:

> I learn best while it is quiet so I can concentrate. I am kinaesthetic. I also learn better in the morning because in the morning my mind is fresh, and in the afternoon I get tired. I also learn best when our atmosphere is funny.

> Sometimes teachers come into the classroom and I have questions. They answer them and they help me understand what I'm doing. I also feel the water in the class helps me because if I'm thirsty it wakes me up. My magic-

circle helps me because if I'm angry or frustrated it gets me out of my reptilian brain and when I work in my Pride it also helps.

I think I learn best when it is quiet in the place I'm working. I am a visual learner, because I cannot work when I cannot see what I am learning about. I think I learn best from pictures. I'm not good when I get things from the Internet because I never read through the information.

The children also articulated their growing confidence, self-esteem and emotional intelligence, clearly indicating future directions for the discerning teacher:

I think our Prides are working and helping us now. First I didn't like my Pride because there were a couple of people I didn't actually like to work with, because they were a bit annoying. But now I've got to know them they are better, and it is giving me a bit more confidence to meet new people.

For the listening and learning teacher, receptive to children's leadership, it meant learning was *facilitated* by leading questions rather than exclusively *delivered* by 'teaching'. The subtle nuances in feedback, meant that the teacher intellectually engaged in these processes, could 'wrap' helpful strategies subtly round the pupil's learning. For example, a visual learner might be encouraged to develop a story plan as a mind map, whilst a kinaesthetic learner might receive support to do this pictorially, with identified sounds, textures and smells. The children's lead ensured learning preferences informed teaching strategies that fitted snugly like a second skin, rather than an ill-fitting 'one size fits all' model.

Children in some schools were also given the lead to assess their individual progress and level their own work, particularly in year 5 and year 6. Working with child-friendly level descriptors, they developed ownership of the next steps to be taken. Close involvement in target setting was the incentive for self-motivation and provided the prompt for feedback to the teacher:

I feel that my learning has improved for me because I can set myself goals, which helped me to achieve much more. (Y2)

I think I've learned a lot, where to put commas, making lists, reading my work. Sometimes I need to put a comma instead of a full stop. (Y2)

I think one particular thing [that helped me] is my targets. My teacher tells me which my targets are so I can achieve them. My friend T helps me in my maths, which used to be my weakest subject, but now it isn't. My weakest subject is science but I like it because my teacher helps.

Children led the learning of peers, parents and siblings

As our growing learners increased in strength and resilience, so they became confident to lead the learning of others. It was the recipients of this support that explained the benefits of their leadership in all its fullness:

> The pupils in my class help me to understand the problem and instead of telling me the answers they explain it very clearly to me. This kind of learning always helps me.

> Children in my class help me by not telling me the answer, but by explaining it to me.

> If there is a long queue to see the teacher, I ask someone on my table and instead of giving me the answer straight away, they explain how they did it and leave it to me to work out now that I know how.

The children learned to be very accepting of the leads they were given from others. The language of their shared explanations was familiar and comfortable. In turn, recipients became adept at leading the leaders, who were providing such valuable support. They adjusted the pace, clarified and asked questions of their peers, in ways that they might not wish to, repeatedly, with their teachers:

> G helps me in maths. He explains it very well too if I get stuck on a question.

> When I ask my friends for help they don't just give me the answer they explain it fully so I understand better.

> When I don't understand something I ask someone and they explain it in a clearer way until I understand.

Paired and shared marking was a feature of this assessment process, and the children became skilled at providing focused feedback to each other, identifying where learning intentions had been met and where developments lay.

It was also pleasing to see children participating in community leadership, and supporting each other in their leading roles. School councils played a major role in this area. Their influence effected changes in a range of pupil services ranging from school meals to healthy snacks, playground improvements to recycling schemes. Playground buddies offered support and friendship for those who might be feeling lonely or left out. Lunchtime helpers supported the necessary routines to ensure the processes ran smoothly.

Children were confident in extending this leadership into the public domain. Performances, festivals, musical, dramatic, artistic and physical skills were regularly celebrated and displayed. Opportunities for celebrating such skills, encouraged others, by their example

Other children were able to apply these leadership skills at home in support of others' learning:

> Learning my sounds helped me. I read to my sister. (RY)

> Learning is important to me because I can use these skills … and help others with that skill, which in turn makes me happy and makes others happy. For example when I learned how to do ratio, I helped my brother on a question he was stuck on.

It was also pleasing to hear from parents, that this influence continued into secondary schooling and beyond. One parent told a headteacher how delighted she was that her son had influenced his older siblings into an appreciation of classical music pieces. This was a direct consequence of his own experiences of listening and responding to a whole range of mood music in primary school.

Children led the learning of teachers and governors

Empowered learners were increasingly confident in expressing themselves, and that provided a rich learning resource for teachers. Some, particularly supply staff, found their leads challenging, for feedback could be quite direct:

Stop shouting! Teachers will lose their voices if they shout too much!

Sometimes what teachers thought was helpful, pupils found a hindrance. This practical suggestion was quickly adopted by teachers before national tests:

In tests, if we are halfway through, the teacher usually gives us little reminders or something, and it puts you off the answer or thing that's in your head, and I think she should just write it on the board.

Children's leadership was ignored only at teachers' peril. For example, when piloting 'close the gap' marking in one school, teachers learned that the children did not like felt-tip pens highlighting their achievements, because the ink seeped through to the next page. It was important to understand apparently minor issues that assumed major importance, because they could get in the way of learning and be put right so easily.

Pupil leadership applied at strategic levels too. One school developed the pupils' voice on the governing body. A link governor for the school council was appointed to meet with the children, and feed back to the governing body. Currently the school is extending this concept further so that the school council can meet formally with the governing body.

The children's voice plays a powerful leading role in our schools.

Conclusion

We conclude by:

- reviewing what we did
- reflecting on what we learned.

Reviewing what we did

We:

- ensured headteachers modelled leadership for learning
- practised joined-up thinking to translate whole-school strategies into practical action in classrooms
- distributed leadership for learning across the school, utilizing and developing the wide range of talents and skills available within our communites
- enabled leadership teams to reflect and learn, and to develop their working practices in order to lead the learning
- provided opportunities for differentiated INSET to meet the leadership and management needs of *all* staff
- enabled children to become leaders of learning.

Reflecting on what we learned

We learned:

- that to build capacity in schools requires long-term strategies rather than short-term tactics
- that the headteacher's role is developing and changing in tandem with the processes of school self-evaluation
- the importance of reviewing learning in order to connect each stage to the 'big picture' of school improvement
- that higher-order metalearning and emotional intelligence are essential skills in leadership and management
- that given the opportunity, children can lead teachers' learning and the learning of others.

As we developed leadership for learning in a distributed way across the school we recognized that to do this requires:

- headteachers to have a fundamental commitment to the creation of a learning organization
- a *'we can if ... '* attitude because leadership for learning involves challenging and changing the culture of the school if learning and teaching is to be transformed
- a recognition that transforming learning and teaching is a process not a package. It requires paying attention to capacity-building strategies that will have a long-term impact on learning and teaching in classrooms and across the school as a whole
- coaching, training and the recognition and valuing of the knowledge, skills and talents of adults and children.

We now return to children's learning. In Chapter 6 we describe the strategies we used to accelerate children's learning. In Chapter 7 we explore the ways in which we kept track of that learning.

6

Accelerating children's learning

Being a good learner is not just a matter of learning a few techniques like mind mapping or brain gym. It is about the whole person: their attitudes, values, self-image and relationships, as well as their skills and strategies. (Claxton, 2002, p. 15)

We can accelerate children's learning if we :

- **heed the health warnings**
- **reflect on and review progress**
- **maintain and enhance inclusive provision for a broad and balanced curriculum**
- **use creative differentiation to support inclusion.**

In our learning journey together we came to recognize that to accelerate learning it was essential to take account of at least four health warnings.

Heeding the health warnings

The health warnings we heeded were:

- accelerating learning is a process not a package
- authority not autocracy rules!
- excellence without exception!
- befriend the barriers to learning.

Accelerating learning is a process not a package

The magical learning potential unlocked by perpetuating 'can-do' attitudes was virtually akin to a professional treasure chest. However, following the route in search of the pot of gold was not as straightforward. Our experiences affirmed that actualizing a 'can-do' philosophy required corporate thought and considerable depths of understanding and commitment from all staff in order to develop such a temperate climate within a school. Tangible strategies that could be replicated fairly easily and superficially were tied to a deeper vision about learning, which informed our policies, practice and pedagogy. In other words, just because our teachers and pupils practised brain gym, listened to music and drank water, it did not automatically accelerate rates of progress.

The development of 'can-do' attitudes was a process not a package. It was a shared language, a belief that became almost spiritual in its intensity, and was simultaneously complex and simple in its application. The particular techniques used were developed gradually but deliberately and were described for readers in Chapter 3.

If we are mindful of Michael Fullan's observations on the simultaneous simplicity and complexity of 'what teachers do', the dichotomies are highlighted here in sharp relief. We wanted to accelerate children's learning – yet without the pressures upon them so inherent in a performance culture. Each school had to find its 'position' on the continuum between learning and performance orientations. Therefore, the fundamental importance of well-established, positive approaches and relaxed alertness in order to accelerate learning could not be overstated. Learning about their learning developed our pupils' emotional intelligence, respect and self-esteem and enabled the growth of resilient, aspiring learners who were more 'connected' to interpersonal and intra-personal understanding. They developed their own learning identities and preferences and became equipped with the skills to further their own learning.

Authority not autocracy rules!

We found that many organizational factors or school systems militated against the development of children's confidence and the fostering of positive attitudes in each individual. Such factors ranged from the timetable to inflexible lunchtimes.

The impact of teachers' traditional position of power was another important factor for us to overcome; for example, 'if you don't do your homework, I will … ' 'you do not answer me back because … '. Simply lowering the power-based barriers between teachers and pupils to function on a basis of mutual respect and tolerance was painful and threatening for some staff who believed that the class/school would go to pieces if traditional discipline and systems were not firmly upheld.

One of the schools, for example, had just emerged from a successful Ofsted inspection prior to the beginning of the project. Whilst the headteacher saw the 'Learning to Learn' project as a vehicle to move forward again, the staff needed to be convinced of the need to change their practice. The headteacher wanted to move away from some more 'traditional' methods and 'open up' the teaching. She wanted to encourage staff to begin to give children open-ended questions, let them work in groups and make a purposeful noise. This was a big step for some. Understandably, some staff were concerned they would lose control and respect.

Undaunted by this, the headteacher was determined 'Learning to Learn' was going to be a whole-school project. The emphasis was put on learning to move to a deeper level of learning than just academic study. Through carefully selecting and introducing some of the practical strategies described in Chapter 3, she created a learning environment of mutual respect for everyone. She actively encouraged the development of emotional, spiritual and ethical intelligence, three essential characteristics of the 'Intelligent School' identified by Barbara MacGilchrist and her colleagues, Kate Myers and Jane Reed (MacGilchrist et al., 1997; 2004).

After the first year when end of key stage test results remained high, staff were more confident and more willing to 'let go'. After the second year, with a cohort of 120, the school had the highest points score almost in the country for this size cohort. It was confirmed for staff and parents that working hard to develop a learning orientation had not compromised any aspect of learning. Instead, it had enhanced the quality and depth of learning which in turn led to the school's second School Achievement Award in three years.

Excellence without exception!

There was no suggestion intended above, that accelerated learning was achieved merely through children and teachers simply being 'nice' to and comfortable with each other, or by tolerance of mediocrity. Praise needed to be given for genuine efforts or high standards achieved, not just for its own sake, otherwise it was not credible. It was important for children to know the boundaries of what was expected of them. Praise needed to go hand in hand with systematic developmental feedback for pupils and rigorous evaluations of progress, achieved by teachers, pupils and parents working in partnership. Just because a car was worthy of praise for its fuel economy, the accelerator could not propel it forward unless a helpful foot was applied to the throttle.

Befriend the barriers to learning

Identifying and overcoming barriers to children's learning were often challenging issues for teachers to manage. Yet, if we ignored them it was at our peril. On many occasions learners simply needed to develop or clarify their knowledge, or rectify a simple misconception, without which learning could be impaired. Unless resolved, however, such difficulties were likely to be compounded from one session to another. Longer-term learning difficulties were often more deep rooted in emotions and experiences. The support needed was to unlock the emotional key, which was preventing access to learning. For example, one school identified that a particular group of refugees became upset every time classroom doors were closed. One can only guess at the emotional traumas attached to such simple everyday acts, but they raised significant learning barriers. Problematic for the individuals – as well as the classes who witnessed the distress – the situation was quickly resolved once the cause was identified and managed sensitively by the teacher.

Whatever the barrier, once identified and managed, it unlocked the key to confident and successful learning. However, reflective and proactive practitioners were required to be aware of and perceptive to these needs. Our discerning teachers related to children and classes on microcosmic as well as macrocosmic levels, in order to break down the barriers and promote 'can-do' attitudes amongst their learners.

Reflecting on and reviewing progress

We reflected on and reviewed progress by:

- reviewing the schools' use of formative and summative assessments
- developing the use of learning and personal targets
- reviewing and revising systems for developmental marking
- working in partnership with parents.

Underpinning our 'we can if ... ' attitude was a determination to review and reflect upon children's learning in a rigorous, systematic way. Chapter 7 describes how we kept track of children's learning. Here we outline the strategies we developed to enable this to happen.

Reviewing the schools' use of formative and summative assessments

With their schools the headteachers considered carefully the changes that would need to be made if we were to establish a culture that genuinely accelerated children's learning, as opposed to use of a 'quick-fix' solution. In so doing, we took some detailed looks at our assessments of pupils' progress, both summative and formative, to consider whether the ethos in our schools, and the systems we were using, were actually improving children's learning.

Issues surrounding summative and formative assessments encapsulated the tensions between learning versus performance orientations, which had preoccupied us. Parents were increasingly aware of the importance and meaning of attaining required levels in the context of the National Curriculum, whilst schools were trying to guard against deflating those pupils who were progressing well, but at lower levels.

Over time, we gradually became convinced of the need to share summative information much more explicitly with pupils and parents on an annual basis, although we knew recognizable difficulties with it had to be resolved. Philosophically however, it took us some time to reach that point. To some extent we had shied away from being too explicit with our pupils – with the best of intentions – because of such divergent needs. We were acutely aware that with high proportions of SEN, EAL and mobility in some of our communities, many of our pupils might have made excellent *progress* but were still *attaining* at below average levels. Sharing such decontextualized information was simply demoralizing and we felt summative assessment adversely affected pupils' self-esteem, motivation and confidence.

We also considered how, alongside our quests to establish a positive ethos and to encourage each child's achievements, the dangers of valuing mediocrity also lurked. We pondered the number of occasions over years gone by, where we had heard 'average' work being praised as 'fantastic', with none or few development points identified. Chastened, we thought carefully about the work of Black and Wiliam on formative assessment (1998; 2003) and each parent and child's entitlement to systematic feedback on progress and achievement. Tempered with a system of formative assessment, summative information enabled pupils to engage and understand exactly 'where they were' and 'what they needed to do next' to improve the standards of their work.

Developing the use of learning and personal targets

The moves we took to develop formative assessment procedures were gradual – one step at a time – but it was not a particularly tidy process. First, we considered what was already happening in the assessment domain.

At that point, summative reports on attainment were published at end of key stages, and annual Qualifications and Curriculum Authority (QCA) tests were employed as a system for the internal tracking of pupil progress.

Formatively, target-setting was restricted to half-yearly occasions during pupil–parent–teacher consultations. At the end of an academic year, these were revised and reviewed with pupil and teacher, and published to parents in the end of year reports. Targets were behavioural or task focused, but not explicitly or systematically linked to National Curriculum level descriptors.

We were also conscious that we needed to find time to *teach* the targets the children were aspiring to. We could not just leave them to meet the target without appropriate support, yet we wrestled to find the time in an already overloaded curriculum. One of our schools had particularly high levels of EAL. Over the years quality monolingual models within classes and groups had decreased sharply, and thus teachers' 'modelling duties' had increased just as sharply. Here, there was a significant additional requirement to teach systematically to the targets.

It was a process that was difficult to manage, because we were finding our way a bit at a time, as many schools were doing across the country. Through 'doing' and 'reviewing', we experimented in order to identify the best way forward for our respective schools.

We concluded termly meetings with parents, as well as mid-year and end-of-year reports, had proved successful in feeding back some sense of progress and attitudes to learning. Yet we readily accepted the need to develop the tangible details about attainment and progress, which parents would find informative, and pupils could engage with, in order to further their learning in school.

Our thinking moved forward with the development of the use of SMART targets for SEN pupils (DfES, 1998), which quickly permeated schools' psyche. Realistically, the manageability of such a process was unsustainable for class teachers. We did not want to overburden them by rushing in, yet the potential benefits of effective target setting were by now very clear to us. Paring down administration was essential. Like many, no doubt, we spent a great deal of time thinking about how we could devote regular attention and teaching time to targets, and incorporate an additional system into medium- and short-term planning. The curriculum was already so tight that nothing else could be fitted in. Something had to give!

So it was, that whilst reviewing its English policy, one school incorporated group target-setting into literacy sessions. Feedback and progress against National Curriculum level descriptors and the National Literacy Strategy (NLS) targets took place weekly, in targeted group work. It was felt the administration of individual targets and feedback was simply unmanageable if the children were to receive the support and guidance they needed from the teacher in order to develop targeted literacy skills.

During guided writing, once per week in rotation, an ability group would bring a piece of work to review it with the teacher in the light of targets set. Students were made aware of the level their piece of work had achieved or the writing features they needed to build in to raise the standard of their work by the next third of a level. The work may have been previously distance marked by the teacher, or pupil self-evaluation and supported editing may have been the intention. Whatever the case, pupils reflected on progress made against their targets, either by themselves or with their peer group. From the accessible descriptions, their targets were drawn so that they knew exactly how to improve their work. The teacher gave individual support and teaching to the target as the work was under way. In this way written and spoken models were always available for EAL learners, making the process tangible, and scaffolding them in, whilst at the same time it opened up mutually supportive pupil working partnerships.

Thus, through the usual methods, children developed their knowledge and understanding of their targets, because they were readily to hand in their class books, or target cards and homework books. They had dedicated time to interact with and respond to teachers' distance marking in order to raise the standards of their work.

Parents were sent copies of these targets, which featured the next one-third level's progress. All this was made possible by the excellent practical work of Redbridge's Literacy Forum. Under the guidance of John Hickman, Margaret Preston and Ian Bennett, the forum analysed and broke down the skills and knowledge required from the National Curriculum and NLS, and then compiled planned activities to meet the targets. It was the breakthrough we had been seeking, in making such a process manageable.

Even so, after a short time, the schedule of teaching to targets each week felt so tight that it had to be relaxed into a two-week cycle. Illness, courses, visits, visitors and the everyday tensions of competing priorities and provision of a broad and balanced curriculum saw to that. However, the targets had the desired effects for the children and parents, instilling awareness and ownership of development points and accelerating learning.

A year 6 pupil's view was:

The targets that you have are very useful because you become determined to fight your way through to your target.

Following an inspection at the school Ofsted judged that:

Pupils [are] beginning to understand exactly what they need to do to improve their work through explicitly shared targets for individual lessons and group activities. (2002, ref. 131013)

Ofsted reported that parents felt:

The teachers know their pupils very well. They closely monitor pupils' personal development and work sensitively to challenge and support their specific needs. The impact of the 'Learning to Learn' project means that pupils know how well they are doing and are involved in identifying and reviewing their own targets both at an academic and personal level. (2002, ref. 131013)

Reviewing and revising systems for developmental marking

We had begun to dabble with shorter target cycles in order to make our systems SMARTer and to accelerate learning. In so doing we revised marking policies and improved developmental marking techniques – whilst also trying to retain the manageability of it all for our staff. Some teachers began to restrict marking to learning intentions, whilst others argued the lost opportunities of such a narrow focus. The following are examples of some of the techniques we introduced.

Using ICT In one of the schools, marking in years 5 and 6 was an onerous task. Initially, to ease the pressure, the school adopted the highlighting approach suggested by Shirley Clarke (1998) in which positive work was highlighted in one colour, and one area for development in another. Comments were also written. Staff still found this time-consuming so the marking policy was reviewed yet again. The school decided to adopt a range of other strategies. For example, on-line marking was used in year 6 through the London Grid for Learning. Children could access this at home and the teachers could mark in school. This was particularly useful in science and proved to be a motivating force for many pupils. The use of whiteboards made a huge difference especially in mathematics. The visual impact of the interactive whiteboard, and the potential it offered to input and interact with information, made it a dynamic assessment tool. For example, in a mathematics capacity topic, pupils saw liquid being poured into a measuring jar, ready for the learners to interpret the measurements. With a flourish of the teacher's pen or finger, quantities were changed and physically moved around on the screen, enhancing opportunities for differentiation and extension of knowledge. Coupled with the teacher's questioning techniques, using approaches akin to the mental oral starter, this became a powerful, as well as labour-saving, assessment tool. With less marking to do teachers had more time to think about varying activities and differentiating the work. However, it was important to bring parents on board to help them understand the rationale for this approach.

Closing the gap Shirley Clarke's more recent work (2001) inspired some of us to revise the ways we provided feedback to our learners. We were reminded of the wasted hours of precious teacher time, when pupils seemingly ignored their developmental 'pearls of wisdom'. Equally we knew how marking could be dreary rather than dynamic. Books peppered with 'good try' or 'well done' were not enabling learning at any level. We reminded ourselves of the maxim we cited in an earlier chapter: 'If you always do what you've always done, you'll always get what you always got!'

Having tried different systems we began systematic 'closing the gap' marking. After the weekly extended writing session on a Friday, teachers marked one group's independent writing, using closing the gap marking strategy. (The size of the group varied according to the literacy model being used.) Dedicated time was built into the timetable on Monday of the following week to allow pupils to respond to the teacher's marking in a designated 'response time'. During the guided writing session that followed later in the week, the teacher conferenced/taught to the targets arising from the marking. Each group had their writing marked in this way, in rotation. The other group's work was peer reviewed. Pupils wrote independently on one side of the exercise book whilst the 'closing the gap' comments and pupils' responses were written on the other side. Another school used Post-it notes to provide the space for upgrading the work. Yet another used asterisks or highlighter pens.

'Closing the gap' marking made explicit to pupils the gap between what they were doing and what they needed to be doing to raise the standard of their work. The marking was informed from the teacher's knowledge of the pupils, gained during the target sessions, and then fed back into the practice of their writing. It consisted of various prompts that aimed to help the child to reach the next stage of development and make some small qualitative improvement. Two examples amongst the many suggested by Shirley Clarke (2001), were:

- a reminder prompt – 'Say more about how you feel about this person.'
- a scaffold prompt – 'Can you describe how this person is a good friend?'

Paired or group marking Less labour intensive for the teacher, this initiative required students to mark each other's work and award 'three stars and a wish'. The stars celebrated achievement, the wish identified an area for improvement. To assist with this process some teachers displayed in the classroom explicit examples of work at different levels, for example, writing in the English National Curriculum. These displays showed the children the standard expected and what they had to do to achieve the level. It was like an 'aha!' for the children. 'So that is what level 5 in writing looks like!' This proved to be a powerful tool to support paired and group marking. The children were honest and open with one another and, because of the 'no put-down' zones in these classrooms, children who were struggling were openly supported and encouraged by their peers. *'We can if ... '* became translated into 'you can if ... ' in very practical ways.

Self-marking This featured more predominantly in mathematics so that children could learn through their own mistakes as they marked their assignments. In one of the year 6 self-marking lessons observed, the learning orientation developed by the school was clearly a key ingredient in the success of this approach. There was no air of competition, no sense of shame at not getting many of the answers 'right'. Instead, children openly told one another the outcome of their marking. Children shared why they had found some questions difficult, others shared the strategies they used to find the correct answer or solve the problem. Learning mentors were identified. For those who were clearly achieving beyond level 4 (the standard expected at the end of year 6), instead of more of the same, focused teaching was arranged using a member of staff whose subject knowledge in mathematics was more advanced than that of the class teacher.

Working in partnership with parents

Parental involvement with children's progress was enhanced as our schools developed the ways to share the targets with them. Several schools began by holding 'Assessment for Learning' days. The purpose behind this was to review each individual's progress against targets that had been set. To facilitate this, one school used supply staff to release class teachers, enabling individual consultations to take place during the school day. Each child in turn was withdrawn from class, to reflect on learning and review progress against targets with the teacher and his/her parent(s). The support and critical friendship of teachers, pupils and parents working together to support learning in this focused way were powerful processes and added another dimension to 'a day's learning'. It also meant that parents' awareness of the differences between progress and attainment was raised, and thus they could share the language of learning that was emerging in our school communities.

The 'Assessment for Learning' days were very successful. Staff had time to sit and talk with the parent and child both present. Together they set targets agreeable to all and understood by all. One year 6 boy said of the day: 'It's good, my mum can't come home and get it wrong anymore!' A parent said: 'Well, now he can't play one off against the other – I know exactly where he is and where he's going.'

Other schools took the actual organization of this concept further, in consultation with a supportive governing body. The first step was to organize an evening meeting with parents that raised awareness of the school's management of children's progress:

> The session was marvellous. I only wish every parent of this school had attended to benefit from the 'wonderful' talk delivered by all four personalities. 'Bravo' for imparting ever so useful information.

> This evening has been unexpectedly fruitful. You have definitely confirmed and given me the confidence to carry on with my style of approach of training my son.

Although it's obvious (now it's been pointed out!) that children learn better when in the right frame of mind, I don't always take the time to ensure this before starting a task. I am going to try to rectify this from now on!

I think today has made us realize how the school is working with us to help our children. My children enjoy being part of a Pride and having a certain role to have responsibility. Also, they enjoy brain gym.

The second step was to close the school to class-grouped learning for the day, whilst remaining open for individual learning consultations between teachers, pupils and parents. Children therefore stayed at home with their parents until their appointment to peruse workbooks and hold their consultations was due. In this way, supply staff were not needed, and the need for additional financial resourcing, and organization of cover was removed. These 'learning surgeries' were valued equally by all participants because of the quality time that could be devoted to review and progress. Pupils helped to draw up their next targets and were clear about what had to be done and why. Parents knew more precisely where their child needed help and support and more precisely how they may be able to provide it. They were also clear about their child's attainment and the correlation with other factors that affect learning, such as behaviour, mobility or attendance. Teachers received valuable feedback on their assessments, their teaching and the benefits of home–school partnership.

Community learning workshops during a similarly structured day, developed the idea further. The education welfare officer managed one workshop, bringing with him a short Powerpoint presentation to advise parents about his role. Informal discussions meant that the school could encourage parents of poor attendees to access advice, and raise awareness of important legal requirements in a supportive and informal setting. The school nurse's workshop offered advice on the management of head lice or medical conditions. Parents who had been attending family learning classes in the school ran another 'stall' to advertise the benefits of such courses, and encourage new participants. An external bookshop was invited, as the school was not situated near a library. School uniform and name-label stalls were also available, as were other learning materials. Refreshments were for sale, and televisions strategically placed in the school hall showed videos of school events, celebrating and publicizing achievements and keeping other family members amused during their siblings' consultations, or at odd moments as necessary. The curricular opportunities were exploited as children enjoyed preparing guidance and informative pamphlets to advertise the event, as part of their literacy sessions.

These initiatives prompted different approaches to community learning, not least in the sense that the school became an epicentre for some community and welfare services. Parental support and attendance was very high. Some parents were not able or particularly keen to take time off work in order to attend an educational consultation. However, enthusiastic take-up of early or late slots was a helpful compromise. The schools also encouraged parents to view these consultations as they would a doctor's –

important for their child's healthy educational development. Visits to 'educational stalls' at the community learning day were variable, but encouraging. The notion of community learning was attractive and undoubtedly sowed benefits for children's learning. This was definitely confirmed by the feedback received from parents.

One school was fortunate to attract funding for family learning from the Basic Skills Agency. Over several weeks parents shared fun and games in support of their children's developing literacy and numeracy skills. Sometimes the classes were run with an open invitation. At other times, likely instances of underachievement within a specific cohort focused the invitation list. At the end of the course, the Mayor of Redbridge presented certificates in a celebration of the learning that had taken place for children and parents in partnership. Parents greatly valued these sessions. For many it raised awareness of different ways they could support their child's learning, without recourse to the formalities of published workbooks. Ultimately, the enthusiasm of participants encouraged some to apply successfully for school-based support work. Three parents advertised the benefits of this learning for other potential recruits.

One of the parents said:

I am a mother of three children of which two of them go to … School, I have always been keen to learn about the education system at primary and secondary level.

Despite having a degree I felt the need to refresh my understanding of new techniques and methods being applied in primary schools.

The family numeracy and literacy courses provided me the necessary knowledge to support my children's education and later on helped me to enhance skills as a bi-lingual assistant at ………. I strongly recommend these courses to all parents.

The other two parents wrote the following:

Dear Mrs …

We feel that by attending these courses we benefited immensely. Now we read and help our children at home in the right way and have confidence that he/she is learning. These courses help all ages of children because the tutor gives advice and leaflets on older children too.

The games we make in the courses are fun, colourful and useful to do at home with your child. The educational benefit is a bonus to you and your child. It was an eye opener to see how numeracy is taught and how we as parents can teach at home without puzzling our children with numbers.

We expected family numeracy/literacy to be boring tedious courses where our nightmares of being back to school. It appeared to be enjoyable and friendly atmosphere which encouraged us to do both numeracy and literacy course for key stage 1.

Yours sincerely,

End-of-year reports were similarly developed to ensure that parents had full information on the attainment as well as the progress of their pupils. Completed as the final part of a sequence of target-setting, parent consultations, teacher assessments and tests, these summative reports not only detailed levels attained, but also progress made within or beyond a level. Parents were advised separately of expected levels of progress and national expectations. In this way, they received the information they needed to monitor and evaluate their child's attainment. They were aware of national target levels and where their child 'sat'. Through the target-setting process they also knew how to help them progress, and through developments in metalearning which we had shared with them, many felt better equipped with strategies to encourage, support or scaffold their child's learning! The parent–teacher partnership was invigorated by a sharper focus on learning. At the same time, accountability for pupil progress – answerable from all three perspectives, pupil parent and teacher – made the process of accelerating children's learning more rigorous and thereby productive.

Maintaining and enhancing inclusive provision for a broad and balanced curriculum

We maintained and enhanced inclusive provision for a broad and balanced curriculum by:

- doing a mileage check to see how far we had come
- considering where to next.

As we have stressed throughout, inclusion and the provision of a broad and balanced curriculum to support lifelong learning were two of the fundamental principles underpinning our project. Part way through our two years together we took stock of where we had got to in realizing these principles in practice and then identified next steps.

Mileage check: how far had we come?

Despite many new national initiatives, which created such demands upon curriculum time, our schools had devoted much thought and effort and workshop time to ensure the provision of a broad and balanced curriculum. Gardner's intelligences (1993; 1999) were a timely reminder that we should be committed to the notion of a wider and wholesome curriculum because each individual has strengths which may not otherwise be valued appropriately in the context of a narrow curriculum.

The consequential impact of a narrow curriculum and singular approaches to teaching and learning were issues managed by all schools in recent years. Adverse effects on self-esteem and learning capacity were concerning outcomes and, like many, our schools grappled to resolve these issues in the best interests of our pupils. We operated a variety of systems for commendation and appreciation of our children's skills to offset the potentially damaging elitism of such policies. We knew our strategies were successful because we could identify many children successfully 'included' in school life. These pupils would otherwise have been disaffected or disruptive if they had not had their opportunity to share their skills and feel valued, and thereby gain the credibility they so needed for their achievements, however small.

We now understood how many of our pupils with identified special educational needs responded to different learning styles. Their capacity to achieve came from ensuring that they had real access to the curriculum through teachers' understanding of how they learned best, and by having a clear understanding and explanation themselves of what was being taught. Our rationale was that in meeting these needs we would enhance learning for all.

There was also a growing sense that the restricted curriculum was gradually imploding because it stifled creativity, narrowed vision and motivation, and was so deeply rooted in performance. We were managing these initiatives as we were 'required' to do, yet, more importantly, as trained professionals, we were also trying to maintain a broader perspective and preserve children's prospects for lifelong learning. Their creativity and tolerance, their motivation and a broader understanding of relationships and the world at large were imperative skills. We gained confidence from our mutual support of each other, but it was challenging for schools to hold on to this belief. Some, in the face of very low baseline entry, high mobility, SEN and EAL, had much to do to raise and maintain standards, particularly in literacy. Like so many centralized initiatives that were insufficiently rooted in research and child development, we reminded ourselves that it could not hold indefinitely. The publication of the DfES (2003) primary strategy emphasizing the importance of creativity and enjoyment confirmed this.

Pupils clearly felt likewise about the restricted curriculum. Though we had enriched our provision, they still thirsted for even more creative and reflective opportunities than we were providing as some year 6 children explained:

> I would like my teacher to give us more free time to draw pictures.

> Let us do more fun and exciting things eg. Art, ICT, D&T, Food Technology etc.

> There are a few things I would like our teacher to do. The first thing is to do more class council and to do more art and show our feelings. Also to do more circle time so we can express our worries.

Nevertheless we had made progress with some lifelong skills which was recognized and valued particularly by new students:

> When I came new here everyone was kind to me. I felt very welcomed and no one behaves rude or unkind. Everyone helps me here. No one lets anyone down.

> Our concentration has improved and our listening skills have grown!

Where to next?

Promoting key skills for lifelong learning Through promotion of key skills we hoped our children would become responsible citizens and motivated and creative learners. Whilst reviewing our policies and practice in line with Curriculum 2000, and translating it through to our schemes of work, we highlighted key skills identifying how these were connected to planned developments. We saw these as:

- communication skills integrating literacy and oracy with other subjects
- working with others in collaborative settings and through Prides
- citizenship, through school councils and Prides
- improving one's own performance through self-review and evaluations in partnership with teachers and parents
- opportunities for developing metacognition, metalearning and emotional intelligence through circle time, Prides, plenaries, no put-down zones, chains of consequence, behaviour targets and so on, as described in Chapter 3.

Curriculum 2000 presented an opportunity to review subject time allocations and to revisit the links between subjects that we had tried to preserve in the face of the Ofsted inspection framework (2000). Learning was planned holistically, and curriculum content was 'blocked' or integrated to ensure in-depth work could take place within the usual time constraints.

Enriching extra-curricular provision and celebrating achievements We built on achievements and further enriched provision with the help, in some instances, of lottery grants to provide larger numbers and a wider range of extra-curricular clubs, from recorders, orchestra, African drumming, Indian dancing, playground games, to drama, rugby, football, art and gymnastics.

As we had done in the past, we celebrated a large number of multicultural, community and charity fund-raising events. Children were presented with multiple opportunities to celebrate and share their many skills and talents, and parents were similarly invited to contribute and share their skills, to provide role models. These included an Afro-Caribbean carnival, historical pageant, a celebration of science through PE, presentations for Diwali, Hanukkah, Eid, Christmas and other religious festivals, and regular promotional events such as Red Nose Day, Children in Need and National Society for the Prevention of Cruelty to Children collections.

We allocated, maintained or created appropriate space for enriched curriculum provision through the development of new libraries and computer suites. Drama/music studios enhanced speaking, listening and music in the curriculum. An activity room housed large play equipment for the development of early social and motor skills or the promotion of collaborative skills. Additional group rooms were set up to make more provision to scaffold or extend children's needs.

Programmes of visits and visitors were continued and developed to enrich curriculum study and ground it firmly in first-hand experience. This included resident community artists and musicians. Clergy and faith representatives enhanced provision for collective worship. Cross-curricular provision was stimulated by visits from staff at the Redbridge Drama Centre and Redbridge Music School.

To support these developments we enhanced curriculum expertise through the appointment of specialist co-ordinators in PE, literacy, music, science and drama. We also ensured the quality of subject leadership, through effective management of subject leaders, which enabled co-ordinators to implement the school's vision and needs in their area. Alongside these curriculum initiatives we also paid close attention to the use of specific strategies to meet the many and varied needs of our children. Creative solutions were called for!

Creative differentiation to support inclusion

Creative differentiation to support inclusion involved:

- supported reading activities
- target-setting in literacy and numeracy
- interactive learning
- booster groups
- mind maps, and
- revision posters.

Several initiatives implemented in our schools over the two-year project aimed to raise achievement for pupils, particularly those with SEN. There was the inevitable and specific focus on numeracy, literacy and science amongst our schools. However, our schools were committed to the ethos that good practice for children with SEN was good practice for all pupils. It was felt these initiatives would have wider implications for whole-school practice – and so they did!

The difficulties we experienced were that some of the initiatives were time-consuming and difficult to fit into a very busy school day. Furthermore, our commitment to provide a broad and balanced curriculum made the time constraints even more challenging to manage. We were aware of these significant tensions at the outset, but felt that it was important to try, given our mantra of 'we can if … '. As usual when the going got tough we reminded ourselves that we were learning, and that we could review and adapt our practice – though, by the same token, we had to work with initiatives for long enough to be able to evaluate their successes. The feedback from children was an important part of that evaluation.

The initiatives included:

Supported reading activities This was an initiative that helped pupils to develop a mixture of phonic and visual reading cues, through an integrated programme involving teaching assistants and the class teacher. Supported and Independent Guidance and Activities for Reading (SIGAR) (London Borough of Redbridge, 2001a) were devised to help pupils with specific special educational needs in Key Stage 2. Most of these pupils, working within level 1, spoke English as an additional language too, and therefore needed focused support in order to gain from the literacy hour. Developed in 2001 by colleagues in the borough, Angela Sheahan SEN consultant, Margaret Preston and Ian Bennett, then literacy consultants, and Tony Davies then borough SEN INSET co-ordinator, it was in part a reading programme, self-esteem development programme and an important survival tool kit for the classroom teacher. Children so enjoyed working on scaffolded activities independently and successfully, whilst the teacher was able to secure undivided time for guided groups:

I'm doing more reading and my work is getting neater.

I learn my spelling words now by:

writing them out
thinking about them
hearing how it sounds
putting them into word trains
listening to them, and
visualizing them.

Target-setting in literacy and numeracy This was used, as described earlier, to help teachers to plan more inclusively, and to refine differentiation. This initiative was in line with guidance set out in Redbridge's *Targets for Guided Reading* (2001b), *Targets for Guided Writing* (2001c) and *Targets for Numeracy* (2001d).

Before I used to ask everyone to help me but I know that if I really try on my own I can pass my target.

Interactive learning Encouraging children and adults to focus on learning and engage more actively with its processes, required their active participation. Interactive learning was encouraged in a variety of ways.

During whole-class sessions, teachers shared clear learning intentions, 'we are learning to … ' (WALT) and success criteria, 'what I'm looking for … ' (WILF) with pupils, so that they knew exactly what was expected of them:

My teacher helps me learn by telling us what we're learning. (Y1)

WALT and WILF helps us to learn because WALT tells us what we are learning to do and WILF tells us how to do it. My teacher reads out the learning intentions and links them to what we are learning. (Y4)

In the Foundation Stage, interactive learning was a natural process, and the sharing of techniques influenced the strategies of other practitioners throughout one school:

• In the hands of expert nursery and reception staff, puppets captivated children – their stories or questions hooked all children into learning. Children communicated with the hapless puppet verbalizing their own learning, thus enabling appropriate teacher assessments to take place.

- Rhymes, rhythms and songs to gentle movements, were precursors to brain gym, for those yet unable to complete cross-lateral movements!
- Stories, integral to themes and schemes of work, acted out by the children, or linked into other areas such as PE, reinforced important language development and positional vocabulary such as 'under, above, below'.
- Large play equipment, water and sand, developed gross motor, social and collaborative skills, and encouraged use of key words linked to specific learning intentions.
- Information letters and key words attractively displayed on the classroom wall were attached with Velcro. Thus when the teachers referred to them, children 'picked' them off the wall, and used them to support their writing or class activities. The VAK and the 'doing' engaged the learner and scaffolded the learning. Colour coding these letters or key words was useful, to help sorting and retrieval, and it simultaneously encouraged the incidental reinforcement of other skills.
- In the nursery, smaller components of the termly 'big picture' were attached using Velcro. This meant children could detach the picture or objects that clearly depicted, for example, mathematical areas of experience. Physically taking it with them to their activity, where they were perhaps involved in a counting or sorting task, helped children to establish this link, and to begin to understand 'what's in it for me?' The VAK and interactive processes involved, supported those who were developing their acquisition of the English language as well as the language of learning.

The children fed back their enjoyment of these interactive processes

Singing helps me to learn maths. (Reception year – RY)

At the table I learn maths … when the children play with me. (RY)

Happy because I like doing stuff. (RY)

Opportunities to raise the quality of speaking, listening and writing were extended with the development of 'VAK packs'. Teachers developed interactive resource packs to support schemes of work. For example, one year 4, planning for science-fiction writing, packaged some 'transportation tablets' that magically rocketed pupils through time and space – Smarties! Different coloured sweets authentically wrapped in plastic became the space traveller's complete meal, and the 'music of the spheres' was inserted via the school's electric keyboard. Lumps of rock from science resources became evidence of meteorites, and a life-size plastic alien completed the props that scaffolded the children's learning. The processes of interactive learning and teaching included sensory stimulation such as touching, visualizing, tasting, hearing and 'moving through space'. This meant that, before writing, children were able to immerse themselves in the verbal constructs required for the task. They accessed a new set of vocabulary, and shared and rehearsed imaginary sets of science-fiction circumstances that they might not otherwise have been able to access, as early learners of English.

In year 3 interactive learning was encouraged during whole-class editing. This gave pupils a chance to learn how to correct work in response to marking and feedback. The positive ethos created by the class teacher ensured the children were confident in editing collectively a piece of their work that was displayed on the projector. Teachers 'taught to' the skills required, but the pupils modelled the processes for each other.

Use of interactive whiteboards was another part of this process, particularly if pupils wanted to extend their own knowledge. A whole range of 'what if ... ?' questions could be actively explored by the pupils with the scope that such technology affords.

> Since I have come into key stage 2 the way I learn has really improved. Now, before we do our work, the teachers explain it a lot clearer and they usually have a child do an example on the board or an OHP.

A Fair Test Planning Board (Goldsworthy and Feasey, 1997) was introduced through INSET for all science co-ordinators delivered by Anne Goldsworthy at Redbridge Teachers' Centre.

The board is part of a practical process enabling children to think through science enquiry in a systematic way. It focuses particularly on independent and dependent variables in science investigation. It provides children with confidence, enabling them to take ownership of planning, carrying out, and making decisions on practical science activities.

It links well to the different styles of learning because kinaesthetic learners can use Post-it labels on the board to highlight the role of variables in an investigation. The post-its can be moved easily from poster to poster. An example of the posters is provided in Figure 6.1.

It also enables the children to work in Prides to discuss and make decisions. It is a very powerful tool for helping children to understand science enquiry.

This initiative was followed by a Literacy Planning Board. This came about from input by a number of sources and was designed by a year 6 team leader. It took account of support from Anne Goldsworthy and Frank McNeil (Institute of Education) who had previously worked with the school.

The school had analysed children's responses to 'close the gap' marking for a term. They found that children were not always clear about its purpose, the audience and key features of the genre they were creatively writing in.

So pulling together the Science Fair Test Planning Board, Frank McNeil's framework for 'purpose of a task' headings, and informed by WALT and WILF, the team came up with the model in Figure 6.2 during editing sessions. It was a powerful interactive tool for learning and teaching.

Year 6 teachers now refer to this in the introduction before children begin to write. It helps the children to refer back to it in the plenaries. Furthermore, with a revised literacy model, the children refer to it again when peer marking and discussions take place in a class.

Booster Groups These were run inclusively for all year 6 pupils three times per week. It was akin to setting, except that it was more fluid and transient. Running from February until May, additional teaching resources were deployed to reduce/

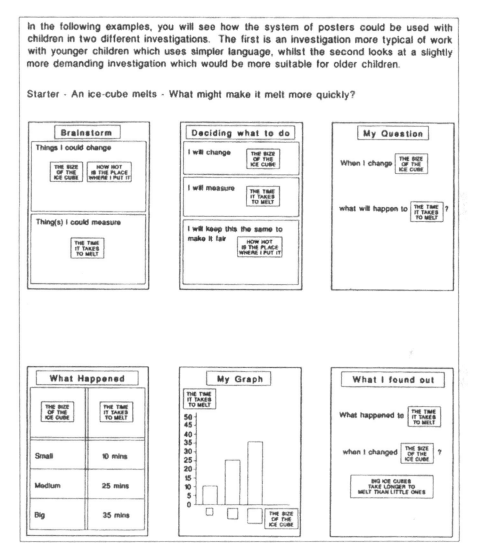

In the following examples, you will see how the system of posters could be used with children in two different investigations. The first is an investigation more typical of work with younger children which uses simpler language, whilst the second looks at a slightly more demanding investigation which would be more suitable for older children.

Starter - An ice-cube melts - What might make it melt more quickly?

Figure 6.1 Examples of posters
Source: Goldsworthy and Feasey, 1997, p.13.

increase the pupil–teacher ratio, and ensure the children received more opportunities for individual and regular feedback on their work. Children moved flexibly between groups as needed:

> I feel that my learning has improved especially in year 6 as we have a once in a lifetime chance to expand our views in our booster groups. This is very helpful because if I'm stuck on a question I can ask my friends. In other schools I didn't have the opportunity to talk or the support teachers who explain to me as clear as they can.

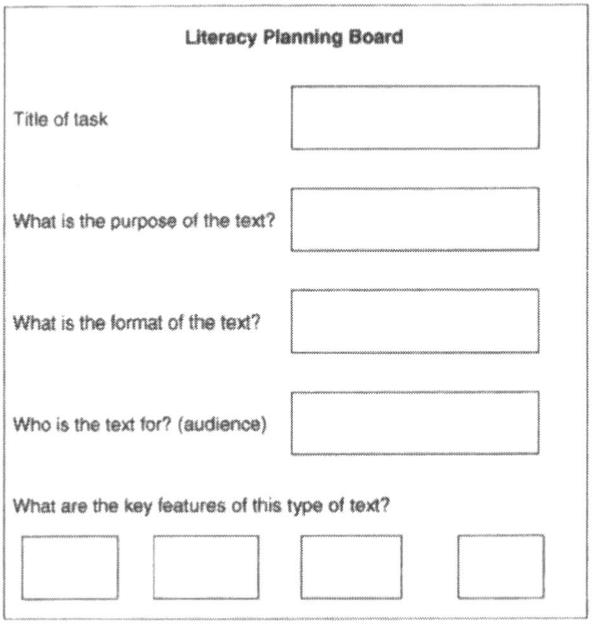

Literacy Planning Board

Title of task

What is the purpose of the text?

What is the format of the text?

Who is the text for? (audience)

What are the key features of this type of text?

Figure 6.2 Literacy Planning Board model

I think my learning has improved in year 6 mostly because we have booster groups. We have booster groups which push you up to the next level. I think this helps for me because normal English and maths lessons do push you up, but all the children are in different levels, so it makes it a little bit harder, because you don't get enough attention for your group. Booster groups have children all around your level which helps a lot because what the teacher says to the children, it's mainly what you want to know, so it's lots of help.

I think my learning has improved for me because of the booster groups. Booster group teachers have taught me much more things than I was learning in the class, not because of the teacher, but because I couldn't concentrate as well in class with all my friends around me. Although in booster groups I have friends in them as well, they don't annoy me or talk to me about non-appropriate matters!

Mind maps Mind-mapping became an important tool for engaging children in the initial stages of new work, particularly in science, history and geography:

Doing our own mind maps tells us how much we are learning and improving. We see how much we can learn from the mind maps and how many different subjects one topic covers.

Mind maps are beneficial for children and for teachers as it helps children to revise and it helps teachers to see how much a child has learned.

Children would work collaboratively to map out what they knew about a given topic at the beginning of the unit of work. This was important information for teachers as they were able to see the extent of the children's knowledge. As the work progressed the map was referred to and at the end of the unit it was updated. This was a powerful tool to boost each child's confidence and very useful for teacher assessment. The maps were either displayed or readily available in pupils' books for constant referral. They were also a powerful tool in the revision process as Key Stage 2 tests approached. In Figures 6.3 and 6.4, we have included two examples of mind maps.

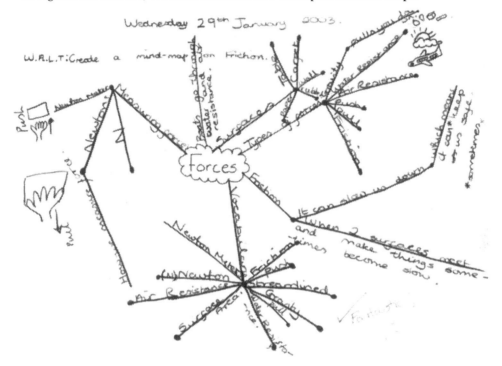

Figure 6.3 Example of mind map (1)

Revision posters and knowledge boards Year 6 pupils developed a whole range of posters for science revision on various topics likely to come up in the national test. All the relevant information was incorporated into the picture in a way that would help the child to remember. An example can be found in Figure 6.5. It was fascinating to observe how each child's preferred learning style tended to dominate the picture and the ingenious ways children recorded information particularly through cartoons and mnemonics. These were displayed in the classroom and the corridor and referred to constantly:

> When we go to school we have posters with useful information that we need to know on the walls. The posters go over the key things and by seeing them all the time we remember the information. They are bold and eye-catching that attracts our attention. They are also in our classrooms so we can use them when we need help.

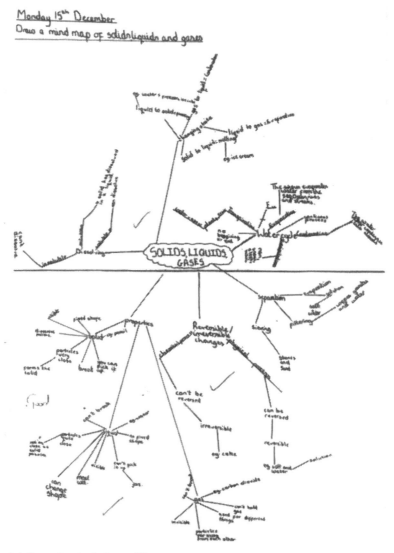

Figure 6.4 Example of mind map (2)

Some teachers used 'knowledge boards' to aid the revision process which children very much appreciated:

> Knowledge boards help us to remember all the things we have learned. So in case we forget anything we can always refer back to the knowledge boards. Furthermore we can use the knowledge boards for useful revision.

> The knowledge boards gives synonyms for different words and interesting words to use. The science board has got information in mind map style. It separates the information into different categories to make us understand it more easily.

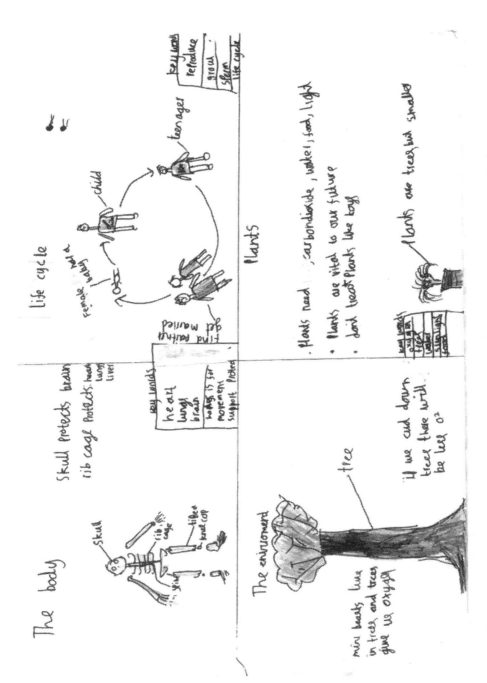

Figure 6.5 Example of science revision posters

Conclusion

We conclude by:

- reviewing what we did
- reflecting on what we learned.

Reviewing what we did

We reviewed our assessment systems to consider whether they were actually improving children's learning. As a result we:

- built targeted group work into literacy sessions once per week for each child
- established an 'Assessment for Learning' day for parent–pupil–teacher consultations to take place during the school day
- developed learning workshops for parents
- used ICT and interactive whiteboards as an assessment tool
- introduced 'close-the-gap' marking to provide systematic and developmental feedback
- involved children in marking their own work and in giving feedback on others' work
- enriched provision of extra-curricular opportunities and curricular workshops, in order to enhance pupils' self-esteem
- introduced supported and independent activities in reading to encourage autonomy and self-esteem
- structured booster groups more flexibly to provide additional opportunities for individual and regular conferencing
- introduced mind-mapping and revision posters to support revision and review processes.

Reflecting on what we learned

We learned:

- that strategies we use to support children in school need to be connected to a much deeper vision about learning, and need to inform 'learning-focused revisions' of school policies
- that children have very clear, and largely accurate, views of their own abilities. The support they respond to most favourably is identifying exactly what they need to do next.
- to evaluate the effectiveness of these strategies by obtaining feedback from children.

The children were keen to talk about the things that teachers did that best supported their learning. They were also very aware that the teachers were tracking their progress and encouraging them to play a part in this process. How the schools did this is described in the next chapter.

7

Keeping track of children's learning

To measure or to learn: that is the question. (Broadfoot, 1996, p. 42)

We can keep track of children's learning if we:

■ identify issues that can inform and have an impact on the tracking of pupils' learning
■ ensure the micro and macro management of quantitative data
■ use a range of qualitative tracking measures
■ track a focus cohort.

Identifying issues that can inform and have an impact on the tracking of pupils' learning

The issues we identified that could inform and have an impact on the tracking of pupils' learning were:

■ the local context
■ shared issues in the tracking of pupils' progress
■ individual issues.

The local context

In Chapter 1 we described the main features of the London Borough of Redbridge. We recognized that for the project to be successful we needed to have a shared understanding of the general expectations that the borough had of its schools as well as the support mechanisms in place. We were keen to maximize the expertise, facilities and techniques available to help us track our children's progress and achievements.

123

Shared issues in the tracking of pupils' progress

The five schools in the project were located in different parts of the borough, and thus whilst they shared several common features, they were also equally diverse. These issues impacted upon our tracking systems and the management of our pupils' progress. We had three particular factors in common.

We were large schools A common denominator, was the fact that all five were large schools – with three-form entry primaries and four-form entry junior schools included amongst their number. Amalgamations or increased standard numbers had occurred in several Redbridge schools following demographic changes within the borough, and our schools were no exception.

Management of large communities of learning needs, unfolded particular issues in the tracking of progress. The schools were concerned to ensure that individuality and equal opportunities were closely guarded rights in such large establishments. This was essential to achieving our inclusion agenda. Holistic tracking of each child's development as a learner was therefore prioritized – attitudes, preferences, areas of confidence and uncertainty. Aware we were subject to the inherent dangers of depersonalizing a child's progress or achievement, simply by virtue of roll size, we worked proactively to counterbalance this.

For manageability, we were also very keen to ensure knowledge and management of every child's progress in a large community was clearly systematized. However, we were concerned that the individual circumstances affecting learning also needed to be 'understood'. Children's progress and attainment were more than a mere statistic or a 'result'. Information gathered required management at micro and macro levels. The potential hazard was that the importance of individual underachievement could become secondary to analysis of 'trends'. Whilst the latter might aid school development, it did not guarantee individual progress. Over the passage of time, record-keeping was carefully tailored to address these concerns and track both individuals' needs and school-based trends.

We celebrated cultural and linguistic diversity Another shared issue was the percentage of pupils in the schools who spoke English as an additional language. Ranging widely from 1 per cent to 84 per cent, however, the management of needs was different within our school settings. In one school, for example, a total of 34 community languages were spoken. It meant it was often difficult to gauge the attainment or achievement of some pupils who arrived speaking little or no English. Though the school employed a variety of bilingual assistants it was not enough to cover the 34 languages spoken. Tracking systems inevitably focused more on securing progress in speaking and listening, and the articulation of concepts in an additional language, for such students. The same expectations of attainment, simply could not be applied – even though the school was shown no such mercies in the league tables.

We were inclusive schools Pupils with SEN ranged from 13 per cent to 30 per cent in our schools. This raised a number of issues relating to the informed use of the management of data:

- P-scales assessments were needed to measure progress. P-scales are assessment criteria for progress below level 1 in National Curriculum programmes of study (QCA, 2001).
- Good progress may have been made but not reflected in attainment, which strengthened the schools' determination to extract value added, even with the confusing dynamics of mobility.
- All were inclusive schools providing support for complex needs among their student body. Information needed for target-setting was not easy to frame up. It was difficult to project from one key stage to another. We had to consider the data we had in the context of mobile populations, gender differences and the circumstances of particular ethnic groups. Answers were not always straightforward.

Individual issues

Beyond these similarities we also had to recognize differences and support one another in the management of these because in their different ways they had an impact on the strategies we used to track progress. There were four in particular that exercised us.

High levels of pupil mobility For one school in the group the effects of pupil mobility heightened the challenges of managing a 'large school'. Created by the development of temporary housing in the area and the influx of migratory residents, there was often repeated turnover for one school place. In the case of the year 5 focus cohort it was 146 per cent since the reception year.

It was challenging to keep track of every pupil's academic records, as movement was so frequent. Staff deployed to this task were beset by the usual frustrations. Often records never arrived, lost in the momentum of continual transit. Frequently, they took a long time to arrive or were incomplete – usually of assessment information! For those speaking little or no English, and subject to repeated school moves, it was bewildering. Insightful assessments were the vital information needed to provide some semblance of continuity for the unfortunate pupil. It also left our database with gaps until teacher assessments could be substituted. Depending on the time of year, these omissions could hold up teacher or whole-school target-setting processes or school self-evaluations.

For class teachers, pupil mobility added yet another dimension to the complexities of widely differentiated planning. Staff were continually managing extra administration, and changing cultural and social classroom dynamics. Additionally there were issues of constant induction, assessment, target-setting and the pastoral support of new pupils, many of whom were in the process of acquiring English. On top of this, teachers were developing the skills of the core group of pupils who had attended the school since the reception year. Implementation of curricular targets became ever more complex as classroom dynamics changed so regularly.

The annual round of governing body target-setting was similarly affected. Increasing difficulties were experienced when making simple predictions from one key stage to another. The process of pupil turnover compromised accurate comparisons of like with like. Instead, the school developed finer predictions either based on performance in year 4 tests or even tracking from one year to the next, to ensure inclusion of the most recent arrivals.

Attendance and extended holidays Two of our schools experienced high levels of absence and lateness. Requests for extended holidays of three to six weeks' duration were also common. This was a challenging issue to address when coupled with pupil mobility and school size. Tracking systems had to be particularly tight and required additional resourcing. Significant progress was made by one school with the allocation of a member of the administrative staff deployed to monitor attendance. A dedicated answer-phone was put in place for parents to inform the school of absence on the first day. Administrative staff contacted families on the first day of absence if the school was not notified of the reason. The governing body published rigorous policies on attendance and leave of absence to all parents, which were applied without exception. The governing body attached a link governor to monitor attendance closely through termly meetings. The link governor and headteacher met regularly to review progress and develop policy and practice. Members of the leadership team met with parents, and weekly focused visits from the education welfare officer ensured proactive support when the school could progress no further.

With an established correlation between poor attendance and low attainment, the school had to consider this additional dimension in its holistic tracking of pupils' progress.

Variable baseline attainment on entry If the reader looks back at the pen portraits of the five schools in Chapter 1, it will be seen that the schools varied noticeably in the levels of attainment of the children on entry. This variability of baseline attainment strengthened the resolve of the schools to focus on value added progress rather than raw results in league tables. It was important for children, staff and parents to learn to interpret and use data in such a way as to celebrate progress and be clear about the difference each school was making.

Issues for a voluntary-aided school One of our schools was a voluntary-aided school. All the children came from the same religious background. The community served by the school had additional expectations and demands that in turn impacted on the curriculum. Tracking progress in this school had to take account of the particular requirements of this community.

These common and individual issues created a backcloth for tracking progress. Our next challenge was how to manage the gathering of 'hard' data – quantitative evidence that we could gather and use to inform future action. In the next section we describe the complexities of this process.

Ensuring the micro and macro management of quantitative data

We ensured the micro and macro management of quantitative data by:

- seeking a computerized tracking system
- analysing the data to set targets and monitor progress
- using the data to develop class profiles
- using 'hard' and 'soft' data to address underachievement
- using the data with parents
- using the data to change practice.

Seeking a computerized tracking system

For our large primary schools the sheer volume of data that needed to be managed was daunting. We needed to account for the individual, managing needs at micro levels, whilst also being responsive to macro trends and patterns which could be addressed through strategic actions.

Technological advances throughout schools in the borough were varied at the time. Planned changes to introduce a borough-wide tracking system for primary schools were near but not quite here. Some headteachers struggled with manual spreadsheets to complete their analysis of performance data. Others used computerized databases, whilst the rest operated betwixt and between. The database that had advanced significantly within one of the project schools ultimately led to the secondment of the deputy headteacher. Her mission was to seek appropriate software to meet our needs. 'Target Tracker' was initially identified as our rescue package. A system devised by Essex County Council, it was flexible to use, was regularly updated and enabled spreadsheets inclusive of baseline assessment right up to the end of Key Stage 2. Colour coding highlighted underachievement and notepads allowed individual inserts on each child. This was one system that helped us to monitor progress in mathematics, English and science. Excel was another.

Analysing the data to set targets and monitor progress

'Target Tracker' was used by one school to store information from Key Stage 1 to Key Stage 2 in reading, writing, mathematics and science using QCA and National Foundation for Educational Research (NFER) data and teacher assessments. It was given to staff at the beginning of each year and they used it to target and/or set children in groups.

In October each teacher set a target for each child in the class from the QCA tests in May. Targets were set for reading, writing and mathematics, using previous data and their own expectations. They then compared their class results with their targets and the previous year's results. Concerns were passed on to the next teacher and the parents as needed.

At the end of each term the Attainment Target (AT) 1 assessments in English, mathematics and science were also added to the data. Tracker showed in graphs how each child/cohort was doing compared with the cohort/national expectation. It indicated in colour whether the child was achieving her or his potential based on Key Stage 1 results and the targets set by the database. It gave details of the percentage of children achieving each level. Achievement was compared between genders, ethnic groups and between classes.

The assessment co-ordinator monitored the data and followed up areas of concern with the relevant staff. The school also checked on the cohort's points score at Key Stage 1 and the expected results at Key Stage 2 for value added – or not!

Using the data to develop class profiles

For another primary school, the complexity of the school's intake entailed fine-tracking systems. The high levels of pupil leavers and joiners, many with early English acquisition or significant SEN, meant that class dynamics changed with regularity. Protracted annual target-setting processes were beset by information that was out of date, no matter how frequently it was modified. The school's data manager worked in close conjunction with the assessment co-ordinator and the leadership team, to develop the school-wide database and tracking systems.

Information was stored from baseline onwards, tracking progress via NFER, QCA and home-made internal tests, through to the end of Key Stage 2. As before, writing, reading, mathematics and science were focus areas. At the beginning of each year teachers were provided with a class profile summarizing the progress and attainment of their class, and SEN and EAL stages. Children who underachieved in the previous year were identified.

Additionally, summaries of SEN, EAL, gender and mobility factors that had an impact on their class were recorded, to provide an overview of needs which could inform teaching strategies. For instance, one year group had a 60 per cent male dominance. Teachers, including NQTs, needed to be aware of the management implications for learning and teaching processes. It was important to redress this imbalance in teachers' planning, to ensure girls had equal opportunities to answer and ask questions and to participate fully and proactively in the learning community. Activities needed to appeal equally to both groups. Planning processes particularly needed to reflect the needs of more submissive and passive learners, so that shared learning from a range of styles could be fully exploited. Class profiles enabled teachers to finely tune their teaching to the needs of a particular cohort or class and set targets for achievement and monitor progress throughout the year. Team leaders, had copies of their year-group's class profiles, raising their awareness of year-group issues and the pace of progress which needed to be managed.

The cycle adopted was:

- September: Class teachers evaluated year-end data and class profiles.
  Team leaders evaluated issues arising for year-group planning.

- October: Class teachers set targets for the following May.

  Leadership group monitored progress.

- February: Class teachers reviewed projections.

  Year-group team redeployed support staff where necessary, to secure the expected progress.

  Inclusion team provided preventative support (February–May) for those identified as potential underachievers.

- May: Data manager processed information to identify any underachievement from Foundation Stage Profile, Key Stage 1 tests, or QCA tests.

  Assessment co-ordinator collated information.

  Pupils banded into groups requiring specific 'types' of support.

  Inclusion teacher investigated circumstances of assigned underachieving pupils.

  Inclusion team provided support (May–July) for those who had underachieved.

  Leadership group met with the school's inclusion team.

- July: Inclusion team support given (May–July) evaluated to see if learning gaps had closed.

  Report on performance data prepared for presentation to governing body.

Using 'hard' and 'soft' data to address underachievement

After QCA and internal tests, a detailed questionnaire was completed in the case of each individual pupil. Class books and test papers were scrutinized as part of the investigation, and the class teacher was interviewed. The pupil was also interviewed in order to gain an understanding of the individual's perspective. The student's feelings about his/her learning and progress helped to inform management of the need. It was an enlightening process in some cases. A year 1 child, whose apparent lack of progress was a mystery to staff, told the teacher: 'It was hard for me to write so I copied my friend'. In the event, his choice could not have been more unfortunate!

Following May interviews with the children and class teachers, some children were removed from the list of underachievers. Performance of some pupils highlighted trends that could be resolved through strategic management, planning and monitoring. Other students were removed in favour of light-touch monitoring to develop their personal accountability. In this case, teachers were doing all they reasonably could, whilst the pupil was not. For other children, however, it was a more complex and individual need – whilst not necessarily a special educational need. Thereafter, each child still considered to be underachieving, and not already receiving support for the identified needs, was attached to a teacher or mentor with responsibility for drawing up and implementing an individual action plan for progress. The inclusion process and the bands are shown in Figure 7.1.

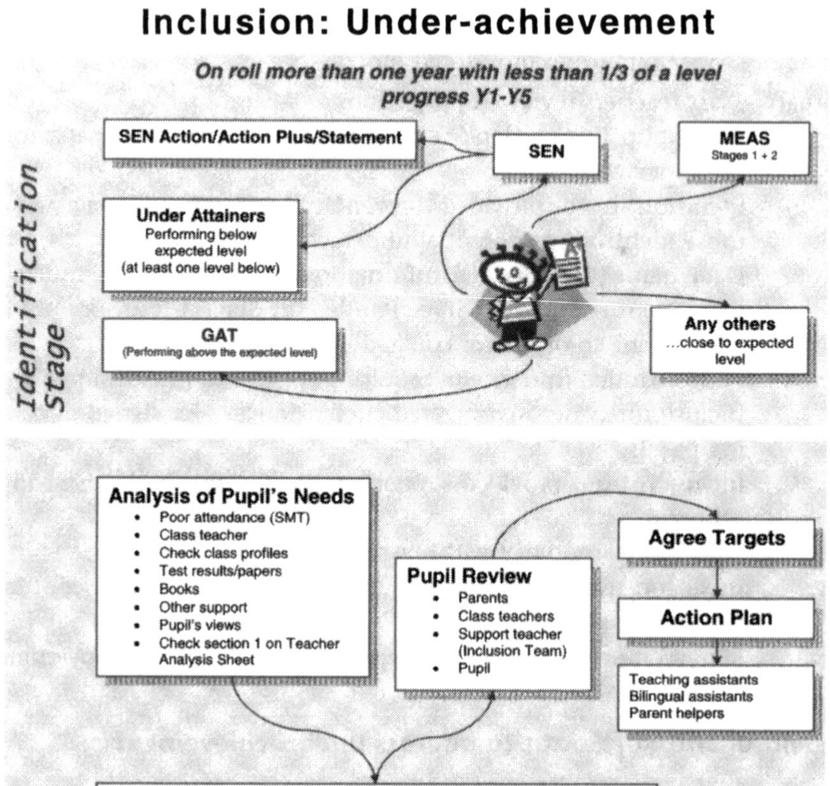

Inclusion: Under-achievement

Figure 7.1 Inclusion process and bands

Using the data with parents

Discussions with some parents were part of the plan, so that those condoning poor attendance or taking extended holidays realized the consequential impact on their child's progress. These were not always straightforward decisions however. Some children were pressurized by extra tuition at home and ended up with a double dose of homework. Some were also confused if, for example, home tutors taught them different and more abstract approaches to mathematics. Sometimes, our pleas on behalf of a child's attitudes to school-based learning were ignored. Over-exerted from private tuition, a pupil had worked with little commitment at school. Thirsting to redress the imbalance of work and play, the student's priority was development of social skills. Other parents held unrealistic or high expectations of their child. Some of these children were genuinely fearful of the consequences of perceived 'failure'. The information we held was sensitive and we made every effort to manage it respectfully, in consultation with the children themselves, whilst also keeping parents informed and involved.

Using the data to change practice

For another of our schools, the management of tracking pupil progress across a cohort of 120 required some creative solutions. Each year group became like a mini-school, but with the same structure. Teachers, year-group leaders, the deputy head and the headteacher all had specific roles to play. Clear tasks were discussed with the year-group leader to ensure monitoring was systematically carried out across the school.

To enable pupil assessment to be carried out properly, the structure of staff meetings changed. They went in cycles of three weeks. Week 1 focused on the curriculum. Week 2 enabled individual completion of assessment. Week 3 focused on individual classroom management linked to 'Learning to Learn'.

Once every half-term there was a meeting for the literacy, mathematics, science and information technology representatives from each year group to monitor the curriculum across the school and to look at standards. Year-group leaders at year-group meetings did book sweeps. Tracking was helped with the use of Redbridge's Literacy Forum publications on writing and reading targets (2001b; 2001c; 2001d).

It can be seen, therefore, that we found the strategies that were best fitted for our own individual circumstances. As a group of headteachers we shared our 'hard' data with one another which helped us to keep going and share good practice. The same was the case with the qualitative (soft) data we used as will be seen in the section that follows.

Using a range of qualitative tracking measures

We used a range of qualitative tracking measures:

- class teaching and learning
- groups of children
- individual pupils
- self-assessment by children
- peer assessment
- teachers' assessment.

Teachers used formative assessment to establish the impact of teaching and learning on children's progress and to identify future planning needs. It was used in a variety of ways for the whole class, groups and individual pupils.

Class teaching and learning

Each lesson was planned with a clear learning intention and success criteria – using Shirley Clarke's WALT and WILF, described in Chapter 3. This enabled teachers to give feedback on learning intentions. It took place in plenary sessions, orally to groups or individuals or in pupils' books as written feedback.

Teachers used formative assessment to evaluate the next stages of planning. It may have been, for example, that periods of time spent on a learning intention were lengthened or shortened, or the approach to a learning intention changed.

Groups of children

All children were divided into ability groups for reading, writing and mathematics. During this time the teacher focused once per week on the particular needs of one group. During these sessions the teacher identified the levels at which the groups were working and worked with them to help them on to the next stage of development. Records were kept of progress in these areas.

Individual pupils

Within the focus group, teachers identified specific needs of individual pupils. Notes were made and targets drawn up. Information was shared with relevant support staff and parents, and the child was involved in deciding the route towards the target, and how successes would be recognized.

Self-assessment by children

As early as possible our pupils were encouraged to evaluate their own progress. In the Foundation Stage the skills were developed through oral discussion and respectful sharing of success. Children were encouraged to evaluate what had made something successful and they started to reflect on their own progress.

By the end of Key Stage 1 pupil self-evaluation became a structured form of formative assessment that was encouraged in a number of ways:

- discussion in the plenary session
- effective teacher-led questioning relating to WALT and WILF
- pupils identifying successful work to include in their profiles
- self-marking for right/wrong answer work
- dedicated taught time to agree and revisit whole-class procedures for self-evaluation.

In Key Stage 2 in one of the schools, self-assessment became integrated into the school's formative assessment procedures. Each class had an assessment file which followed the class through the school. This file was completed manually although the school was hopeful that Target Tracker would eventually make this unnecessary. Along with this assessment file the following practices were introduced which proved very successful:

- All classes displayed level descriptors for English and mathematics. This meant each child knew where he/she was and what she/he needed to do to achieve the next level.
- When children marked their work, or the work of others, they looked at the sheets and decided what level it was.
- The children then wrote their own targets for improvement.
- The level achieved was written on the work.
- The open policy of marking did not upset the children, rather it made it clear that they understood the level they were working at and what they needed to do to improve on that.
- Staff backed this up with detailed, focused marking once a term.
- In the sets for mathematics staff took to highlighting areas completed for the set to see.
- Lesson objectives linked to tasks in the levels were written in the books so progress could be tracked.
- The school was honest and open with the children and this allowed each child to move forward.

Peer assessment

Our pupils were also encouraged to provide support for one another. Some found it of immense value to get feedback from a partner. In one of the schools pupils used Post-it notes to stick on peers' books to help them develop their work.

In another school paired marking took place using 'three stars and a wish' which we described in Chapter 6 (page 106). Working with a partner, pupils were sometimes asked to present their work on the left-hand pages of their books. Evaluating on the right-hand side of the book, the peer was asked to star three achievements, and identify one development point, by drawing a wand. The marker needed to write feedback and share it with the partner. Children used the success criteria for a given task to make their judgement.

Teachers' assessment

Verification through moderation A vitally enriching process to ensure accuracy and rigour in teachers' assessment, moderation was important at two levels.

First, in checking the accuracy of the whole-school assessment processes. During October, teachers in one school reviewed each pupil's progress in line with attainment in the previous year's (May) QCA tests. This ascertained, at an early stage in the new academic year, whether the pupil's current class work was reflecting progress. Exceptionally, if the teacher felt the child's class work belied the level previously attained, the assessment coordinator investigated the matter. Occasionally, this process highlighted school-based, as well as pupil- or parent-based issues, to be followed up. This process moderation clarified discrepancies so that expectations of progress were explicit for all those involved.

Secondly, moderation was the vital tool for verifying teachers' assessment of individual work samples. The process elicited a shared understanding of programmes of study and level descriptors. Teachers' assessments and expectations of pupils' work were developed and honed through their shared learning.

The same process was also used to evaluate the effectiveness of assessment initiatives. Could we 'see' in the children's books if these initiatives had actually worked to raise standards? For example, one school completed this scrutiny for 'closing-the-gap' marking. The involvement of staff in this exercise, enhanced opportunities for teachers' moderation of their own marking and feedback techniques, as well as identifying pupil progress. Figure 7.2 is an example of this exercise.

Questions
- How many positive points about the quality of the writing (as opposed to grammar or spelling) have been identified?
- How many development points about the quality of the writing have been identified?
- How many spellings and grammatical errors have been 'corrected?'
- Do you think the balance between these three is right? What needs to be addressed?

- Have development points been identified that will specifically enhance creativity and style? What is your evidence for this?

- Is the feedback given in relation to WALTs or specific or general WILFs or LBR Targets, or simply in response to the child's work?

- Do the teacher's prompts ensure that the comment can be acted upon?
  Has the child had *time* allocated to respond?
  Did the child understand what needed to be done?
  Was the feedback appropriately differentiated?
  Any other comments?

- Did the improvement/edit fit exactly back into the piece of work?

- Did the child have an opportunity to read the edited piece to see if it made sense?

- What are the issues for teachers' and pupils' learning, arising from the question above?

- Has this feedback *actually made a difference to the standard of the child's work?*

- What is your evidence for the question above?

- Do you level activities marked in this way? If so where do you record it?

- When and how do you track progress in writing?

Figure 7.2 Scrutiny of children's work and teachers' feedback to consider the effectiveness of 'closing the gap' marking

Assessment books In one of the schools, National Curriculum AT 1 activities were completed in assessment books termly in English and maths and twice yearly in science. The work was levelled and formative comments written. The book went with pupils through the school.

Speaking and listening assessment Every half-term in another school, minority ethnic achievement staff (MEAS) identified a focus group. The teacher set individual targets and language aims for each child in their focus group and applied these targets to other satellite pupils with similar needs. The teacher reviewed the language aims and targets of their focus groups each half-term. The information was shared with class teachers and parents, which enabled them to plan and support appropriately.

'Closing the gap' marking This was a worthwhile though demanding strategy that our schools used, with varying degrees of success because of the time constraints. One school tried to build it into literacy sessions. After the weekly extended writing sessions, the teacher marked one group's work using the 'closing the gap' marking strategy described in the previous chapter. During that group's guided writing time the following week, the teacher conferenced the group about the marking and gave them time to make the necessary improvements. Prompts helped the child to reach the next stage of development and make some small improvement to her/his work. In this way each group benefited from detailed developmental marking and feedback at least once per half-term.

Conference marking This tracking strategy was used more particularly though not exclusively, in the Foundation and first key stages. Related to the learning intention that was shared with the children it was achieved by:

• reinforcing successful work as children worked on a task
• using the plenary session to share success and difficulties that the children incurred during the task
• sharing a piece of work and suggesting ways to improve it
• pupils marking their own work with the teacher in a plenary session
• use of a guided session with children to evaluate and feed back on completed work.

Tracking the focus cohort

We tracked the focus cohort by:

■ combining different kinds of data to assess the impact of the 'Learning to Learn' project.

Combining different kinds of data to assess the impact of the 'Learning to Learn' project

To make the project manageable, in our early days of data management, the research information was focused on pupils who began year 5 in September 2000.

This was agreed despite the fact that all schools had chosen to implement the 'Learning to Learn' project as a whole school. It made the process of data analysis more manageable, and the project more finite, in that it allowed a two-year research focus, informed by end of key stage outcomes.

Pupils, their parents and teachers, provided qualitative information about their attitudes towards schooling and learning, via a baseline questionnaire. Also, during the project, the views of children, staff and parents were regularly sought, as were the views of certain visitors such as our mentors and educational psychologists.

We drew on a range of documentary evidence to help us to track the cohort. The evidence included:

- children's work
- teachers' planning and their reports on children
- headteacher progress reports written during the lifetime of the project
- written comments on 'Learning to Learn' by teachers
- the outcome of an action research project conducted by a group of teachers in one of the schools.

Four of the schools were inspected during the two years by Ofsted so we were also able to draw on the subsequent reports to help with our evaluation, not just of the cohort's progress, but also of the impact of the project across the schools as a whole.

Quantitative information, gathered on the children's performance at the end of year 4, was reviewed and analysed at the end of year 6. As well as each school analysing their own data, Bob Percival, retired from the borough and now an external consultant with access to the borough's database, was able to provide us with comparative data. This enabled us to compare the national test results of the cohort at the end of Key Stage 2 with schools across the borough.

By combining these different kinds of data we were able to assess the impact of the project on this particular group of children. We were interested in the value added not just in tests results but also in the children's attitudes and beliefs about themselves as learners and their efficacy in learning.

Conclusion

We conclude by:

- reviewing what we did
- reflecting on what we learned.

Reviewing what we did

We:

- shared each school's approaches to issues we had in common, in order to develop assessment practice, and enhance the connections for learning and inclusion

- developed assessment databases (in 2000)
- developed and enhanced assessment calendars to provide an overview of the annual round of assessment, and made the formative processes explicit
- banded the needs of pupils identified as underachieving, and provided focused support to close the gap
- developed children's involvement in assessing the quality of their own work.

Reflecting on what we learned

We learned

- to see data, be it quantitative or qualitative, as a friend not a threat
- how to be more discriminating in our use of data so that it was 'fit for purpose'
- how to make the monitoring of progress a shared responsibility between adults and children
- how to bring formative and summative assessment together so that each informed the other of next steps in learning for individuals and next steps in strategic planning for the school as a whole
- that a focus on value added across all aspects of learning for each child enabled our commitment to inclusion to be realized.

Over the two years we went on a steep learning curve as our mentors pressed us to be rigorous and focused in our collection of evidence about learning. Our collective capacities for school self-evaluation were honed, broadened and deepened.

We still have much to learn about ways of streamlining our tracking procedures but, without doubt, our schools are much more data rich than they were in 2000. Our mentors pushed us hard. Two of their questions in particular were a driving force for improvement:

- Are you making a difference?
- How do you know?

We now feel in a much stronger position to answer the last question than we did at the beginning!

So, did 'Learning to Learn' make a difference? The answer to that question is an emphatic yes, not just because we think so, but because we know so, as a result of analysing and evaluating the data we gathered. Chapter 8 describes the outcomes of those evaluations.

8

Evaluating the impact of the 'Learning to Learn' project

He who asks questions cannot avoid the answers. (Cameroon proverb)

> **We can evaluate the impact of the 'Learning to Learn' project by:**
>
> ■ **analysing test data to assess the value added by the schools**
> ■ **taking account of objective external validations**
> ■ **obtaining the perceptions of children, teachers, parents, governors and others.**

Throughout the project we concentrated on the metalearning of pupils and teachers. As we described in Chapter 3, our intention was to develop a learning orientation to counterbalance the performance orientation engendered by the target-setting and testing regime of recent years. We were of the view that by doing this we would:

* improve the academic progress and achievement of the children
* maintain and develop further a broad and balanced curriculum
* improve children's motivation and engagement in learning
* enhance children's understanding of themselves as learners, and their mastery of a range of learning strategies.

To evaluate the impact of the project on children's progress and achievement, we evaluated the progress made by the 2002 year 6 cohort. We paid particular attention to the value added, by the project, to children's learning. We were rigorous in our analysis of data we gathered.

Analysing test data to assess the value added by the schools

Individuals schools collected and analysed their school-based data. These included QCA optional test results, NFER test results, and the results of national statutory tests and assessments at the end of Key Stages 1 and 2. We chose to focus on the value added data from four out of five of the project schools because of the particular circumstances surrounding the fifth school's short placement in 'Special Measures', at the time.

We wanted to evaluate the schools' progress in the context of externally verified and nationally published data. The method of measurement we used was the value added measure, published for the first time in 2003. A score of 100 means pupils gained the number of National Curriculum points that would have been predicted from their performance at the end of Key Stage 1. A score of 101 means they performed one point better than this. One point represents about one term's progress.

We looked at Key Stage 2 published data for 2002 and 2003. We compared the progress pupils had made from the end of Key Stage 1 in the project schools, against those in the rest of Redbridge Borough's primary schools. Although the value added measure was first published in 2003, we were able to use the technical information published at www.dfes.gov.uk/performancetables to calculate a measure for the previous year.

We analysed the data to:

- compare the progress of each of the four project schools with the average progress for the rest of the schools in the borough in 2002 and 2003
- compare the progress of *all* the pupils in the four project schools with the rest of the schools in the borough in 2003
- compare the rates of progress in English, mathematics and science of pupils in the four project schools with the rest of the schools in the borough in 2003
- compare the progress of particular groups of pupils in the four project schools with the rest of the schools in the borough in 2003
- provide a case study of the value added to the 2002 cohort in one of the project schools.

Comparison of the progress of individual project schools against the borough average

Figures 8.1 and 8.2 compare the progress of all pupils in each of the project schools against the average progress for all pupils in the rest of the borough's 37 primary schools. Figure 8.1 shows progress in 2002, at the end of the project. The progress in each project school was equal to or better than the average of the rest of the schools.

Figure 8.2 shows progress in 2003. Pupils in the project schools made more progress than the average of the rest of the borough schools. The comparison confirmed that the progress of each project school was at least equal to, but in most cases better than, the schools in the rest of Redbridge. Moreover, this rate of progress was sustained and improved after the project ended.

For our further analyses and comparisons, we focussed on the published Key Stage (KS) 2 2003 value added measure. We wanted to ensure our analyses were supported by robust data with a high rate (93 per cent) of pupil coverage (pupils with both Key Stage 1 and Key Stage 2 results), and a verifiable stability rate (78 per cent) (where pupils sat both Key Stage 1 and Key Stage 2 tests within the same school) across the borough.

Comparison by earlier achievement: all four project schools against borough averages

We analysed the data to scrutinise the progress made by *all* our pupils, regardless of their levels of attainment. We wanted to evaluate the success of the strategies we had used to promote inclusion. Had the focused support given to pupils had an uneven impact, or had the initiatives added value evenly and inclusively?

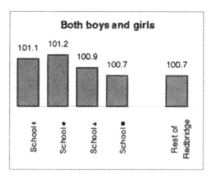

Figure 8.1 KS1 to KS2 value added, summer 2002, boys and girls

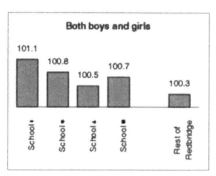

Figure 8.2 KS1 to KS2 value added, summer 2003, boys and girls

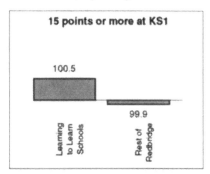

Figure 8.3 KS1 to KS2 value added, summer 2003, 15 points or more at KS1

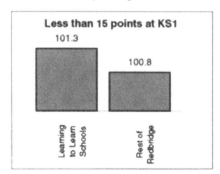

Figure 8.4 KS1 to KS2 value added, summer 2003, less than 15 points at KS1

Figure 8.3 illustrates that pupils in project schools whose average point score was the nationally expected 15 points or more at Key Stage 1, made greater progress than the rest of Redbridge schools.

Figure 8.4 shows similar rates of progress for those whose average point score was less than 15 points at Key Stage 1. The results of this comparison endorsed the inclusive approaches that the schools had adopted. Value added to the learning of *all* pupils in the four project schools was effectively half a term's progress.

Comparison by subject: all four project schools against borough averages

We then analysed the progress in English, mathematics and science made by pupils from the four schools, to establish if our 'Learning to Learn' strategies had added value in each of these core areas of the curriculum. The results of the comparison

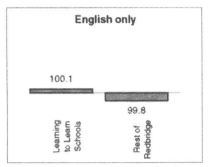

Figure 8.5 KS1 to KS2 value added, summer 2003, English only

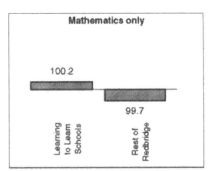

Figure 8.6 KS1 to KS2 value added, summer 2003, mathematics only

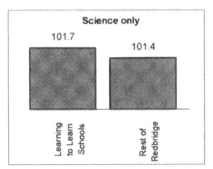

Figure 8.7 KS1 to KS2 value added, summer 2003, science only

shown in Figures 8.5, 8.6 and 8.7 confirm that the rates of progress in each National Curriculum subject were indeed greater in project schools than in the rest of the borough schools.

Comparison of all four project schools against borough averages for particular groups of pupils

We collated the published data of the project schools and made further analyses to establish whether particular groups of pupils made more progress than others. The data showed that the inclusive practices developed by the schools had worked well to enhance the progress of the pupils.

Comparison by gender: all four project schools against borough averages We scrutinized the data to compare the progress made by boys and girls in relation to other Redbridge schools. Figure 8.8 illustrates that the average progress of boys in the project schools in 2003 was greater than the average progress of boys in the rest of the borough schools. Figure 8.9 shows similar, though slightly less marked, progress of girls.

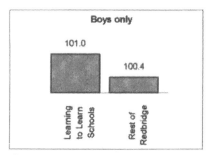

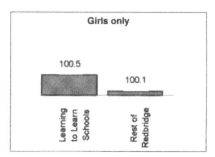

Figure 8.8 KS1 to KS2 value added, summer 2003, boys only

Figure 8.9 KS1 to KS2 value added, summer 2003, girls only

Comparison by ethnic group: all four project schools against borough averages We compared the average progress of different ethnic groups in the project schools, against borough averages. Here, one graph needs to be compared with the other.

In the project schools, about 31 per cent of the cohort was Asian or Asian British, 9 per cent was Black or Black British and 47 per cent was White. For the rest of Redbridge, the figures were 33 per cent, 10 per cent and 43 per cent respectively.

Figure 8.10 shows the progress by each ethnic group for pupils in the project schools. Figure 8.11 reflects the progress of those groups in other Redbridge schools. Average progress in each ethnic group was greater in the project schools than the average for the rest of the borough schools.

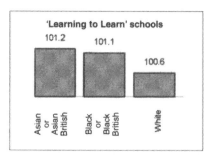

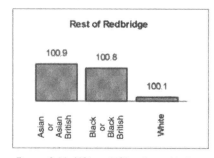

Figure 8.10 KS1 to KS2 value added, summer 2003, 'Learning to Learn' schools

Figure 8.11 KS1 to KS2 value added, summer 2003, rest of Redbridge

Case study of value added for an individual school: school ■ year 6 cohort 2001/2

School ■ year 6 cohort 2001/2: comparison of progress in reading, writing and mathematics As shown earlier, progress made by pupils in English, mathematics and science was better than expected. An exemplar of this progress is reflected in data collected from one school. This was prepared in the context of a forthcoming Ofsted inspection, hence the data were not gathered consistently for the other schools. However, whilst the school's attainment profile was below the national average, the points added during year 6 were almost double what was expected. This high level of progress was despite the fact that levels of mobility in the school were high. The overall mobility rate (both leavers and joiners), for this cohort during the project was 27 per cent, between Key Stage 1 and Key Stage 2 this was 78 per cent, and since reception year 156 per cent.

Figure 8.12 shows the progress of the cohort in school ■ between the end of year 5 and the Key Stage 2 tests. During the course of the year, pupils made a gain of six National Curriculum points in both reading and writing and five National Curriculum points in mathematics. The number of points added during year 6 was almost double what was expected.

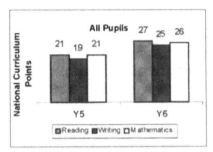

Figure 8.12 School ■ Year 6 Cohort 2001/2, all pupils

School ■ year 6 cohort 2001/2: comparison by gender In the same school, patterns of excellent progress were similar for both boys and girls, reinforcing the successes of the school's inclusion strategies.

Figure 8.13 shows that boys at school ■, between the end of year 5 and the Key Stage 2 tests, made an average of five National Curriculum points progress in reading, six in writing and five in mathematics.

Figure 8.14 shows that girls at school ■ made an average of five National Curriculum points progress in reading, writing and mathematics.

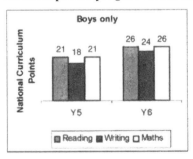

Figure 8.13 School ■ year 6 cohort 2001/2, boys only

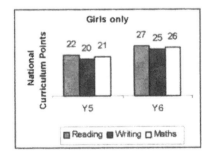

Figure 8.14 School ■ year 6 cohort 2001/2, girls only

School ■ year 6 cohort 2001/2: pupils with a known entitlement to free school meals
A further endorsement of the school's strategies to support inclusion was the fact that progress of pupils with known entitlement to free school meals was better in reading and writing than the progress of the rest of the cohort.

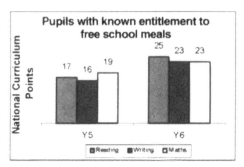

Figure 8.15 School ■ year 6 cohort 2001/2, pupils with known entitlement to free school meals

Figure 8.15 shows that pupils in school ■ with a known entitlement to free school meals, made an average progress of eight National Curriculum points in reading, seven in writing and four in maths.

To complement the analysis of test data, we drew on a range of objective external validations of our school improvement efforts.

Taking account of the outcomes of objective external validations

We took account of the outcomes of:

■ Ofsted inspections
■ awards from different agencies.

The outcome of Ofsted inspections

During the lifetime of the project four of the schools were inspected by Ofsted. The following extracts from the reports on these inspections illustrate some of the significant developments identified by Ofsted inspectors during their visits.

School ●

This is a very good school ... Improvement since the school was last inspected ... is very good. The overall quality of teaching has improved and standards, as measured by national tests are significantly higher ... The school is very well led and excellently managed. All staff have a clear understanding of the school's philosophy and expectations ... There is a very strong emphasis on meeting the pupils' personal needs ... Relationships are very good, with a strong sense that success is possible with working together. The outstanding feature of the curriculum is, however, that it is planned and taught in a way which not only meets National Curriculum requirements but also, as far as possible, is fun. (2001, ref. 102826)

School ▲

This is a very good school. Good teaching means pupils learn quickly, achieve well and reach high standards by the time they leave. Calm and effective leadership and very good teamwork help to put learning at the heart of the school's work. The school is very well led and managed. The headteacher provides a strong yet thoughtful lead and is assisted well by her deputy and senior staff. Management systems are very effective and ensure good communication and a strong commitment towards improvement. The school has improved greatly since it was last inspected. It has been successful in raising standards in English, mathematics and science as well as in many other subjects. Teaching is good throughout the school and this is the main reason why pupils are making such rapid progress and reaching high standards in many subjects ... relationships are very good and there is a high degree of racial harmony. Pupils respect one another's values and cultural beliefs. (2001, ref. 102813)

School ■

This is a very good school with many excellent features. It is outstanding in establishing a harmonious, caring and supportive school community. Teaching and support staff work very successfully together to ensure that pupils are valued and included fully in all aspects of school life. The headteacher provides excellent leadership to give clear direction to the work of the school. She is supported very well by effective senior management, a strong staff team and a supportive governing body. Pupils have very positive attitudes to school and good teaching helps them to make good progress. Pupils' attainment is improving, and promoted effectively by the school's involvement in the Learning to Learn project. The school's provision for pupils' personal development is excellent. It fosters respect and promotes excellent relationships. It enables pupils to have a clear sense of right or wrong. The school is excellent in promoting pupils' understanding of their own and other cultures. (2002, ref. 131013)

School ▬

The school is improving ... Provision in the Foundation Stage is very good and children under five achieve well. The quality of teaching is very good in the Foundation Stage where the school has been able to maintain greater stability in staffing ... but teaching and learning are unsatisfactory overall ... turn over of staff has been high. This has had a major impact on the quality of education provided ... Despite stalwart efforts made by the headteacher, who has set a clear direction for development and steered the school in the right direction, constant changes in staffing have severely curtailed the impact of the good leadership provided by her and the governors. (2002, ref. 102847)

Awards from different agencies

School ◆ was inspected by Ofsted in 1999, a year before the project began. The report stated that:

> This is a very good school ... which has rapidly improved since the last inspection. The leadership of the school gives clear direction to the raising of standards, and this is having a marked effect on the attainment and progress of pupils. The leadership provided by the headteacher is excellent. She is well supported by a very able deputy and a well-informed and competent governing body who share a clear vision for the future of the school. Results of National Curriculum assessments show that attainment in English and mathematics was well above the national average ... and in science above average. The overall quality of teaching has significantly improved since the last inspection. The close attention paid to the spiritual, moral, social and cultural dimensions of pupils' lives enriches most of what they do. (1999, ref. 102824)

It would have been tempting for the school to 'rest on its laurels', but instead, the headteacher was determined to move onwards and upwards so as to build on the success to date. It was for this reason that she joined the project. During the lifetime of 'Learning to Learn' the school did go from strength to strength. The Department for Education and Skills (DfES) awarded two achievement awards in recognition of the outstanding results year 6 children achieved in national tests. The Basic Skills Agency awarded the school a Quality Mark for standards achieved in literacy and numeracy. The Arts Council awarded the school Silver, and subsequent Gold, Artsmarks in recognition of the quality of creative arts.

School ● was successful in its bid for Beacon status for teaching and learning with a high focus on creativity and thinking skills. It now works with partner schools to disseminate good practice. The school was also awarded Healthy Schools status by the DfES as was school ■.

Over and above these objective validations, we wanted to obtain the perceptions of a wide range of people, within, or linked with, the schools' communities, to help with our evaluation of 'Learning to Learn'.

Obtaining people's perceptions of 'Learning to Learn'

We obtained the perceptions of:

- children
- teachers
- parents
- governors
- others.

All the schools developed much more profoundly than a snapshot from any Ofsted report or the receipt of a particular award can reflect. They became learning communities focused on learning and teaching, school self-evaluation, and maximizing achievement and self-esteem. Some of the qualitative evidence of the impact of the project is contained within the following evaluations.

Children's views

We gathered children's views about their development as learners, through their involvement in 'focus group' discussions with our mentors, and through the use of questionnaires. The children provided us with such rich data that we decided to devote the whole of the next chapter to them.

Teachers' views

We gathered teachers' views about the impact of the project through staff meetings, questionnaires, discussions with our mentors, written feedback, and an action research project. In earlier chapters we have included some of the teachers' views. Here, therefore, we include two pieces of evidence about impact on teachers. The first is in the form of written feedback from four teachers. The other is an evaluation of an aspect of the project by teachers in one of the schools.

The following is an extract from the reflections of a senior teacher in one of our schools in response to a questionnaire:

> For me, 'Learning to Learn' has been the mediator in ensuring constructive communication between myself and the pupils. It ensures that I do share goals with the children through the 'big picture' but even more so through the focused objectives taught through WALT and the success criteria taught through WILF. They have empowered each and every lesson to strive to the highest expectations.
>
> It has also helped me to refine various management skills. An obvious example is the different techniques used to gain children's attention when required for class discussions or the plenary without having to strain the vocal cords!
>
> It has made children more independent in their learning and thinking. It has provided children with the opportunity to share the same diet as their teachers; the same focus, the same purposes.
>
> It also allows children, particularly the younger ones, to build up routines more efficiently, which effectively allows teachers to concentrate on the teaching rather than having to spend a lot more time in organizing children into groups, the general tidying up times at the end of plenaries and even the time for getting started and remaining on task. Examples are the use of music, and various moods and styles, to mark different times in the day and different moods during the day, and the use of brain gym to maintain levels of concentration. It has made children better timekeepers!
>
> One of the real challenges I encountered in getting started was probably having the confidence to 'deliver' 'Learning to Learn' as a support teacher, particularly in knowing which techniques individual teachers had presented to their children and attempting to adhere to the same ones. A couple of simple examples are the various techniques to stop a class for attention when releasing a teacher. Usually I ask the younger children how the teacher stops the class when needing to speak to them. Obviously, the older children can

respond to a different technique to the one that they are used to.

Music is another example. Certain songs are played at certain times of the day, but the children are very good in ensuring that the teacher taking them for the day is aware of the system.

Also, I have found that, as a support teacher, 'Learning to Learn' has been easier to deliver in the frame of a context. Thus, for example, when I teach science to a class, 'Learning to Learn' has been one of the tools that has enabled me to 'deliver' science more effectively in gaining children's attention, maintaining that concentration, and sharing with them the purposes and the 'big picture', including the emphasis on key words.

I do think differently about the children. I now never use the word 'try' because of 'we can if ... ' which means that my expectations for *all* children have risen. It means they can *all* achieve and therefore my whole approach from 'delivery' of teaching to simple small discussions with children, means I now provide the opportunities and confidence with which children can strive to achieve their goals.

Through 'Learning to Learn' I have become very open with children, and so I feel that if children are not working to their best standards, we have the tool now to be able to say, 'you can do better' and question why, if children do not meet their targets.

A deputy headteacher's views about the 'Learning to Learn' project were as follows:

The 'Learning to Learn' project has been the most powerful catalyst for improving the school. Not only did it create a fine tuning on the processes of teaching and learning skills, it permeated into every aspect of school leadership and management. We became more creative, and willing to take risks, when developing new systems. If something didn't work out we were comforted with the 'there's no failure, only feedback' presupposition which we were instilling in our pupils and we tried something different, learning from our mistakes. We encouraged the staff to apply this in many different contexts. The NLP training was the most useful and practical of all the INSET. It made us more effective in communication at all levels and in all situations. In a large school, nothing could be more important.

Sharing our own research and reading became increasingly more acceptable and staff swapped titles of recommended books, videos and websites, eager to learn more. Daniel Goleman's work on emotional intelligence enhanced teachers' behaviour management techniques and helped pupils to understand and control their own behaviour. Understanding about different learning styles not only helped the staff to become better teachers, but also to become more efficient learners, team members or leaders. This became evident in year group and staff INSET meetings. The 'we can if ... ' motto with which we launched the project has stayed with us. It developed creative problem-solving tactics and lateral thinking – what more could a school manager want?

Next, is feedback received from an advanced skills teacher in one of the schools during the project who has now moved on to a new school. She was one of the teachers who went on the Canadian visit:

The 'Learning to Learn' project fundamentally transformed my teaching. I know this because I can't remember how I used to teach, nor can I imagine teaching without the tool kit of strategies acquired during the last four years. My learning can be categorized into a series of 'inspirational gems'. They make so much sense that you wonder how you ever survived without them.

As a new teacher, I felt the constraints of the NLS, the NNS [National Numeracy Strategy] and Curriculum 2000. 'I haven't time for art or music', 'I can't do circle time or class council because there isn't any space on my timetable. I have to teach' were common staffroom complaints. School became an arena for 'I can't' and an institution of moaning. For stressed out teachers the aspects of education that should have felt so right had, in practice, become something wrong.

With an NLP diploma under our belts, I was party to a school changing this philosophy. Emanated from our head, and picked up by the staff, conversation changed from 'we can't' to a concerted 'we can if … '. It's quite amazing to watch what happens with such a seemingly small language change. Attitudes change. More importantly, things change. Because they can.

Better still, our classroom language changed. Dialogue with the children made explicit the importance of changing the 'we can't gremlins' into 'we can fairies'. They understood because it makes sense. The children in our classes now know that if they are to succeed in anything at all they have to have the right mental attitude. The belligerent voices in our heads have to make positive statements for positive things to happen.

Suddenly mistakes became the most desired object in the classroom as the root of the best learning. Challenging work was the most motivating because new learning was just around the corner. Children cheered each other on to gain swimming certificates, 'You can do it!' Self put-downs were frowned upon and, without adult prompts, they gave each other, and their teachers, reminders that negativity was deconstructive … it wasn't a school thing.

School was transformed at many levels, although this didn't mean life was a bed of pink roses. Management meetings put us outside our comfort zone by tackling core issues head on. This was the key factor behind the positive changes that occurred at our school. Meetings became a forum for open and professional discourse. Children became the focus. This enabled professional dialogue without personal grievances … most of the time anyway! The icing on the cake was that as middle managers we had a real voice, we were empowered and aware of whole-school issues. We could see the school was changing for the better.

My second gem came from a very simple diagram and explanation of the reptilian brain. This stated that if children were not in the right state for learning, learning would not occur. Armoured with this physiological knowledge and understanding, my instinctive feeling that the classroom environment was all important and that the little people in my class had to feel safe, content, fed, watered and valued now had real scientific back up. Neuroscience had allowed me to invest time in what I consider education to be about. In tandem with their academic learning, we should be equipping children with the skills they will need for the rest of their everyday life. Namely, compassion, empathy, tolerance, self-efficacy, resilience, co-operation and the ability to compromise. It was Prides which provided me with a structure to facilitate the learning of these skills.

Prides is a process and rewards are not reaped overnight. I used to feel annoyed when teachers complained that they couldn't have their children working in Prides 'because the children didn't get along'. This was for me the very essence of why we need to give children opportunities for this style of collaborative learning. My intolerance for such attitudes subsided this year. In a new school, I know that had Prides not been my absolute passion, and if this passion had not manifested itself in a stubborn faith that Prides would work, I would have given up putting the process into practice months ago.

Fortunately, I write this after two terms of chipping away at a block of *anti-co-operative* children. I am finally being repaid for my persistence and reaping the rewards I so desired. We're by no means the model class but the Prides philosophy is embedded. 'Shut up' is a swear word! Children can delegate tasks and work collaboratively to produce high quality work in which each child has played an invaluable role. There is a new level of tolerance, sniggers have subsided, and every child feels valued, and their achievements appreciated. Children have the vocabulary and a level of emotional intelligence to discuss their learning, their own behaviours and that of their peers in a manner that displays self and mutual respect. The children themselves set the expectations of their peers and these expectations are gradually becoming higher and higher. I never stop being amazed, and I'm so proud, that every time I hand a little more over to the children they continue to exceed my expectations.

Mine is not the perfect classroom and I am nowhere near the perfect teacher. We all have good days and bad days. I have days at school when I know I have the best job in the world. These are punctuated with frustrating days. The photocopier doesn't work, I have a hundred unmet learning objectives, and I'm astounded at why they just can't be kinder to each other. Days when I am filled with the disheartening acknowledgment that I haven't completed all my termly assessments.

What is consistent is a delight in my own conscious incompetence. The knowledge that there is *so* much I don't know and *so* much to learn. Moreover, when I think I have learned it, how on earth do I bridge the gap between academic understanding and how it reflects in the classroom? The 'Learning to Learn' project set the challenge of seeking answers to these questions.

At recent conferences about Learning there is frequently a 'guffaw' response about the fact that learning is *not* about water, music, big pictures and brain gym. I wholeheartedly agree it is not only about this. Yet I would never go a day without these things being an integral part of a lesson – the children wouldn't let me. In retrospect it was those new-fangled ideas several years ago which opened the dialogue between academics and practitioners, teachers and their learners. That was how the journey started for me.

Now I am more tolerant of others and thrive on co-operation between colleagues, schools and boroughs. I relish the fact that I learn from my mistakes and desire to be outside of my comfort zone. Learning is the most fascinating subject in the whole world and I know that I have to battle with the gremlins in my head that so often shout 'you can't'.

Imagine if someone had taught me that at primary school.

Finally, this is an extract of the views expressed by one of the class teachers:

Using co-operative learning groups transformed the ethos of the learning community. Mine was no longer a classroom whereby I delivered and the children absorbed, but was far more interactive. Learning became something that we all did together and participation was increased significantly, as every pupil had a role and was instrumental to the team. Often it was noisy and learning outcomes were occasionally changed by the nature of the process, but this is what made it for me. To see a class of 8-year-olds self supporting, role allocating and task managing was utter bliss, I felt as though I had suddenly stumbled upon what true learning was all about.

Next, we include a research project evaluation about an aspect of 'Learning to Learn' by teachers in one of our schools. The project focused on the impact of creative differentiation to support school-based initiatives for inclusion. A number of practical strategies implemented in one school were evaluated for their impact. These activities were

- supported reading activities
- use of target-setting in literacy and numeracy, to help to plan more inclusively, and to refine differentiation
- interactive learning use of success criteria for all activities, and giving pupils a chance to correct work in response to marking and feedback
- use of skills of metalearning.

There had been little time to reflect on the impact of these qualitative measures until the school took advantage of a research project that attracted some funding. As a result of the opportunity, each year-group leader was given one day out of class to collect evidence of the four initiatives. Classroom observations, work samples and pupil interviews formed the basis of the research evidence, which was collected from eight pupils in each year group from reception to year 6. In summative assessments, half the pupils were recorded as having made good progress over the last 16 months and the other half were recorded as having made poor progress.

After recording their observations and results, year-group leaders were asked to draw together their findings and report back to the leadership group and the special educational needs co-ordinator (SENCO) to identify year-group patterns and trends. The information was recorded in a chart of the eight pupils, and whether they had scored positively on the initiatives. For example, successful completion of the SIGAR programme described on pages 113–14, and positive appraisal of the programme by the pupil, was rated as a positive mark in connection with the initiative. Poor attention and incomplete work rated as a negative. Scoring was standardized, and at the end of the project, 56 pupil ratings were made in response to each initiative. These responses were organized in relation to the two groups to identify if there was any correlation between high/low progress groups and involvement in the initiatives. The results were as shown in Figure 8.16.

The exercise revealed the successes of the initiatives, some of which were under consideration for review, cut back or reform. However, this evaluation made the case for continuing the initiatives and developing consistency of practice. It was also clear from the data that a significant percentage of pupils were not successfully participating in the four initiatives. This was perhaps because of their emotional or learning circumstances or because they were new to the school. Alternatively it was perhaps because of staff turnover, the need for staff training, and monitoring implementation of initiatives. Issues identified for future investigation were helpful in moving the school forward following the evaluation.

Parents' views

In the previous chapter we included some of the views of parents following the introduction of workshops and consultation days for parents. We also included in the section on inspection in this chapter, the views of parents. Below, therefore, we have reproduced in full, three written responses from parents to provide an overview of parents' perceptions about the impact of 'Learning to Learn':

Dear…

My thoughts about the 'Learning to Learn' project as a parent. Please feel free to quote. My apologies that it is not very coherent.

The learning environment has always been a strength I feel at … Every classroom is attractive, tidy and well ordered and provides a stimulating and supportive environment for learning. The school feels happy and welcoming. Seeing the children's work displayed attractively celebrates their personal achievement and my children have always been proud to point out their pieces of work. The 'big picture' is another area that my children are always keen to show me in their classroom. This is complemented by the termly plan that is given to us which is both informative and provides a focus for our support.

Speaking and listening, performing and celebrating are given a high profile at the school despite the pressures of the curriculum. Not only do the school cele-

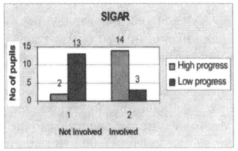

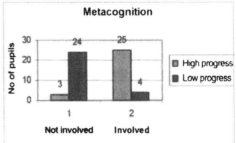

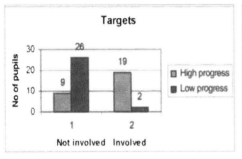

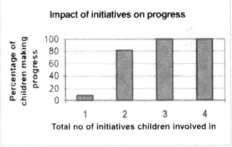

Figure 8.16 Research project response evaluation

brate the main festivals but also they regularly celebrate learning. Weekly commendation assemblies are a highlight of my children's week. One time that one of my children was commended sticks in my mind particularly – that was when she had helped someone that was upset in the playground and she explained to me how she had included her in her friends game. It all sounded very complicated – Nobel peace prize spring to mind! The celebrations culminate in a grand festival in the summer term which always makes me very proud to be a parent at …

My youngest child has probably benefited most from the 'Learning to Learn' project. She is in the good habit of drinking lots of water and it is second nature for her to take water to school. She enjoys movement and actively participates in brain gym exercises. Her favourite is the duck one. Explaining the process that she has gone through to get to an answer is as important to her as getting the right answer. This is particularly the case with number problems, where she has been able to make explicit her mental strategies from an early age. In reception she used to put her hands on her head as if she was holding the number there and then count on. I feel that through supporting the development of visual, auditory and kinaesthetic channels of learning she has grown to be a well-balanced learner.

My middle daughter however has benefited in other ways. She has always been less self-assured and has grown in confidence as a result of teaching strategies such as allowing thinking time, paired sharing of ideas and answers, moving from known and familiar into new knowledge. She also likes to know what her work needs to include and how it should look at the end. Visualizing the end product and the WILF has helped her in this. When doing some homework recently she could visualize and explain to me the fair test planning board for science which really helped her to plan and record her experiment. She has also gained a lot of confidence through working in prides and learning co-operatively. She now happily takes a leading role in her pride and feels that she has always got ideas and a valuable contribution to make to the work of the group. For personal reasons she has recently found separation from me difficult. She has successfully used NLP strategies (a paper clip in her pocket at one point to act as a hook) to help her to overcome her anxiety. Most successfully though she has learnt to verbalize her concerns to a friend and this has helped significantly.

A second parent had this to say:

A parent's perspective of 'Learning to Learn'
Since 'Learning to Learn' was introduced within .... school, my son has benefited through some of the approaches adopted within the class. Involving him to identify and work towards individual learning targets made a difference to his learning – this enhanced his self-confidence.

The introduction of Brain Gym, children working in PRIDES, No Put Down and positive thinking within the learning environment made a further impact on involving and building on his self-esteem.

Furthermore, with joint working partnership and strategies he adopted, he maintained his progress, and continues to do so in High School. In my personal opinion I would like to add that 'Learning to Learn' has created a very positive outlook on children's behaviour. This is displayed through children's behaviour and respect for each other's learning abilities and contributions, thus enrichening the school ethos of mutual respect. I'm extremely fortunate that my son had the opportunity of being able to benefit from learning in a learning to learn environment.

A third parent wrote the following:

Dear ...

As a parent of a child at ... I felt compelled to write to you to express my concern about the national and unfortunately local preoccupations some parents have with SATs [Standard Assessment Tests] and more importantly SATs results. As some parents place so much emphasis on these results not only do they ignore the excellent work carried out by teachers, but they fail to recognize the progress made by their own children. More and more children are being made to feel failures by parents because they did not achieve the 'required level for their age' in school tests. For a parent to do this to their child is in my opinion tragic, who wants to be labelled a failure at either 7 or 11 or in fact at any age? Is this what we send our children to school for?

My child has had an extremely happy and successful time at ... and is sorry to be leaving. However despite later success it has not always been easy, as you may recall.

In year one I was called into a meeting to discuss my child's progress, as it was causing slight concern. This concern continued into year two and my own prognosis that my child was dyslexic was confirmed by the school. From that moment my child received specialist and appropriate support which continued throughout his time at ... More importantly I was involved at every point receiving regular pieces of information and advice. I was also listened to by teachers and support staff who were always willing to try out different and new ideas to help my child. Never once did I feel patronised or my opinions undervalued. Year two SATs came and went with my child being awarded W/1 (working towards level 1) in most subjects. Years three and four were fantastic years, with the appropriate support in place the level of progress was astounding – my child learned to read and by the end of year 3 was producing well thought out and imaginative stories, although spelling was and still is 'interesting'. Numeracy also improved and with every term something else fitted into place. Not that I care, but for those who do, my child 'did not reach the expected level for his age' in either year 3 or year 4 tests. The specialist support continued for the rest of my child's time at ... The meetings continued, however by this stage were an exchange of ideas – still very informative and supportive. I knew that my child had made significant progress in year five and did in fact read the Harry Potter series with ease and confidence, something I would not have thought possible a year before. Numeracy also became a regular talking point with my child being 'moved up a group' at the start of the spring term. My child's progress continued to improve and I received regular updates from both my child and teachers, both formally and informally.

The amount of progress my child made at ... can not be measured by SATs or any other exams, if you remember many parents would have thought him a failure at the end of year two. The progress my child made was down to early intervention and recognition of his 'disability' and the subsequent support and excellent teaching. As a parent I recognise this and would congratulate and thank ... for helping to produce a happy, confident and able child. This is what ... does well and you must be congratulated.

One day I hope that more and more parents will feel like myself and begin to value their children for themselves and congratulate them on their achievements, irrespective of their test results. School is not just about SATs, tests and league tables and it is about time more parents realised this.

Yours faithfully,
A very happy parent!

P.S. Oh yes, for the record my child is leaving ... after, how is it phrased? Having exceeded the expected level for his age this year.

Governors' views

We did all we could to involve governors in the project. They became part of our distributed leadership strategy. Below is the feedback we received from a governor about 'Learning to Learn'.

The impact of 'Learning to Learn' on the school performance and the school community has been really important. From a governor's perspective, when our contact with school is limited, it's not always possible to separate out the impact of a single strategy, but this one really seems to have significantly changed the school and the way learning happens.

Children's performance has improved, particularly using added value measures. As importantly it's changed the atmosphere of the school. Governors who have been on monitoring visits repeatedly report on how well children behave, how self discipline is the norm, and how teachers manage the classroom without the need for raised voices or overt control.

As a school we have always been committed to supporting and developing teaching and non-teaching staff, encouraging them to remain in school and take on additional responsibilities. 'Learning to Learn' appears to have accelerated this process. Governors have noticed and supported, the ongoing development of school management and a leadership culture based on trust and delegation, encouraging all types of staff to contribute positively to school development.

The views of others

Throughout the project our mentors provided us with feedback about the impact of the 'Learning to Learn' project. They did this following termly visits to the schools during which they observed classroom practice, talked with teachers and with children. Their views have informed the writing of this book.

During their joint visits to each of the schools, the LEA and HEI mentors always took time out to meet with a 'focus' group of children to talk about their learning and the progress they felt they were making. Barbara and Melanie were struck by the perceptiveness of the children and by their increasing willingness to talk about themselves as learners and what they needed to do next to improve. As the schools became imbued with the language of learning and became much more explicit about progress and the standards expected, the children mirrored these developments. As one child put it:

I feel that my learning has improved for me because I can set myself goals which helps me to achieve much more, and I can take myself into my visual memory. Knowing that I can learn more makes it more easier, not much more harder. It makes it easier because I know that I can do everything if I put a bit of effort into it. The atmosphere makes it much more fun and easy.

We also sought the views of others who visited and supported our schools. We have included here the written feedback from an educational psychologist who was a regular visitor to one of the schools:

> The pupils at the school show awareness of learning in a way that is highly unusual for pupils in the primary phase. They show that they know that learning is the purpose of being in school and expect activities to have an outcome in terms of adding to knowledge and/or skills.
>
> In assessment of pupils, they make frequent references to their own learning and that of other pupils; often in outlining the reasons why they find things difficult. This also extends to group work – they are conscious and aware of members of the group. The older pupils, in particular, are aware of their learning style and refer to this in discussions.
>
> The greatest impact/change from an assessment perspective is evident in the way pupils of all ages respond to the question:
>
> 'Tell me how you do that?'
>
> This is a difficult question for most children who will happily 'show' they find it impossible to 'describe'. The familiarity of the vocabulary of learning gradually permeates their conversation and allows them access to a range of constructs not generally accessible until the upper primary and lower secondary stages.

Conclusion

School self-evaluation requires the rigorous use of evidence, be it quantitative or qualitative. It needs to be supported by objective, external evaluation, and to be set within a local and a national context.

The quantitative evidence presented in this chapter indicates that over the two years of the 'Learning to Learn' project, the value added to the end of Key Stage 2 national test results of the cohort group in four of the schools was equal to or, in three out of four cases, better than the LEA average for the rest of the primary schools in the borough. The value added by the four schools was sustained and improved even further the following year. The children in the four schools made greater rates of progress in English, mathematics and science compared with the rest of the schools in the borough, and exceeded expectations. The above average progress of boys, and pupils from different ethnic groups, confirmed the positive impact of the inclusive approaches to learning adopted by the schools. The detailed value added case study of the test results for one of the schools illustrates the significant gains made.

These outcomes provide evidence that a concentration on learning does enhance performance as researchers, such as Paul Black and Dylan Wiliam (1998; 2003), have been telling us for some time. The evidence from a range of external agencies confirms the importance of the schools' commitment to inclusion through the provision of a broad and balanced curriculum. The comments from teachers, parents, governors and others, and the strong views of the children described in Chapter 9, provide additional evidence to support the work that we did and the principles that underpinned our practice. We knew we could, and we did, make a difference.

9

Growing learners – children's views about learning

Good learners like to wonder about things. For them, it often really is a wonder-ful world. The phrases 'How come?' and 'What if?' are never far from their lips.
(Claxton, 2002, p. 25)

Transforming children's learning through transforming teaching is at the heart of this book. In previous chapters we have described the various ways in which we went about this transformation. The children were central to this process. Throughout the 'Learning to Learn' project we listened to children, we consulted them and we used their feedback to enable teachers and others to modify their practice. We have threaded through the book some of the feedback we received from the children.

The purpose of this chapter is to assess the impact of the project on the children. To do this, we step into their shoes and enable the reader to get some insight into the children's perceptions about learning and themselves as learners. We provide some examples of the many responses children gave to the questions asked of them at the end of the project. In the conclusion we reflect on the feedback from the children and draw out some of the key messages.

We asked the children:

- what does learning mean to you?
- what does it mean if you learn something?
- how do you learn best?
- how do you feel learning has improved for you?
- are there particular things teachers, support staff or other pupils do which help you to learn?
- how do you feel about the 'no put-down' zones?
- what gets in the way of your learning? How do you try to sort this out?
- are there things you wish your teacher would do that he/she does not do?
- what is it like to be a learner in your class?

We now take each of these questions in turn and give a flavour of the responses we received.

What does learning mean to you?

The importance of learning

- Learning is important to me because I can use these skills later on in life to help me move on and help others. I know I've learned something new because when I come across it again I can do it easily. When I find something difficult to do it keeps me motivated to try again.
- Learning is important to me. It's really vital to learn new things, a lot of the time it's what I live for. I enjoy it too. You never stop learning.
- It means to me that I have gone up a stage in my brain and the more you learn the easier it is to learn in the future. For example I learned how to multiply with big numbers in my mind and all of a sudden I learned to divide big numbers in my head in a short time.
- Learning to me is knowing something I didn't know before. So when I learn I feel it's an achievement so I feel proud. Learning is exercise for your brain. You never stop learning but some people learn quicker than others. Learning information means that I can apply that information and sharing it is what teachers in our school do.
- Learning means to have the knowledge, to find out new facts, and benefit from them, as well as keeping them in your mind. Learning means that I can get better marks in tests and use the same input for other tests in the future. Therefore I will keep on using this information until I don't need it anymore. Learning is a step to success. I have learned many things, and am still learning. We all learn something new everyday. Learning enriches your life. If you didn't learn, then you wouldn't have good qualifications, a nice house, money, and a peaceful life! Even adults are still learning!
- To me, learning is an understanding of the world I'm in which grows larger as I grow older. It is also like a precious gift that can be shared with everyone in turn.
- Learning helps me in several different ways. It could help me to get a good job. Not only does it help me, it makes me feel I have achieved something. It also helps me feel more comfortable in lessons when a teacher asks a question. Also I believe I can do it, it makes me feel proud. It helps me to trust people and feel more confident. There's a saying we say in class: 'We know it, we can do it, we are the best.' This helps us feel confident too. Learning also allows us to pass on what we know to others. Even if you don't understand something and you're determined to learn, you should keep on trying until you do understand. People learn in different ways, but eventually understand. People keep on learning everyday. This helps us communicate with others.

Learning and the emotions

- Learning is sometimes easy for me and sometimes difficult. It makes me sometimes happy if I'm doing something I like and sometimes a bit moody if I'm doing some-thing I don't like, but then again I get over it after a while. I like it when I learn something new, for example I didn't used to like ratio because I used to find it annoying and hard but then when I learnt how to do it properly I loved it and I got every single ratio question right, I wanted to do it over and over again.

- When I learn I feel really happy, then the next time I'm doing something and it comes up, that's the time I feel really proud and I think from now on this is going to be very easy, that's one problem gone.
- When I learn something new I feel very proud of myself because it becomes something that I can't fail in and it's like only I can do it.
- When I learn something I feel very happy because I know that I can do better next time.
- I feel happy and know that I can do it so I feel I can do anything.
- When I learn something new, the next time I do it I feel confident.
- Learning to me is making me feel happy because I am developing my reading skills. I have made huge progress and each time I have done it, it makes me feel more con-fident to do it again and that makes me feel excellent as I know I can do it.
- Learning means to me everything, because if you didn't learn you will get sad. If I learned something I will discover something else. If you learn you won't get in bad temptation on your work. If you learn people will respect you. If you learn you feel happy by being clever. If you learn you will be proud of yourself.
- To me, learning is fun and enjoyable. It helps me to be more comfortable in lessons because if I didn't learn I wouldn't be able to keep up with the lesson. When I've learned something, I feel happy and proud, because I know I've achieved something good. It gives me confidence and understanding, and it makes me feel like I'm progressing. Learning is good for me as it helps me to co-operate in lessons and keep on trying. When I come across someone who doesn't know something that I do, I feel important, and like a teacher because I can tell them. For this reason, I can be good to everyone else and they can teach me as well. To be able to learn well, I have to believe in myself and have trust in me, my teacher and everyone around me. I get a lot of encouragement from everyone else so I need to trust them.
- When I learn something it makes me really proud of myself that I've achieved something. If someone younger asks me a question and I don't know then I will feel really embarrassed but if I know the answer it builds up my confidence. All the teachers and assistants help people to understand the work we are doing. They give us direct instructions and we would follow them. If we do we feel more comfortable in the work, so we progress to help us with the tough world and jobs. Not only that, we have posters up everywhere saying things to encourage us such as, 'we know it, we can do it, we are the best'.
- When I achieve something I always feel very proud of myself and it makes me believe that I can do it. The more I believe I can do it, the better grades I will get, the more good grades I get the more relieved I feel, which helps me relax and not

rush my work. But I will always have trust in myself, my teacher and everyone in my class, whatever we're doing. Plus my teacher will feel relieved as well, plus she'll be happy for us because we worked hard. Now I'm improving a lot and I hope I will carry on like this.

What does it mean if you learn something?

- It means to understand the world and the difficulties in it; also it isn't just about knowing your sums but learning other things like music because that is still learning.
- It means understanding things that you didn't know before. It can also mean getting a better understanding of something you already know, from the price of a Mars bar to the distance between the planets.
- To me, learning is an excellent opportunity for me to understand things I never knew before; I also believe that if we all just knew everything learning wouldn't mean anything at all to anyone.
- Learning means to me that you learn to understand educational things you didn't know before. Once someone told me that you learn something every day and I believe that. Also we learn social skills, such as how to cooperate.
- Finding out something that I didn't know before. Being able to work something out. I can make sense of things that I was muddled about. We can learn in lots of different ways and it doesn't always have to be written down.
- Learning means to me that I look forward to going to school and I feel excited that I don't know what is going to happen the next day. My brother has special needs so I feel really proud for when I learn something and he doesn't know how to do it. So I help him and I put trust in him that he can do, so I encourage him. Sometimes when I don't really get something my friends put confidence in me and make me achieve my targets as well as the teachers and the LSAs. I like to do experiments because I feel real understanding and it helps me learn when I do the activity, touching and investigating things so I get good results.
- When I learn something it makes the work easier. It makes me feel happy and excited. I am proud of myself. If I learn something I can teach someone else and they learn things. I can tell my mum and dad about my learning and they are pleased. Learning gives you a better job when you are older.

How do you learn best?

The importance of the learning environment

- I learn best in a friendly, cool, classroom with lots of friendly people and a kind teacher; in nice surroundings and with a simple timetable.
- I think the way I learn best is when the teacher speaks properly in a learning, like-able way. I also think I learn best when the teacher explains the work better. I also

think that I learn best when I'm around my friends.
- Good listening in a quiet classroom.
- The atmosphere needs to be calm and relaxed in order for me to achieve a good amount of quality work. Luckily, this is what it is like in my class, most of the time! In discussions the atmosphere is lively and my teacher makes sure everyone gets a say.
- The friendly atmosphere has helped me to learn.

Working in Prides

- I like being in my Pride because it makes the atmosphere in the class more calmer and quieter and less hyper, and then we absorb all that goodness and take it into our magic circles. It makes our lives more easier to handle in our Prides.
- When we are sitting in Prides if you make a mistake they don't laugh at you. They tell you how you do it and which method to use.
- I learn best when I work in my Pride because all of us work together and we finish the work quickly and we explain the answers to each other if the members of the Pride don't know how we found the answer.

Working alone and with friends

- I can work well silently, but even better when I'm in a group, because we think about things, and I get better.
- I learn best when I'm alone but someone has to sit next to me so if I get stuck they can help me.
- I think I learn best when my friends are around me because we know each other's strengths so that if anybody's stuck we know who to turn to. I also like a challenge.
- I learn best when I talk it over with a friend, you don't copy each other, you just share your ideas, which makes your work better and more full of ideas.
- I learn best with people whom I feel like and respect me, when there's someone to help you.

Learning preferences

- I feel I learn when there's laughter. I think I'm an auditory and kinaesthetic learner.
- When I learn something if a question comes up, I can go back in to my visual memory and answer the question like in science.
- I learn best in a half visual, half kinaesthetic way – luckily the teachers provide all three ways of learning; visual, aural and kinaesthetic. Sometimes it is nice to work in silence to concentrate properly and sometimes it is nice to talk to share ideas. Three examples of all types of learning are: visual – looking at pictures and drawings; aural – listening to tapes and writing sounds, feelings etc. and kinaes-

thetic – doing activities and tasks.
- I learn best by discussion, because it makes me see what others think about the subject. I am an auditory learner but I like learning in many different ways.
- I learn best by seeing questions written on the board because if I didn't understand something that my teacher was saying then I could still look on the board and answer the questions.
- I learn best visually watching it done before I do it, so I know a lot before I do the activity.
- Touching and feeling what's going on, you understand it more.
- I learn best actually by doing the experiment and seeing things.
- Kinaesthetic is my way of learning because I need to see it or actually use it and I know this because I have tried other methods like hearing it but it just doesn't stick in my mind.
- I am a kinaesthetic learner. I find it easier to work with people I know well and people of the same ability. I like to work in a calm atmosphere with music and silence, but sometimes I prefer to work in groups.
- We learn best when we do kinaesthetic activities. We find this fun, and it's good because our teacher teaches like this a lot. We also learn best when we do a thing called brain gym, which refreshes our minds every now and then. We do this for about 2 minutes every lesson, and feel much better afterwards.

Learning prompts

- I learn best when teachers make it fun and reward us. Also when we have a brain gym, (dancing to *Night Fever* and singing) refreshes our brain. We have a variety of signs to encourage and help us, also when our teacher describes it really well. Finally when we co-operate together we work well.
- By discussing with other people and listening to their opinions. Doing our teacher's brain gyms helps our mind work more clearly. Being involved with the lesson by asking loads of questions helps you think. There are a variety of things around the classroom which helps us remember things and encourages us. Our teacher does activities to help us remember the things we have learned, for example mastermind. Our teacher makes learning fun by telling us jokes to do with the subject we are learning. Our teacher is normally positive which helps us to feel good about ourselves.
- Sometimes you can learn in more depth when you do work by kinaesthetic methods and get involved, instead of verbal and looking. You can also learn well when you have a different teacher, because you can do extra-curricular activities and learn in different styles. We can also memorise by mnemonics. You can also learn when our teacher, comma, speaks like this, full stop. You can then, comma, understand well, full stop. It is also useful when you have prompt posters to encourage you to use them and learn what they say. Often, when you get homework, it can help you understand what you learned in class. If you are in groups,

you can learn well because you can bounce ideas off each other and get good ideas. Sometimes you can use computers to do research and learn.

- I learn best when it's quiet so then I can focus on what I'm doing. When the teacher gives a good explanation I understand what I'm doing so I can get my work done. When we share ideas it helps you with your work. It also helps with pictures and labelled diagrams to show the information that we are learning in the class.

- I can learn better when someone gives me a method that I have to follow to solve a problem. Also if they give me questions I learn good as well. Additionally we have WILF which stands for what I'm looking for. This helps me because on the board under WILF my teacher writes the method which makes it easier. If I explain the method back or to someone, it makes it settle in my head.

- Figure 9.1 is a mind map produced by three children in response to the question.

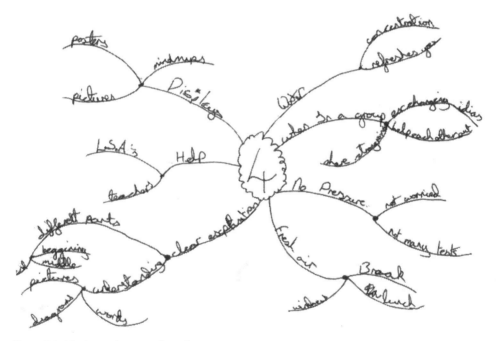

Figure 9.1 Mind map: how you learn best

How do you feel learning has improved for you?

- I feel that I have improved a lot because in year 4 the world of English just seemed to be gobbledegook and a load of talking that confused me, so I didn't even attempt most things that looked almost as if it was baby language.

- I'm very slow to learn, but when I was in year 5 and in year 6 we started booster groups. Then I got a bit better at my work and know what to do.

- I think I've improved rapidly with my work. Last year in the tests I didn't get the grades which were my level but now I've become much better.

- I think like in maths I didn't understand what the teacher was trying to say but now I whiz through my work and enjoy it as well.
- When I started this school I felt down at maths, but when booster groups started I felt confident at maths.
- Learning has improved a lot for me. There were some things that I couldn't do good, but slowly I am getting better in things that I couldn't do good before.
- When we never had booster groups I was slow with my work, but when we had booster groups I was improving.
- I can listen properly now.
- I can even learn at home now like at school.
- I feel my learning has improved by my friends and their understanding and co-operation for example, at first, I never believed that my English skills would ever improve but it was my friends that were always there beside me, beckoning me on and creating an excellent environment for my learning.
- I think my learning has improved because, in my class maths group, if I need any help I have 13 people to help me, I just need to ask if I think I couldn't do something, and by the time I got my results for my maths test I was two questions away from 5c.
- My learning has improved through music, mostly. I have an outlet to tone down my emotions.
- I, as a person, have learned how to co-operate with my classmates and not always take control. My teachers have helped me tremendously in this in all subjects especially maths where I have learned different strategies and other ways to attack my problems.
- I know how I have improved something because before I didn't understand a part of maths and I taught my mum and she got surprised and I didn't know that I actually had improved.
- My learning has improved because last time I got all level 5s and before I got level 4s so it's boosted up my confidence. The atmosphere inside my class is wonderful and I can focus, but when I can't focus I look around and I see people focusing and start to think why can't I focus, so I get determination to keep on going and think I can do it.
- I think learning has improved in the way that no one feels nervous to put their hand up. I think that even though I do not like practice papers they really help. I think all children are good at something and this school gives those children opportunities to extend their abilities.
- I think that to have travelled from tiny words such as 'bat' and 'ball' with no meaning to greater sentences that help us express our feelings and communicate with the rest of the world is my greatest learning achievement.
- Learning has improved for me by being more fun. By enjoyable learning, I found myself achieving higher grades in tests, and actually liking learning. I think more children will like to learn like I do. In school children have had more

opportunities like trips, lectures and maths road shows. The weak subjects of other pupils can improve. Pupils with different skills have been given the chance to stretch their knowledge. Everyone is good at something and this school has proved it.

- I think my learning has improved a lot because the atmosphere in the class encourages me. When I can see other people in the class learning why can't I learn? For example, I could see I was struggling, then I was determined to make huge amounts of progress in my levels and in my way of learning.
- How I think I have improved in my learning is when I think I can do it and never give up on my work, and if other people can do it, I can do it.

Are there particular things teachers, support staff or other pupils do which help you to learn?

Class teachers

- My teacher makes it interesting and tells us how much time we have. I like lessons where we do lots of different ways of doing the same thing. When we do a mind map to see how much we know and then another one and I see I know more.
- Miss … helps me because when she teaches the class and I don't get how she does it, she explains to me how she did the methods on the board.
- Teachers and support staff encourage a quiet environment that helps me to concentrate.
- Teachers give some tips to help me. They show me different methods like the grid method, chunking method and many more. Teachers help me by giving challenging sums. Learning helps me because other people have different learning skills and they can share their skills to help.
- My teacher always does funny mnemonics, such as how to remember the planets in order and the seven life progresses.
- My teacher helps me to learn to sit quietly so I can hear her when she reads a story.
- They give me general support. They give you friendship and honesty, no one knows you like your teacher. They also give me space if they're real friends, or really good teachers. They can help with the atmosphere; it's nice to have the right atmosphere for learning.
- Our teacher is one of the best teachers we know. She always has time for us, and would never give up on us. In our classroom we always have a relaxing atmosphere, so we don't feel tensed up, this helps us to concentrate more. Secondly, our teacher is always willing to help, if you don't know the answer, she'll make sure you do by the end of the lesson. If we still don't understand by the end of the lesson, she'll stay into playtime for us. Also, she also makes us believe that we

are responsible for our own learning and if we think we can do it she always tells us we will. Next, she puts up encouraging posters and phrases to make us feel confident and positive in ourselves, one of which is:

We know it

We can do it

We're the best

Finally, in our class lessons, she does things like brain gym to relax us and clear our brains. Not only this, she always makes lessons fun. All of this helps us to learn with confidence and know she will always be able to help.

- In our class, we have fun, but we also work hard. In most of our lessons our class would do a 2-minute brain gym, such as: answering as quick as a flash questions, or a distress dance. Our teacher helps us visualize our piece of work by reading it slowly, with expression. At the end of a lesson our teacher would recap the whole lesson, to make sure that everyone understands, which helps us to remember, so we can move on to the next stage.
- There are lots of things that our teacher does to help us learn. She helps us by: brain gyms – we have two special brain gyms. One is *Night Fever*, and the other is an Italian song. It gives us a chance to have a break from our complicated work. Music – we have our own clear-up song, and by the time that it has finished we have to have cleared everything away. Also, our teacher sometimes puts on the radio while we are doing our work. This helps us by being able to relax while we're working.
- Enthusiasm is a big key to learning to me. I get this a lot from my classmates and teachers. I can promise you that without enthusiasm I would never be as far as I am today. Advice is also important because then, without it, I wouldn't know how to improve. I am very grateful for my teacher, Mrs ... , and her long, pageful of nothing but advice and enthusiasm.

Support teachers

- When I'm stuck Miss ... and Miss ... couldn't be more welcoming to help. Some of my friends and fellow students try and help too. There is always a nice atmosphere in the classroom, and very rarely a word to dishearten. Always encouraging and helping with my stress.
- Teachers help by taking children out who need help a lot and children help by sharing their methods.
- My teachers encourage me to work and help me in my science and they read me the questions, it helps me a lot because in a child's way I don't understand, but in a teacher's way I understand.
- Teachers are very helpful. They find the most easiest way to help us in working out a sum. They understand that everyone needs a time to talk to someone about the problem, so in nearly every lesson, they give us a chance to do that. The pupils in my class help me to understand the problem and instead of telling me the answers

they explain it very clearly to me. This kind of learning always helps me.
- Our LSA gives us confidence and our teacher supports us in everything we do. Other children help us.

Friends

- Others help me learn by co-operating and encouraging others and me. Pupils even help me by commenting on my work and telling me how to spell difficult words.
- Changing classes has helped me as I've been with different people with different levels. If I was stuck or didn't know something they wouldn't just laugh in my face, they would explain it again and show me different methods. So being able to trust my classmates, male or female has helped me.

Prides

- What helps me learn is that we have Prides which are groups of five mixed children (boys and girls). What helps me is that sometimes we have to work at a question on a sheet. Everybody writes down their method and explains it to us. Sometimes my method is not the best and there are methods done by my friends that are much easier, so it helps me a lot especially when other children explain it to me.
- My Pride is the people that help me because the cheer leader says 'come on, we must not give up' and another person explains everything clearly when we are stuck.
- My Pride helps me not to have a nervous breakdown because I always think that I never can do it, but my Pride use this phrase to go against me and say 'you stop to think that you can't do it, but you can'.
- My Pride helps me to learn. All the members of my Pride encourage me to learn. They make me feel jolly which puts me in the right mood to learn.
- My Pride helps me to learn because I can always share my ideas with them. They always cheer me on. They always help me to do the right thing. My teachers help me because they always help me out. I have to know my teachers properly if I want to talk to them about something, so that I feel comfortable.
- Yes, my Pride helps me very much because we have a mixture of culture and different personalities. Teachers encourage us to answer the questions because they know we are capable of doing it.

Learning strategies

- Using a number line to help figure out maths sums. Using brainstorms for story ideas and science. When we get up and move around it makes learning maths fun. When Miss asked a question in maths, I didn't get it, but when it was drawn/explained on the board I got it.
- The WALT and the WILF helps me, so sometimes if I come late to school it helps me because the teacher just says a little bit.

- Get together everyone's opinions, going on the board and doing different methods and finding the easiest method. Going through answers and hearing how people get to that answer.

How do you feel about the 'no put-down' zones?

- The no put-down is good because it reminds you in your class. If you listen attentively to people they will do the same and share it. It also helps you in making new friends and knowing them better. Also next time you can make friends much better from the other experience.
- It is so easy to put your hand up and get the answer wrong but the good thing about it is no one laughs. I think no put-down is lovely. It should receive a peacemaker certificate. They make our classroom a lovely place to work in.
- I feel like a better person and happy to be in a class with no put-downs. We all clap when somebody has achieved something.
- I think no put-downs are a good thing because it keeps the class a happy environment. An example of this is an appreciation.
- I think we have not really needed it in the class, but if someone puts someone down I think when we show them a claw they don't do it again.
- I think no put-downs works because all children agree and stick to their rules, but if somebody accidentally says a put-down people give a signal to stop it.
- I feel very happy because we don't feel upset. Nobody says horrible things they say kind things. If there are no put-downs, we can trust everybody to not say horrible things. I also feel that I am part of my class. Instead of my class giving put-downs they give great put-ups. They make you appreciate each other. That makes you feel great.
- When we never had put-down, people used to put down each other, but now when people get a question wrong, and another person got it right, they don't put them down, they just say good try.
- I think it works very well because first lots of people gave lots of put-downs but they don't now, and now many people don't say a single put-down because the teachers and the children have tried to avoid that. So this worked well.
- It makes you feel welcome.
- I feel happy because no children will be nasty, for example, this boy in my class said 'shut up', everyone turned around and gave the claw, we were really shocked.
- It's worked well in the playground – no one gets into fights.
- I don't like put-downs, because it can make you feel sad and alone. But it's good if your friend is getting bullied, then you can sort it out without getting into trouble. You give them the sign.
- Before they had the no put-down zone I gave put-downs to people, but now that I know what put-down is, I don't give any put-downs, I keep the whole thing to myself.

What gets in the way of your learning? How do you try to sort this out?

Classroom behaviour

- When children in class are talking too much which distracts people from learning. To sort this out people shouldn't always sit next to their friends. Also when something amazing has happened such as a person's favourite football team won in a match or there was a fight during playtime. For this to be sorted there should be a rule like once you have stepped in the classroom then you can't talk about stuff like football.
- People often get distracted if other children or teachers come into the classroom and ask for something which is not to do with school work. To sort this out, none of the children or teachers should be allowed to go in other classrooms.
- When your teacher tells you to send something to classes it clashes with your class time and you may miss some vital information.
- If you have joined a club, your club tutor may often call you out of your class for a lesson which will cause trouble, as you would have missed a lot of information.
- I don't like sitting near some children because they mess around and it stops me from learning. I find it very hard to listen so I have to sit near people who will help me. It is hard if you have a different teacher and they tell you to do things in a different way.
- Sometimes people burst into the classroom and say that a club has been cancelled or something like that. The problem is that immediately whatever we're doing is stopped and all the ideas go out of my head because of one small interruption.
- Sometimes noise gets in the way of learning. I try to prevent it by asking people to be quiet or ringing the chimes which is a signal for the class to be quiet.
- When we come in from lunchtime, most of the time there is a problem with people in our class. Our teacher takes us out of the room, he doesn't shout he speaks in his normal voice, and sorts it out. At the end of the day we are all very happy.
- If it's noisy some people just keep talking and I have to say can everyone just talk in their heads.
- When children stop me when they're talking. When somebody talks next to me, I tell you straight away. When people be noisy and I can't hear – I say keep your noise down a little bit I can't hear the teacher.
- When people talk about something else and I try to concentrate and try to block it out of my mind.
- Whenever there's a real noise behind me and I've got a good idea what to write in my book, the noise distracts me and I completely forget what to write. When I try to sort it out I act like I'm wearing ear-muffs.
- Noise gets in my way when I study and all the words get muffled up.
- I find it difficult to work with noisy and naughty children. My teacher does not tolerate this behaviour so that is how my problem is solved.

- Noise stops me learning. I can work, but the rate of me actually working is slower, so I don't get things finished. To help me concentrate I think of all the high marks I will get in SATs if I work hard.
- When I'm given a question and other children start to whisper the answer in my ear, which makes me lose my concentration. It makes me angry because I think others think that I'm dumb but I try to learn myself so I tell them to not tell me the answer and not to talk while I'm concentrating.
- When I am doing some work and somebody comes and talks to me but I don't want to talk I have to say please don't interrupt me.
- People talk to us and it puts us off.
- We learn best in a quiet and a little talkative class.
- We learn best also in a classroom in an educated school like this one.
- If people talk over the top of us we can't learn.
- If teachers continually talk during lessons it stops me concentrating. When this happens I just stop working until he or she stops talking. Sometimes we have to stop working and that means that I get distracted and I cannot write as easily as before we stopped. I sort this out by doing brain gym when I get back to class so as to get back into the flow of writing.

Personal distractions

- When something comes in your mind that you are worried about.
- What puts me off is whenever I'm doing my work and something is out, I have to go and put it away, then I can do my work.
- I think people who are unfamiliar to me stand in my way because I wonder who they are, and I can't work. Also if something is out of place in class, I have to correct it or I can't work. Another thing is time because sometimes I don't have enough time.
- I think when I put my hand up for a long time to answer a question, when a teacher asks me for the answer I forget it. It really frustrates me and I go into my reptilian brain for a few minutes. To make me calm down, I fiddle with my ring on my hand and then I calm down.
- The thing that gets in the way of my learning is anger. I used to get very very angry and not learn and be moody. I sorted this out by talking to my teacher more often. I tried to be nice and that helped. I made a best friend and I made other friends. So now I don't get angry a lot.
- If we are learning something boring I start to daydream and I cannot concentrate on what our teacher is talking about. I try to sort this out by trying hard to keep focused.

Friends

- Friends sometimes get in the way of my learning. I often sort it out through communicating, which helps them and me understand.

- What gets in the way of my learning is when I am at school and my friends are not my friend then I do not like work anymore and I solve it by saying to myself be calm.
- Normally, the things that get in the way of my learning are friends trying to interest me in things having nothing to do with my work and other children criticising it. I believe the best way to be rid of these things, is to ignore all of these terrible distractions.

Outside distractions

- When I am really concentrating nothing can distract me unless it's the voice of a teacher. If I'm concentrating as much as I can, outside lessons such as PE can take my attention away from some thing, as it is quite noisy.
- Sometimes there are loud noises because our classroom is right near the motorway. Also if we are talking about a boring subject I start to fidget and I get hold of my absent mind.

Home

- When I do my homework my brother tells me my favourite programme's on so if I want to finish my work I tell him to go away so I can do my work.
- When I am at home and studying in my room I always think about my favourite programme that is coming on. I always rush my work and get it all wrong. I stop myself from doing this by forgetting about the programme, and plus it will come on again.

Are there things you wish your teacher would do that he/she does not do?

General classroom behaviour

- When my class is having a discussion I would like my teacher to write key points on the board so if we miss anything we can always pick it up again.
- I think my teacher should stop WALTs and WILFs because it wastes time in our work when we have to write it down. I think there should only be a title.
- When you know the answer and you're the only person with your hand up Miss gives them clues instead of picking you.
- I wish the teachers would have two groups in a class; one that learns by the method of kinaesthetic and actually doing the work and one other group that prefers the method of auditory so in that way we all learn best.
- Sometimes it gets noisy and I get distracted, so I would like my teacher to write 'be quiet' on the board.
- What I wish my teacher to do and she is not doing is more games and more PE and extra play and more ICT (lots of these!).
- I wish she would give out personal whiteboards to everyone for, for example, a

mental starter for a maths lesson. It stops me cheating and is a fun way to learn.
- Play more team games. Cooking and painting lessons.
- I wish my teacher would let us work with our friends because we would co-operate more and get more work done. Also I think it would be good if we could play more educational games such as Bingo.
- My teacher talks a lot and sometimes I just want to get on with my work! I like it when we do things in lots of different ways but sometimes the teacher doesn't do that.
- Yes there are things that I wish my teacher would do. These include having more circle time because when we are feeling upset we can talk about it openly and the class can help find a solution to your problem. I would also like to have more history and geography lessons because I feel they are important to our work because we should know about the past and things all around the world.

Keeping to the subject

- Not really. My teacher is very fair and understanding, sometimes she drifts off the subject, but it's nice to have a break, even though she always refocuses. She knows how to handle any problems you might have, she's a good listener too.
- Are there things you wish your teachers to do that they don't? Not really though I would like teachers to keep to the facts.
- I sometimes wish that my teacher would be more concise because we would be talking about an important subject and then he would go onto a different subject so sometimes we don't finish in time.

Talking during tests

- I wish she would stop talking in the middle of tests. This is a good help but if people who have got the question in their mind and are trying to solve it, the whole thing goes out of your mind.
- Don't talk in tests because when we are in the middle of the test and the teacher talks it gets the idea out of my head.

Finally

- I am very happy with my teacher and there is nothing I dislike about her teaching.

What is it like to be a learner in your class?

Feelings

- We feel that to be a learner in our class is like the title on a book and if that title wasn't there we wouldn't know where we were.

- Great, happy, fun, more grown up.
- Happy! I think to myself that I've done good!
- It feels good to be a learner in my class because I am very happy with my class and teacher. They are kind and enthusiastic.
- It's enjoyable because there are always new things to learn and do. There is also a lovely atmosphere to work in.
- It's FUN! Because you learn new things and I like it when we are in our literacy group.
- It is very enjoyable to work in this class. I feel very safe and accepted. Sometimes however I do not feel challenged enough.
- It is fun and enjoyable because our teacher teaches in a good way. She teaches in a good way because every now and then she uses music in lessons and it inspires us. We find that our lessons can be fun or boring depending on the way we are being taught.
- Happy and brilliant. You give us things a bit harder than nursery or reception. In Yr 1 it's a bit like Yr 2, you get hard work.
- I feel safe in my class. I also feel that I have a balance of people to work with because they have different skills and abilities. I also feel happy in my class.
- It's very enjoyable to work in this class. I feel safe and accepted.
- I feel very happy being a learner in my class because I can put my hand up to answer the question and if my answer is wrong no one gives me put-downs everyone gives put-ups. I feel very happy when no one gives put-down because if they don't give me put-downs I don't be shy to answer a question in the class even if it is wrong.
- It's a bit fun, because they make learning more fun by saying jokes and making us feel safe and encourage us.
- It is very exciting being a learner in my class because I feel very safe. That also makes me feel confident.

Learning in class

- I like to be a learner in this class because in the past couple of years I wasn't sure on what we were learning. But in Yr 6 because we were doing actual tests I know what is coming up in the tests, and I know that I've taken a big step in improvement.
- In this class in this year the tasks have become harder. And I feel positive being a learner now that I get harder work so I can get prepared for the hard questions in my SATs test.
- In this class it's very challenging, because when we do tests everyone competes with each other. This puts pressure on me but in a good way because I just want to have a high mark. Also because I try hard and get high marks I look forward to tests and feel positive.
- It gives me incentive to learn. And it feels good to be a learner as I get a brilliant teacher. She helps by giving out positive things. She also warns you about all the

things you have to concentrate on so it's brilliant to be learning in this class.
- Lots of people to help us. We can work in different groups with different people.
- It's like a challenge to be a learner in my class.
- I feel challenged but it is good to be challenged because you will learn new things in your subject.
- Because if you learn a lot so you can get good results so when I go high school so you can do well and in booster group it helps me.
- It feels pretty good to be a learner in our class but can be stressful for the talented ones as the teachers mainly trust us with helping other students out even if we are still trying to get on with our work that the teacher has laid down for us.
- I really enjoy it because we do a lot of work as a group or in pairs. My teacher has lots of strategies that help me learn like never give up and writing little memos at the bottom of our page. I really enjoy being in my class.
- In my class the two teachers use various methods of teaching and learning, creating a good working atmosphere with stimulus for everyone.
- I had a fun teacher – she played music I liked – when the work was difficult she helped me – when it came to learning she was serious and helped you understand it. This helped me to learn – she came round and told me what to do.
- In my class it is fun to be a learner because the atmosphere is calm and so everyone else is calm as well. This helps everyone to work hard and be positive towards their work. It is also good to be a learner in my class because we have the benefit of a teacher who lets us have water in class and music on. I find it easier to concentrate when the music is on and if I have water in class this refreshes my mind.
- When I am in my class I find it an enjoyable experience because everyone in the class co-operates and finds ideas out from each other which helps them. I also find it good because it is not normally very noisy so I can get on with my work. The teachers I've had as well have been very helpful because although we do our work they make it fun so we focus and concentrate better. It is also good because sometimes after lessons we perform (if we had just done drama), or share what we have done with the class.

Peers

- In my class, to be a learner is a great opportunity to meet and bond with pupils. It is also great to be part of a whole and know that to achieve great heights everyone needs to work as a team.
- It's pretty pleasant to be a learner in my class. There's a good atmosphere and a lot of people I like. There is a small amount of peer pressure, but I think the amount of what I've learned makes it seem tiny in comparison.
- I feel like if you get a question wrong people won't laugh because they are kind.
- It is very good because the people in the class are kind and the atmosphere keeps me happy.
- It is a great joy to be in this class with people I trust and know.

Conclusion

We believe that the comments from the children more than demonstrate the positive impact of 'Learning to Learn' on them as learners. Our aim was to develop a learning orientation in the children in such a way that all children were motivated to learn. In Chapter 3 we drew on Chris Watkins et al.'s summary of the characteristics of children with a learning orientation:

- belief that effort leads to success
- belief in one's ability to improve and learn
- preference for challenging tasks
- personal satisfaction from success at difficult tasks
- problem-solving and self-instructions when engaged in task (Watkins et al., 2002, p. 2).

It was these characteristics that we wanted to inculcate in the children. The children's story about learning embodies these characteristics. *'We can if ... '* comes out very strongly. So too, does their enthusiasm, motivation and desire to engage as learners. Of particular note is the constant reference by the children to the importance of the emotions in learning, the learning environment, support for learning and encouragement to learn. Their affirmation of the importance of a broad curriculum, and of the need for teachers to use a range of teaching methods and learning prompts, confirms the value children placed on teachers and others paying close attention to these issues.

The feedback from the children, combined with the evaluations in Chapter 8, enabled us to identify the main lessons of our work for schools. We draw out these lessons in the next chapter.

10

Transforming learning and teaching – lessons and key principles

Transformation requires everyone to learn: constantly, openly and quickly.
(Hargreaves, 2003, p. 73)

Writing this book has been an important learning experience for us all. It has forced us to stand back and reflect on the journey we took together as we went about trying to transform learning and teaching in our schools. In this final chapter we draw out the lessons learned from previous chapters as a result of our reflections. We then reflect further on these lessons to identify a set of principles that needs to underpin the transformation of learning and teaching.

Lessons learned

We have identified seven lessons from our 'Learning to Learn' project.

These lessons concern how to develop:

- a networked learning community
- a learning orientation
- teachers as learners and researchers
- leadership for learning
- accelerated learning for children
- ways of tracking children's learning, their progress and achievement
- rigorous self-evaluation.

We now look at each of these lessons in turn.

How to develop a networked learning community

Chapter 2 describes how we learned a great deal about the factors that appear to enable schools to collaborate with one another effectively. We were able to identify at least 12 characteristics of an effective networked learning community.

We learned that an effective networked learning community demonstrates:

- commitment
- confidence
- trust and respect
- shared values and beliefs
- knowledge about one another
- knowledge creation and transfer
- clarity of purpose
- robust working practices
- risk-taking and working beyond the 'comfort zone'
- supportive challenge
- rigorous data-gathering and evaluation
- sustainability.

These characteristics are interrelated. When used in combination, they enabled our group of schools to focus on transforming learning and teaching through learning together in a rigorous but creative way. The combination of the characteristics enabled us to engage in what David Hargreaves (2003) calls 'disciplined innovation'.

We learned that whilst our network of schools needed to start by taking small, practical steps, we needed to 'think big' if we were to go beyond incremental change and really transform learning and teaching. Our commitment to the development of a learning orientation was an essential part of this process. How to put this commitment into practice is the second lesson we learned.

How to develop a learning orientation

Chapter 3 describes how we developed our teaching practice to develop pupils' learning. We learned that if we were to move from a performance orientation to a learning orientation we had to do at least four things.

We learned that you can develop a learning orientation if you:

- encourage thinking skills and learning skills
- develop the language of learning in classrooms and across the school as a whole
- stimulate the learning brain
- develop emotional intelligence.

Throughout Chapter 3 we describe how we did this. It will be seen that we worked on these four issues simultaneously using a range of strategies. All important was the need to connect the strategies we chose to use to the 'big picture' – in other words to the values and beliefs that united us as a community of learners, in particular, our commitment to inclusion.

We learned that teachers needed much support and encouragement to step outside the 'comfort zone' and to move beyond a focus on performance and a set curriculum to be 'delivered'. They needed to be given time and space to try out new ideas and to have the confidence to take risks and learn from mistakes. This led us to our third lesson.

How to develop teachers as learners and researchers

We learned that you can develop teachers as learners and researchers if you:

- enable teachers to be learners
- coach managers in the skills of leadership for learning
- provide induction programmes for newly recruited staff and NQTs
- invest in high-quality training opportunities for *all*
- embed support and development within school improvement plans.

Chapter 4 describes the wide range of strategies we used to support teachers' learning and the learning of other adults in our schools. It was through the use of these strategies and our reflection on their impact that we learned, as we describe at the end of Chapter 4, that:

- there is no 'one size fits all' approach to professional development
- CPD opportunities need to be built on a shared set of values and beliefs about learners and their learning
- simply relying on LEA and nationally prescribed in-service provision is not the answer to school improvement. Such provision has a role to play but it is only one part of a much wider strategic approach to changing practice in the classroom
- however good external provision may be, it has to be complemented and integrated with a planned approach to in-school professional development opportunities.

An important part of this planned approach to CPD was encouraging a wide range of staff, and the children themselves, to take on leadership roles. This takes us to our fourth lesson.

How to develop leadership for learning

We learned that you can develop leadership for learning if:

- headteachers model total commitment
- leadership is distributed across the school
- deputy heads become the 'levers' of school improvement
- middle managers and teams become leaders of learning and learning leaders
- we develop leadership roles amongst other members of staff
- children become leaders of their own learning and the learning of others – peers and teachers.

Chapter 5 tells the story of how we developed leadership for learning and how, as we distributed leadership, the headteachers had to learn to have the confidence to 'let go' so as to enable others to lead in different ways. We began to learn to build capacity through recognizing and valuing the range of knowledge, skills and talents represented by the adults and the children in our respective communities. We needed to coach and train leaders to enable them to put our mantra of *'we can if … '* into practice. The headteachers had to learn to be team players, and to trust in the leadership of others. The pay-off was enormous as we unleashed the talents of staff and children. We also had to work hard at sustainability by learning to 'grow' new leaders to take the place of those who moved on. A key focus of this leadership was the enhancement of children's learning which led us to our fifth lesson.

How to develop accelerated learning

We learned that you can accelerate children's learning if you:

- recognize that accelerating learning is a process, not a package
- examine organizational factors or systems that can get in the way of learning
- have high expectations
- provide rigorous feedback for learning
- are sensitive to the personal and emotional barriers that can get in the way of learning
- reflect on, and regularly review progress with children and their parents
- maintain and enhance inclusive provision for a broad and balanced curriculum
- use creative differentiation to support inclusion.

Chapter 6 describes the different ways in which we went about the challenge of accelerating children's learning. In many respects it was the children themselves who taught us the lessons we have identified. We quickly learned that to promote metalearning it is important to create regular opportunities for children to talk about their learning, and to become self-regulators of their own learning. We learned a great deal from them. Their perceptiveness about what can get in the way of their learning, and what can best support their learning, was impressive, and at times, humbling. The children became central to enabling us to keep track of their progress and they contributed a great deal to our sixth lesson.

How to develop ways of tracking children's learning, their progress and achievement

We learned that you can keep track of children's learning if you:

- identify issues that can inform and have an impact on the tracking of pupils' learning such as mobility, attendance and the range of special needs
- ensure the micro and macro management of quantitative data
- use a range of qualitative tracking measures
- track a focus cohort.

Chapter 7 describes the strategies we used to keep track of children's learning. We learned to draw on the experience of others and to adapt their ideas to suit our own contexts. We learned the importance of being rigorous in our pupil tracking, and of involving the children and their parents in the process. As we describe at the end of Chapter 7, it was through the strategies we shared and refined, that we learned:

- to see data, be they quantitative or qualitative, as a friend not a threat
- how to be more discriminating in our use of data so that it was 'fit for purpose'
- how to make the monitoring of progress a shared responsibility between adults and children
- how to bring formative and summative assessment together, so that each informed the other of next steps in learning for individuals, and next steps in strategic planning for the school as a whole
- that a focus on value added across all aspects of learning for each child enabled our commitment to inclusion to be realized.

As we tracked children's progress, there were two questions that helped to push us up our steep learning curve:

- Are you making a difference?
- How do you know?

It was our two mentors who kept asking these questions in a challenging but supportive way. They made us value the importance of having external critical friends to move us forward. They helped us to learn our seventh lesson.

How to develop rigorous self-evaluation

In Chapter 8 we describe the ways in which we evaluated the impact of the 'Learning to Learn' project through a combination of internal self-evaluation and external scrutiny. We learned that for self-evaluation to be rigorous we needed to do at least four things.

Rigorous self-evaluation requires:

- evidence to be gathered at different times for different purposes
- different kinds of evidence to be gathered simultaneously
- different people to be involved for different reasons
- external reality checks.

We gathered data at three points in time. At the beginning of the project we gathered 'baseline' data. This enabled us to know the current levels of attainment of our cohort of pupils, and through the use of questionnaires, the current perceptions of children, teachers and parents. These data enabled us to assess the value-added of the project over the two-year period. They helped us to answer the question, 'have we made a difference?'

At regular intervals during the two years we gathered 'progress' data for formative purposes. We used the evidence, be it from children or adults, to help staff share good practice, change the things that were not working, and try out new ideas. We also used the evidence with children to help them to self-evaluate and self-regulate their own learning. We used the data to strengthen the dialogue about learning between children, teachers and parents.

At the end of the project, we gathered a range of 'summative' data. These data enabled us to make a comparison with the baseline data to evaluate the potential value added of the project. These data, combined with our progress check data, enabled us to answer the question, 'How do we know we have made a difference?'

We simultaneously gathered quantitative and qualitative evidence to enable us to develop a broad picture of the changes that took place. We learned, as we described in Chapter 7, how to become much more rigorous in the use of test data to enable us to track individual, group and whole-school progress. We drew on people's perceptions through questionnaires and face-to-face dialogue. We looked carefully at documentary evidence. We observed in classrooms and across the school as a whole. We kept a careful record of changes in children's and teachers' behaviours. By pulling together these different kinds of evidence, we gathered a detailed and rich picture of changes over time.

Self-evaluation requires different people to play different roles. For the purposes of our project, children needed to play a central role in evaluating their own progress and in telling us the ways in which we could best support them as learners. Teachers needed to learn the language of learning to enable them to be more reflective on their own practice, and the impact it was having on children's learning. Other staff needed to evaluate the role and importance of their contribution to learning. Parents' views, and their knowledge of their children, were also important parts of the equation.

Using external sources of evidence to check out, confirm or challenge our own self-evaluation proved invaluable. Although not planned at the outset, Ofsted inspections provided us with a necessary external perspective as did the validation of other external agencies. Visitors to the schools provided another objective viewpoint, in particular that of our mentors.

Writing this book has also made an important contribution to our shared evaluation of the journey we took together. It has been a good discipline having to record what we did, why we did it, and how.

We are only too well aware, however, that the journey is by no means over. To help us look forward, we have reflected on the lessons learned and applied our metalearning strategies. As a result, we have drawn out a set of principles that we believe need to underpin the transformation of learning and teaching.

Transforming learning and teaching – key principles

Arising out of our reflections, we have identified nine key principles.

The principles concern the importance of:

- a 'can-do' culture
- transformational leadership and management
- the learning environment
- ensuring a broad and balanced curriculum informed by assessment
- enabling children to have a greater say in their learning and in the management of the school
- taking emotional intelligence seriously
- assessment for learning
- strengthening the learning dialogue between children, teachers and their parents
- learning from the 'irritations' between summative and formative assessment.

The importance of a 'can-do' culture

We can transform learning and teaching if there is a shared belief that *all* children (and adults too) have the capacity to learn. A commitment to inclusion needs to underpin this belief. It can be translated into everyday reality through engendering a *'we can if ... '* attitude. Underpinning this 'can do' culture is the importance of promoting a learning orientation in the context of a competitive system.

The importance of transformational leadership and management

We can transform learning and teaching if there is a transformation of leadership practices and management arrangements. These practices and arrangements need to have as their focus, developing the capacity of the school as a whole, of teams of teachers and individual class teachers to learn about learning and how to sustain and accelerate the learning of children. It requires leaders and managers to have a deep-rooted conviction of *'we can if ... '*, and to model this in practice. It also requires the courage to challenge those who say 'we can't because ... ' and to lead and manage that process. A concentration on metalearning enables this to happen. It means headteachers have to create time and space for teachers and support staff to try out new ideas, and to let go, whilst always keeping their eye on the 'big picture'.

The importance of the learning environment

We can transform learning and teaching if the learning environment supports the cognitive, social, emotional and physical needs of young people, so as to promote a learning, rather than a performance orientation. It needs to be the kind of environment that takes the different learning preferences and potential emotional barriers to learning into account. It also needs to be the kind of environment that develops the language of learning and uses display to support, encourage and enhance learning.

The importance of ensuring a broad and balanced curriculum informed by assessment

We can transform learning and teaching if a broad and balanced curriculum is provided in which *all* children can be given opportunities to succeed through an inclusive approach to learning. Such an approach requires the regular assessment of children's progress, which, in turn, enables teachers to plan and modify the curriculum to meet the learning needs of *all* children.

The importance of enabling children to have a greater say in their learning and in the management of the school

We can transform learning and teaching if children are at the heart of the process. This requires the use of a range of strategies to enable children to learn the language of metalearning, and the skills of self-regulated learning. It means that children need to be encouraged to provide feedback to teachers on what best supports their learning and what gets in the way of their learning.

The importance of taking emotional intelligence seriously

We can transform learning and teaching if we pay close attention to the power of the emotions in motivating or inhibiting learning. Motivation and engagement in learning require a *'we can if ... '* attitude and a recognition of the importance of intra-personal emotions and interpersonal relationships. Emotional intelligence in action encourages the confidence to take risks, work outside the comfort zone, and persevere in the face of adversity and challenge. It enables higher-order shared learning, through the giving and receiving of feedback, in ways that develop and enhance the learning of others.

The importance of assessment for learning

We can transform learning and teaching if teachers and children develop a range of strategies to enable children to understand where they are and where they need to get to in terms of next steps in learning. The feedback given to children needs to be clear, practical and honest. To take full advantage of this feedback, children need to be shown how they can improve, and the standards expected and required. They also need to be given the time and space to review and reflect.

The importance of strengthening the learning dialogue between children, teachers and their parents

We can transform learning and teaching if opportunities are created for children, their teachers and their parents to talk about learning and next steps in learning.

This requires traditional approaches to parents' days and evenings to be transformed to enable different kinds of conferencing between all three parties to take place on a regular basis.

The importance of learning from the 'irritations' between summative and formative assessment

We can transform learning and teaching if the different purposes of summative and formative assessment, and the interrelationship between them, are understood. Summative assessment provides a reality check. It offers a snapshot of where the school is at. Formative assessment is an ongoing process of review and feedback for learning. The way in which these two processes come together is critically important. At times, they flow together and support one another. At other times, one can jar the other, acting as an 'irritant' to force a rethink, thus taking the school out of its comfort zone.

Conclusion

At the micro level of the five schools we have drawn out lessons and principles concerned with the transformation of learning and teaching within our own communities and across our learning network. We asked ourselves whether these lessons and principles are transferable at the macro levels beyond the school. We think they are. We invite the reader to revisit our story and substitute LEA, the DfES and other agencies in place of 'school'.

We did this ourselves, which led us to ask a set of questions when considering the relationship between the micro level of practitioners and the macro level of policy-makers locally and nationally.

In the macro world of policy-makers:

- Are core values rooted in learning?
- Are there shared views about learning?
- Is metalearning valued and promoted?
- Is risk-taking encouraged and supported?
- Is leading for learning encouraged and supported?
- Is there a regular dialogue about learning?
- How and by whom is learning evaluated?
- Are children leading the learning?

For us, the children led the process of transformation, enabling us to learn with and from them. Therefore, we feel it is only right and proper that we leave our growing learners to have the final word through a poem written by a group of children in one of the schools.

The Growth of Learning

We were made for a purpose ...
To learn from our mistakes.

We can, if...

...We take the first tiny steps.
Our learning journey
Gives us independence as we take our place in the world.

...We grow our learning roots on earth.
The more we practise, the more our roots anchor,
Supporting our future in life.
Roots absorb our learning, as we journey on.
Branching out,
We share our different skills for
Cooperation and collaboration, and
Different talents for
Solving a sum
Writing a story
Running a race.

...We grow our shoots, reaching for the light
Rocketing towards our goals.
Scattering the seeds of our wisdom.
Growing now into something beautiful,
A new skill unfolds its leaf at the end of each branch.
As we discover our budding talents
We start to bloom.
Our unfolding petals make the world a sunny greater place,
As we learn from teaching others.

Our learning tree might be hidden away in the forest of life,
But our wisdom will live on forever
In others we've touched.

Composed by: Imran Ramay, Arsal Shah, Farzana Mannan, Alejandra Garcia-Gardener (year 6Fx); Uneesa Zaman, Kira Francis, Sharanja Rajalingam, Muhammed Siddiq-Pate, (year 6Wm); Tayibah Seedat, Hana Sodawala, Adil Khokhar, Amarjeet Chaggar (year 6Ch).

Glossary

ALPS	Accelerated Learning in Primary Schools
AST	advanced skills teacher
AT	Attainment Targets
CPD	continuing professional development
CMT	curriculum management team
DfES	Department for Education and Skills
EAL	English as an additional language
GaT	gifted and talented
HEI	higher education institution
ICSEI	International Congress for School Effectiveness and Improvement
ICT	information and communication technologies
IEP	Individual Education Plan
INSET	in-service training
ISEIC	International School Effectiveness and Improvement Centre
KS	Key Stage
LEA	local education authority
LPSH	Leadership Programme for Serving Headteachers
LSA	learning support assistant
MDA	midday assistant
MEAS	minority ethnic achievement staff
NCSL	National College for School Leadership
NFER	National Foundation for Educational Research
NGfL	National Grid for Learning
NLP	neuro-linguistic programming
NLS	National Literacy Strategy
NNS	National Numeracy Strategy
NPQH	National Professional Qualification for Headship
NQT	newly qualified teacher
OFSTED	Office for Standards in Education
QCA	Qualifications and Curriculum Authority
RY	reception year
SATs	Standard Assessment Tests
SEN	special educational needs
SENCO	special educational needs co-ordinator
SIGAR	Supported and Independent Guidance and Activities for Reading
SIP	School Improvement Plan
TA	teaching assistant
TIPDP	Teachers' International Professional Development Programme
TLC	tender loving care
VAK	visual, auditory and kinaesthetic
WALT	'We are learning to … '
WILF	'What I'm looking for'

Bibliography

Assessment Reform Group (1999) *Assessment for Learning: Beyond the Black Box.* Cambridge: University of Cambridge, School of Education.

Black, P. and Wiliam, D. (1998) *Inside the Black Box.* London: King's College, School of Education.

Black, P. and Wiliam, D. (2003) 'The development of formative assessment', in B. Davies and J. West-Burnham (eds), *Handbook of Educational Leadership and Management.* Harlow: Pearson.

Broadfoot, P. (1996) 'Liberating the learner through assessment', in G. Claxton, T. Atkinson, M. Osborn and M. Wallace (eds), *Liberating the Learner.* London: Routledge.

Centre for Studies on Inclusive Education (CSIE) (2000) *Index for Inclusion.* Bristol: CSIE Ltd.

Clarke, S. (1998) *Targeting Assessment in the Primary Classroom: Strategies for Planning, Assessment, Pupil Feedback and Target Setting.* London: Hodder and Stoughton.

Clarke, S. (2001) *Unlocking Formative Assessment.* London: Hodder and Stoughton.

Claxton, G. (2002) *Building Learning Power.* Bristol: TLO Ltd.

Dennison, P.E. and Dennison, G.E. (1994) *Brain Gym.* Ventura, CA: Edu Kinaesthetics.

Department for Education and Skills (DfES) (1998) *Supporting the Target-setting Process: Guidance for Effective Target Setting for Pupils with Special Educational Needs.* London: DfES.

Department for Education and Skills (DfES) (2003) *Excellence and Enjoyment – A Strategy for Primary Schools.* London: DfES.

Dweck, C. (1986) 'Motivational processes affecting learning', *American Psychologist,* 41: 1040–8.

Fullan, M. (1991) *The New Meaning of Educational Change.* London: Cassell.

Fullan, M. (2004) 'Leadership and Sustainability', Ontario Institute for Studies in Education, University of Toronto, prepared for Hot Seat, Urban Leadership Community, England.

Gardner, H. (1993) *Multiple Intelligences: the Theory in Practice.* New York: Basic Books.

Gardner, H. (1999) *Intelligence Reframed: Multiple Intelligences for the 21st Century.* New York: Basic Books.

Gibbs, J. (1995) *A New Way of Learning and Being Together.* Sausalito, CA: Center Source Systems LLC.

Gipps, C. and MacGilchrist, B. (1999) 'Primary school learners', in P. Mortimore (ed.), *Understanding Pedagogy and its Impact on Learning.* London: Paul Chapman Publishing.

Goldsworthy, A. and Feasey, R. (1997) *Making Sense of Primary Science Investigations.* Hatfield: Association for Science Education.

Goleman, D. (1996) *Emotional Intelligence: Why It Can Matter More than IQ*. London: Bloomsbury Paperbacks.

Goleman, D. (1998) *Working with Emotional Intelligence*. London: Bloomsbury Paperbacks.

Gray, J., Hopkins, D., Reynolds, D., Wilcox, B., Farrell, S. and Jesson, D. (1999) *Improving Schools: Performance and Potential*. Buckingham: Open University Press.

Greenfield, S. (1997) *The Human Brain: A Guided Tour*. London: Weidenfeld and Nicholson.

Hannaford, C. (1995) *Smart Moves: Why Learning Is Not All in your Head*. Arlington, VA: Great Ocean Publications.

Hargreaves, D.H. (2003) *Educational Epidemic: Transforming Secondary Schools Through Innovation Networks*. London: DEMOS.

London Borough of Redbridge (2001a) *Supported and Independent Guidance and Activities for Reading*. London: London Borough of Redbridge.

London Borough of Redbridge (2001b) *Targets for Guided Reading*. London: London Borough of Redbridge.

London Borough of Redbridge (2001c) *Targets for Guided Writing*. London: London Borough of Redbridge.

London Borough of Redbridge (2001d) *Targets for Numeracy*. London: London Borough of Redbridge.

MacGilchrist, B., Myers, K. and Reed, J. (1997) *The Intelligent School*. London: Paul Chapman Publishing.

MacGilchrist, B., Myers, K. and Reed, J. (2004) *The Intelligent School*, 2nd edition. London: Paul Chapman Publishing/Sage Publications.

MacGilchrist, B., Foster, M., Buttress, M., Hagon, L., Marchant, H. and Skelton, J. (2003) '"Learning to Learn" – The Redbridge Experience', paper presented at the International Congress of School Effectiveness and Improvement, January 2003, Sydney, Australia.

McGuinness, C. (1999) *From Thinking Skills to Thinking Classrooms*. London: Department for Education and Employment.

McNeil, F. (1999) 'Brain research and learning – an introduction', *NSIN Research Matters*, no. 10. London: Institute of Education.

Mosley, J. (1996) *Quality Circle Time in the Primary Classroom*. Wisbech: LDA.

Office for Standards in Education (1999) *Handbook for Inspecting Primary and Nursery Schools*. London: Office for Standards in Education.

Office for Standards in Education (2000) *Inspecting Schools: The Framework*. London: Office for Standards in Education.

Qualifications and Curriculum Authority (QCA) (2001) *Supporting the Target Setting Process*. London: Qualifications and Curriculum Authority.

Rogers, B. (1997) *The Language of Discipline: A Practical Approach to Effective Classroom Management*. Plymouth: Northcote House.

Rogers, B. (ed.) (2002) *Teacher Leadership and Behaviour Management*. London: Paul Chapman Publishing.

Rudduck, J., Chaplain, R. and Wallace, G. (1996) *School Improvement: What Can Pupils Tell Us.* London: David Fulton.

Smith, A. and Call, N. (2000) *The ALPS Approach: Accelerated Learning in Primary Schools.* Stafford: Network Educational Press.

Stoll, L., Fink, D. and Earl, L. (2003) *It's about Learning and It's about Time: What's in it for Schools?* London: RoutledgeFalmer.

Watkins, C. (2000) *Learning about Learning: Resources for Promoting Effective Learning.* London: Routledge.

Watkins, C., Carnell, E., Lodge, C., Wagner, P. and Whalley, C. (2001) 'Learning about learning enhances performance', *NSIN Research Matters*, no. 13, Spring. London: Institute of Education.

Watkins, C., Carnell, E., Lodge, C., Wagner, P. and Whalley, C. (2002) 'Effective learning', *NSIN Research Matters*, no.17, Summer. London: Institute of Education.

Index

Printed in Great Britain
by Amazon

58741657R00120